CLOSING THE QUALITY GAP

Lessons from America's Leading Companies

A Book from
The Conference Board
by Alexander Hiam

PRENTICE HALL
Englewood Cliffs, New Jersey 07632

Prentice-Hall International (UK) Limited, *London*
Prentice-Hall of Australia Pty. Limited, *Sydney*
Prentice-Hall Canada, Inc., *Toronto*
Prentice-Hall Hispanoamericana, S.A., *Mexico*
Prentice-Hall of India Private Limited, *New Delhi*
Prentice-Hall of Japan, Inc., *Tokyo*
Simon & Schuster Asia Pte. Ltd., *Singapore*
Editora Prentice-Hall do Brasil, Ltda., *Rio de Janeiro*

© 1992 by

PRENTICE-HALL, Inc.
Englewood Cliffs, NJ

10 9 8 7 6 5 4 3 2 1

Library of Congress Cataloging-in-Publication Data

Hiam, Alexander.
　Closing the quality gap : lessons from America's leading companies
/ by Alexander Hiam for Prentice Hall.
　　p. cm.

"A Conference Board book."
"March 1, 1992."
Includes index.
ISBN 0-13-138413-9
　1. Total quality management—United States.　I. Conference Board.
II. Title.
HD62.15.H53　1992
658.5′62—dc20　　　　　　　　　　　　　　　　　　92-19584
　　　　　　　　　　　　　　　　　　　　　　　　　　CIP

ISBN 0-13-138413-9

PRENTICE HALL
Professional Publishing
Englewood Cliffs, NJ 07632
Simon & Schuster. A Paramount Communications Company

PRINTED IN THE UNITED STATES OF AMERICA

CONTENTS

Acknowledgments

This book was made possible by the unprecidented collaboration of The Conference Board and many of its member companies. It is most unusual for any organization to open its doors and files to an independent author to the extent that they have. Melissa Berman, vice president, planning and product development for The Conference Board, was instrumental in making the collaboration possible, and Larry Schein, program director, quality research for The Conference Board contributed generous amounts of time and advice to the project. Thanks to both of them and their organization for these efforts and for their helpful reviews of the manuscript. Tom Power and his team at Prentice Hall have also gone to great effort to make this a better book.

Thanks are due to the subjects of this book, the leading U.S. practitioners of total quality management. We received contributions and assistance from so many managers and companies that I must refer readers to the text of the book for details. Many managers and companies have shared their information, time and ideas most generously.

Finally, special thanks are due my wife, Heather White, who provided a valuable sounding board for many of the ideas in this book due to her studies of management at MIT's Sloan School. She, along with my sons Eliot and Paul, made many sacrifices so that I might write this book.

INTRODUCTION:
THE QUALITY IMPERATIVE

In the course of researching and writing this book, I have come to see that quality is a well to which companies must travel repeatedly for sustenance. The first visit is the most exciting, provided you manage to get all the way back home without spilling everything first. Like irrigation on a desert, however, the first doses of quality are quickly dissipated in the traditional business organization. It takes a great volume of quality to penetrate the stiff, dry conventions of yesterday's management and bring anything new into bloom. Even when this has been accomplished, and the company can step back from its new quality programs and say with guarded pride that they are a success, the well must still be visited. In fact, it seems to become more important to tap into the well-springs of common experience and wisdom on the subject of total quality once you have a quality program up and running. The more acreage you bring under irrigation, the more water you must put into the system. The same is true with quality.

Traditional management methods are failing us. Today, companies that want to compete globally are taking on the challenge of continuous quality improvement and by so doing, are discovering an entirely new philosophy of management. Companies without quality improvement programs are eventually passed by competitors who *have* adopted this new management technology. The only way to meet the challenge is to adopt the new management technology too . . . to join the revolution. And that is what a growing number of U.S. companies have done. (As Baldrige Quality Award winner Globe Metallurgical's chief executive, Arden Sims, puts it, "Our backs were up against the wall, we were on the defensive, and I saw total quality as a way to save the company from going out of business."[1])

These home-grown responses to the Japanese *kaizen* or quality programs started in earnest in the early and mid-1980s (Globe's began in '85). They are, on average, about five or six years old. This may not seem like much of a history compared to Japan's 40 years, but it has been an extremely productive and exciting period. U.S. (and many European and Canadian) companies have taken advantage of the Japanese models to jump-start their programs, and are moving down the learning curve very rapidly. For example, Florida Power & Light's management logged many months on visits to Japanese companies in the early years of their award-winning quality program, and Xerox benefitted greatly from the successful bid for Japan's Deming Award for quality by its Japanese subsidiary, Fuji Xerox.

A uniquely American version of continuous improvement is emerging out of this first generation of American quality programs. *Any* company or organization can benefit from this new revolution in management technique. Yet many find the new techniques difficult and frustrating. A recent Ernst & Young study of quality improvement efforts at 584 U.S., Canadian, Japanese and German companies concluded that, "among most U.S. companies, virtually no quality-boosting practices have reached lasting and meaningful levels," and that "the results seem even worse when compared with quality programs abroad."[2] Despite the fact that total quality programs and customer service programs are spreading rapidly now in the U.S., few companies can claim complete success with them. Only a handful of U.S. companies have reached critical

---

[1]Bruce Rayner, "Trial-By-Fire Transformation: An Interview with Globe Metallurgical's Arden C. Sims," *Harvard Business Review*, May–June 1992, p. 118.

[2]Gilbert Fuchsberg, "Quality Programs Show Shoddy Results," *The Wall Street Journal*, May 14, 1992, p. B1.

mass in total quality management. By and large, the first generation of U.S. quality practitioners *has* learned how to make total quality management work in the U.S. business environment, and it is their programs that provide a meaningful demonstration of the potential of total quality management, not the many fledgling programs surveyed in the Ernst & Young study.

The experiences of the first generation are of vital importance to those who follow them, and there is no group better than The Conference Board to tell their story. The Conference Board's quality councils include almost all of the first wave of U.S. quality innovators, and these companies have been extremely helpful and cooperative in describing and analyzing their experiences for this book, allowing it to examine many of the best practices that have emerged in U.S. quality programs. (And a number of other companies, including Bausch & Lomb, Conference Board member Hoechst Celanese, and Humana, also contributed to the project.) While the contributions of Quality Council members varied, thanks are due to all of them for their assistance with this and previous Conference Board research:

The Conference Board's U.S. Quality Council

3M
American Express Company
Corning Incorporated
Dun & Bradstreet Software
  Services, Inc.
Florida Power & Light (and its
  Qualtec Quality Services
  subsidiary)
Ford Motor Company
Hospital Corporation of America
International Business Machines
  Corp.
Johnson & Johnson
Milliken & Company
The First National Bank of Chicago
The Proctor & Gamble Company
Westinghouse Electric Corporation
Xerox Corporation

U.S. Quality Council II

Allied-Signal Inc.
Analog Devices, Inc.
Baxter International, Inc.
Caterpillar Inc.
Eastman Kodak Company
Equifax Inc.
Hershey Foods Corporation
KPMG Peat Marwick
Metropolitan Life Insurance
  Company
Morton International
Texaco Inc.
University of Michigan Hospitals
Weyerhaeuser Paper Company
Whirlpool Corporation

The 13 elements found in our analysis of Conference Board member companies are the essential foundation for quality efforts in any organization:

- A clear, compelling vision of what quality means in the organization

- Quality plans and a quality planning and management process

- Company-wide customer focus

- Company-wide process-improvement focus

- Innovation in all aspects of the business

- Employee participation in management and change

- Healthy competition to improve performance

- Strong participative leadership from the top of the organization and throughout it

- Dedication to training and learning, for both employees and managers

- Use of teams for many improvement projects

- Benchmarking against superior role models

- Measurement of the costs of bad quality and the results of quality improvement

- Extensive use of process management methods and tools

THREE ORGANIZING THEMES

When you look closely at this set of best practices emerging from the leading U.S. quality practitioners, several organizing themes emerge. First, and most obvious, is how the quality programs are managed. In its broadest sense, management encompasses everything that goes on in a firm, including its quality programs. But as a practical matter, the main contributions of management are in the areas of visualizing, planning, organizing, and directing the work of the firm and its employees. Management needs to spearhead the quality effort by creating a detailed, workable plan of action and by focusing the company's quality improvements on customer needs. And management must kick-start continuous improvement by focusing on improving the many individual processes through which the firm adds value for its customers. These subjects are treated in Section 1, The Management of Quality Programs.

The second major theme is the importance of corporate culture to the success of a quality program. The existing corporate culture is an impediment to quality progress. Period. This is as true at a company that has never implemented total quality as it is at a leader of the quality revolution. Corporate culture cannot stand still. A number of the elements of success are closely related to the whole knotty issue of corporate culture and form Section 2 of this book: innovation, participation, competition, leadership and training.

Finally, a hands-on, practical approach that gets everyone engaged in implementing quality daily is also an essential theme. Quality is a hands-on effort, and must become part of everyone's daily life. There are a number of elements of successful quality programs that have to do almost exclusively with the details of how quality programs are implemented. These are the tools, techniques, and concepts that give individuals the power, alone or in groups, to understand and work on quality problems or come up with clever quality innovations. They include use of teams, benchmarking, measurement, and process management.

These three themes and the thirteen elements that make them up will become required knowledge for every employee and manager as Total Quality Management spreads outward from the successful programs described in this book.

The quality revolution is reaching an important juncture, as the baton is passed from a small number of pioneers to thousands of second-wave companies all across the continent. The thirst for knowledge among this second wave of quality adventurers is great, and there is much they can learn from the companies profiled in this book. Further, I have come to realize that this material is equally valuable, perhaps even more valuable, to those pioneers who are on the second or third phases of their quality programs. They need to return to the well, and can benefit from their visits as much as can the more recent recruits.

One final introductory note, on the 'best practices' philosophy of The Conference Board that I have tried to implement in the following pages. This is the pragmatic philosophy that managers can learn and improve their organizations most readily by looking at the best success models from other companies and industries. It strikes a resonant chord for me, since I have focused on collecting and interpreting best practices in two of my previous books. And it resonates strongly with modern quality programs, for the benchmarking techniques they utilize also search for best practices and success models wherever they may be found. In a sense, The Conference Board's best-practices approach anticipated modern benchmarking.

Many of the individual practices reported in the following pages will provide useful models or starting points for readers. And, beyond the one-to-one correspondence between one company's problem and another's solution, there is also much to be learned by looking at a broad sampling of best practices in the field of quality improvement. Certain common elements begin to emerge, and it is possible to make useful generalizations based on the themes that run through dozens of successful quality improvement efforts. In fact, this kind of analysis holds forth much promise for the future, and can begin to define the signposts for the next steps in the evolution of American quality programs. I have endeavored to tease out some of these themes in the coming pages, identifying the factors that are associated with successful quality improvements at leading quality practitioners. I trust readers will take this process even further as they implement their own quality improvement efforts—in their own work and throughout their organizations.

Alexander W. Hiam
Amherst, Mass.

FROM THE CONFERENCE BOARD

This book relies heavily on the participation of executives in The Conference Board network whose companies have traveled the farthest down the Total Quality path. On behalf of both The Conference Board and Prentice Hall, I want to express my appreciation for their willingness to allow others to benefit from their experience.

Total Quality Management is prominent among The Conference Board's key areas of focus. Our involvement in Total Quality began in 1985, when a group of executives leading the Total Quality effort in their firms met under Conference Board auspices. That group began meeting regularly, and formed The Conference Board's first council on Total Quality—the U.S. Quality Council. There are now three Total Quality Councils, each composed of top corporate-quality executives who meet regularly to exchange information and ideas.

Currently, The Conference Board holds national and international conferences in Total Quality, and cosponsors Regional Baldridge Award Conferences. The Conference Board is launching a Total Quality Management Center. Members of the Center will have access to specially tailored roundtables, seminars, information services, and research programs in Total Quality.

Conference Board activities in Total Quality Management largely benefit only the companies that are Associate Members of The Conference Board. We are pleased to join with

Alexander Hiam and Prentice Hall in making practical information on this crucial subject available to a broader audience.

Preston Townley
President and CEO
The Conference Board, Inc.

February 1992

1

MANAGING QUALITY
PROGRAMS

Quality is an entirely new approach to management of companies, or any organization. Quality programs initiate new ways of thinking about work and new ways of organizing the activities of workers. They provide an antidote to heightened global competition and are perhaps the best hope for revitalization of the U.S. economy. However, when a quality program is initiated, many things have to happen before the full promise is realized. Quality programs do not necessarily change the *status quo*. Sometimes they fall prey to it instead.

At Conference Board companies, successful quality programs are aggressively managed from the top. Senior management starts the ball rolling by visualizing what a new, quality-focused, change-oriented organization ought to look and feel like. This vision is translated into specific quality plans. These plans are not documents *per se*; they are more process than product. The planning *process* turns out to be essential, and when it enlists everyone in the organization, and touches everyone in their daily work, then the plan takes on transforming power and rapid improvements begin to emerge.

Part of the art of quality management is knowing how to let go of decisions and allow participation to flourish. But management must replace hands-on decision making with leadership-by-example and a constant emphasis on two key areas of focus: customers and processes. Quality programs need to focus everyone's improvement efforts on customer needs and perceptions. And they need to concentrate change within specific, well-defined business processes. Management's role is dual; first, to keep everyone focused on the customer; and second, to show everyone how a deeper understanding of what drives quality can be achieved by visualizing the entire company as made up of discrete processes that are subject to modification and management by the people who work within them.

Chapter 1

WHY THE MAGIC
STOPPED WORKING

> Westinghouse became interested in quality in the 1970s because our magic stopped working. The Westinghouse management model had begun to lose its effectiveness—drastically. Understanding that we had to do something radically and quickly, Westinghouse decided that a quality process spread across the total business enterprise was essential.
>
> *—Jack Fooks, vice president, corporate quality, Westinghouse Electric Corporation[1]*

Why did the Westinghouse management model lose its effectiveness? And why was a quality process the answer to this failure of traditional management methods and beliefs? The answers to these questions are vitally important to American managers today, because Westinghouse was not the only company to find that its magic stopped working. In fact, the drastic loss of effectiveness Jack Fooks reports in the introductory quote is a common experience across American industries and services. (Arden Sims of Globe Metallurgical, the first small

---

[1] Jack H. Fooks, "Culture Change and the Quality Organization," speech at The Conference Board's Third Annual Quality Conference, April 2–3, 1990, New York.

business to win a Baldridge award, tells a similar story: "It became clear to me that the old approach to controlling costs had serious limitations; no matter how much I cut and restructured, Globe would never be competitive. . . ."[2]) Traditional management paradigms are failing us. Some companies felt the impact of this failure in the 1970s and 1980s, and others are just beginning to feel it now. For all of them, the solution Westinghouse chose makes sense: A quality process spread across the entire business enterprise. However, this process requires both broader and deeper changes than most of these companies have ever undertaken. As Preston Townley, president of The Conference Board, describes it,

> Today, theorists and practitioners are prescribing continuous quality improvement for companies that aspire to world-class products and services. We know that continuous improvement requires vision, leadership, a learning environment, and the empowerment and participation of all people in the organization. And this means change.[3]

Before we move on to the specifics of how this change is effected, it is important to consider the context that has created the need for change, and to explore what the quality process is and why it has been prescribed. The obvious place to start is with a definition of quality. But, just to be contrary, I am going to ask another defining question instead, "What is the *opposite* of 'quality' "?

The reason this question is interesting is that there is no simple answer! Our language does not provide us with a good antonym. And that is a surprising and puzzling thought. After all, most words have at least one obvious opposite—in fact, on the simplest level, we understand concepts through an appreciation of their opposites. Black and white. Good and evil. Fat

---

[2]Bruce Rayner, "Trial-By-Fire Transformation: An Interview with Globe Metallurgical's Arden C. Sims," *Harvard Business Review*, May–June 1992, p. 120.
[3]As quoted in Conference Board Report Number 979.

and thin. But quality and—what? If we can answer this question, we will achieve a deeper understanding of quality than any dictionary-style definition could provide.

What about synonyms? Again, we are hard pressed to place the word quality. Quality control, the traditional effort to catch bad products *after* they have been made, is at the opposite end of the spectrum from total quality. Excellence is the best of a bad lot in the average thesaurus entry, but excellence, while a laudable goal in management, lacks the external yardsticks of customer perception and competitive position that quality, as managers use it, now evokes. As a nation we went in search of excellence in the early 1980s, and thought we had found it within the walls of some of our leading corporations. When the dust settled, this notion of excellence did not prove as durable as we had hoped. The excellence that managers found did not move customers or competitors—instead, the marketplace chose a surprising variety of upstart competitors, many of them from Japan and, here in the United States, from the ranks of entrepreneurs more often than the Fortune 500. Quality refers to the startlingly revolutionary management innovations that many of these success stories have in common. Their results literally turn our traditional notions of excellence upside down.

A dusty old volume called *Manual of Excellent Management 1957* caught my eye at a book sale a few years ago. I expected to find within it an unfamiliar, antiquated view of business management, one that might reassure me of the progress we have made in the interim. I was shocked to find an approach fundamentally the same as that which is now taught in business schools and practiced in most corporations. The audit's analysis of success factors in areas such as corporate structure, research and development, fiscal policies, production efficiency, sales vigor, and so forth, had a startlingly modern ring to it. The fundamentals, and most of the details, of evaluating management effectiveness have not changed. The volume provides graphic evidence of the stability of management practice in the U.S. Excellence meant much the same in 1957 as it does now.

The American Institute of Management subjected thousands of companies to a careful screening process. If it were not for the date on the cover, the written description of this audit would satisfy today's typical management consultant. It is full of modern-sounding advice like, "The quality of the product or service and its cost to produce or give are fundamental to the financial well-being and to the permanence of the company's success."[4]

As a rough measure of this permanence, I cross-referenced the names of the 399 excellent U.S. corporations from the 1957 list against a current directory of U.S. businesses.[5] How many of these companies still survive in recognizable form, either independently or as separately managed subsidiaries of other companies? By my analysis, *only 54%* survived the three and a half intervening decades. A shocking 46% have disappeared.

How good were the leading management experts of 1957 at picking winners? Apparently not good at all. But to be fair, we ought to look separately at their Top 20 list—the companies that received the highest ratings in their management audits. Surely these should provide less mortal, yet the statistics are not much different. Only 13 of the 20 still answer their phones; a 65% survival rate.

Is this a valid analysis, based as it is on the chance finding of an old book? Other, more strenuous studies do lend support to my finding that companies are far less permanent than they seem. For example, two consultants from Arthur D. Little's San Francisco office found in 1990 that, "Thirty-seven percent of the companies of the 1979 *Fortune*-500 list no longer exist now as they did then."[6] A study in the 1970s reported at the

[4] American Institute of Management, *Manual of Excellent Managements 1957*, New York, 1957, p. 33.

[5] The National Directory of Addresses and Telephone Numbers 1991, General Information, Inc., Bothell, Washington. (This directory was chosen because it includes all businesses that have U.S. telephone listings, making it more complete than other readily available sources.)

time that, "Of the thousands of firms in the United States during the Revolution, only 13 survive as autonomous firms and seven as recognizable divisions of firms."⁷ So much for management excellence.

And so much for our traditional notions of management. If quality means nothing more than excellence, it is another red herring. When you take a close-up look at the leading American practitioners of total quality, what you see is a sharp break from the management traditions that have defined excellence in business management. Quality has almost nothing to do with excellence. It is too revolutionary to have any good synonyms.

But why no antonyms? This question puzzled me for several months, until a simple answer occurred to me. The opposite of quality is the *status quo*, the norm, our current paradigms of management. Quality is something completely different. It stands in opposition to everything else in the world of business management. It is a new management paradigm, holding as much potential for the 20th century as the industrial revolution held for the 18th century.

Excellence refers to the best of the traditional practices. But the traditional practices no longer suit the business environment. Managers and their constituents—employees, owners, customers, suppliers, and communities—are in desperate need of alternatives to the existing coda of management thought and practice. The only well-formed, field-tested alternative presently available is quality.

AMERICAN PROSPERITY: THE END OF AN EMPIRE?

The nation is struggling to shrug off the effects of a deep recession. No one, not even politicians, is pretending that

---

⁶ John Forbis and William Adams, Corporate Victims of the Eighties, *Across the Board*, December 1990, pp. 15–21.
⁷ America's Oldest Companies, *Nation's Business*, July 1976, pp. 36–37.

America's economy is headed for a period of robust expansion. If we can get the patient out of bed, this will be victory enough. The prospect of getting it into the weight room seems absurd.

This weakened condition puzzled economists throughout 1991 as they sought signs of a clear end to the recession. First declared over in May of 1991, the recession was given new life, and later ending dates, with each new quarter's economic results. By the end of the year, Robert Hall of Stanford, who heads the National Bureau of Economic Research's committee in charge of dating the recession, worried that, "In terms of economic fundamentals, it's hard to think of any that are particularly bad. But there is this gloom hanging over the economy."[8] At an October 1991 Conference Board meeting on the state of the economy, this gloom translated into one of the more negative forecasts from managers ever. As Lennox Brown, the chief executive of Teleflex Inc., recalls, "The economists started talking about a recovery. But we all said, 'Hey, you're not being realistic. The economy has stalled.'"[9] The real issue, then, is not whether the economic pendulum is swinging the other way yet, but whether the clocks themselves need rewinding. Economist James Smith of the Rand Corporation sums it up with this sobering observation: "The real question is whether our incomes are going to grow at a faster rate than inflation. If not, or if the gain is only 1 percent a year, who wants to wait 20 years to feel better?"[10]

There ought to be light at the end of the tunnel, no matter how distant. At least that is what the optimist believes. However, it is increasingly clear that, whatever light the end of the tunnels reveals, it will not be shed by the same sun under which America prospered in previous decades, and it will not illuminate the same landscape in which each generation was

[8]Alan Murray, "Clouded by Gloom: Economy in the U.S. Isn't Nearly as Sour As the Country's Mood. *The Wall Street Journal*, November 4, 1991, p. A1.
[9]Ibid.
[10]Louise Uchitelle, Optimism Is Disappearing for a Solid Recovery Soon. *The New York Times*, August 11, 1991, pp. A1, A20.

able to say with confidence that it expected to do better and live better than the generation before it. The pessimists and, increasingly, the realists are concerned that there is a long-term decline underlying the more superficial cycles of recession and expansion. Some of the fire may have burned out of America's sun. There is even talk of "imperial overstretch"[11] and hushed illusions to the fall of the Roman empire. Is it possible that the great engines of economic growth and social prosperity have finally run down? When close to half of the best companies in the country can disappear in 35 years, presumably taking many thousands of jobs with them, it seems eminently possible. This is the broader context in which we need to place the U.S. quality movement, and it is helpful to explore it briefly before we move on to the specifics of the first generation of American quality programs.

THE POWER OF JAPANESE COMPETITION

When America casts about for explanations of its own decline, its eye is easily caught by the glint of Japan's rising sun. The statistics are enough to make many a manager's blood boil. A recent *Fortune* analysis of the computer industry is illustrative:

> In 1980, all the major producers of materials and equipment used to manufacture semiconductors were American. By 1990, four of the top five companies in this critical $22 billion subindustry were Japanese. In the interim, Japan surged past the U.S.

[11] Professor Paul Kennedy of Yale has advanced a theory of imperial overstretch that forecasts the decline of American power and prosperity. His viewpoint is strenuously disputed by Michael Novak, of the American Enterprise Institute, who argues that, "Mr. Kennedy counts mostly military and economic power, which today are losing salience. Other classic forms of power—let us call them faith, ideas, morale, spirit, vision, culture—are gathering force." In general, I hate lengthy footnotes. But in this case it is illuminating to take note of the counter-argument to the declining empire theory. Because unless you relish the thought of a future characterized by impoverished idealism, you will find the oppositions' acceptance of declining economic power an unexpected and alarming support for the decline theory. (See Michael Novak, The Game's Not Over, *Forbes*, August 20, 1990, p. 56.)

to become the world's No. 1 maker of computer chips and its No. 1 buyer of chipmaking equipment.[12]

The future seems to hold forth a continuation of this trend. Frank Carrubba, speaking from the heart of Silicon Valley in his role as Director of Hewlett-Packard Laboratories, puts it this way; "When we look down the road, we see the possibility of losing ground rapidly and completely."[13]

DISPLACED BY A NEW EMPIRE?

To those who call such concerns sensationalist, there are two strong rebuttals. First, as Charles Ferguson of MIT (and a former manager with IBM) explains, while U.S. market share of the world computer systems industry has only fallen a bit, from 70% in 1980 to 60% today versus Japan's 20%, these statistics do not tell the full story. The problem is that market share, as measured in gross retail revenues, ignores the fact that, "U.S. and European companies have been paying an increasing fraction of those revenues to vertically integrated Japanese components and hardware suppliers, who are also their primary future competitors." By Ferguson's calculations, "Japanese industry may well control more than 50% of the hardware content of world-wide personal systems markets within five years."[14] And this will make it the dominant player in the entire computer industry, realizing Frank Carrubba's worst fears.

The second rebuttal is even stronger: many industries have already fallen. The computer industry is just the latest cornerstone of the American economy to feel the power of Japanese competition. Many of the missing companies from the 1957 list were in steel, paper, textiles, rail, and other old-

---

[12] David Kirkpatrick, Who's Winning the Computer Race, *Fortune*, June 17, 1991, p. 58–68.

[13] Ibid.

[14] Charles Ferguson, Computers and the Coming of the U.S. Keiretsu, *Harvard Business Review*, July–August 1990, pp. 55–70.

line industries. Global banking fell quietly to the Japanese over the last two decades (even as domestic banking fell to poor management and misguided regulation); the five largest banks in the world are Japanese, and Citicorp., now struggling vainly to hold onto its number one position in the U.S., has dropped to eighteenth globally.[15] In fact, when the ten largest companies in the world are listed, four of them are Japanese banks, and a total of six of them are Japanese.[16] Toyota comes up seventh—the Big Three U.S. auto manufacturers don't even make the list. And of course production of steel, followed by televisions, stereos, and other consumer electronics, has long since migrated to Japan and points East. But the auto industry's experience tells the story of Japanese industrial development, and U.S. industrial difficulties, most clearly.

THE AUTO WARS: THE ROLE OF LEARNING

Most people do not remember Toyota's first entry into the U.S. market: the Toyota Crown, the very first Japanese auto import in 1958. By 1960 it had been withdrawn from the U.S. market—for quality problems! Today Toyota is number four in the U.S., just behind the Big Three in sales, and some industry observers rank the company number one in quality and productivity.[17] Most recently it has established a strong position in the luxury car segment at a time when traditional segment leaders have been withdrawing some of their models.[18] It is

---

[15] Don't Expect Citicorp to Play Copycat, *Business Week*, July 29, 1991, p. 26. Randall Smith, Big Bank Mergers Come as Boon to a Wall Street Thirsty for Deals, *The Wall Street Journal*, August 16, 1991, p. C1. Fred Bleakley, As Big Rivals Surge, Citicorp's John Reed is at a Crossroads. *The Wall Street Journal*, August 16, 1991, pp. A1, A2.

[16] The World's Largest Public Companies, *The Wall Street Journal*, September 1990, p. R28. (Based on an analysis by Morgan Stanley.)

[17] Alex Taylor III, Why Toyota Keeps Getting Better and Better and Better, *Fortune*, November 19, 1990, pp. 66–79.

[18] The Luxury Car Market: Arrivals . . . and Departures, *The Wall Street Journal*, August 16, 1991, p. B4.

perhaps difficult to remember that Toyota was a very different company only a few decades ago.

In 1960, Japanese factories were relatively inexperienced. Toyota was wrestling with problems, like high-speed vibrations and overheating, that Detroit had ironed out years before. And remember the experience curve? First developed by U.S. strategists in the 1950s and 1960s, this theory held that costs per unit go down as a function of number of units produced. Why? Because experience increases with each unit produced, and the company with more cumulative experience will have learned more, and will be able to build a better quality product for less cost as a result. This theory, supported by hard data from aircraft manufacturers, automakers and eventually many other industries, indicated that the Detroit automakers had a major advantage over Toyota and other Japanese producers. Detroit was farther down the experience curve by millions of units, and its costs and quality were way out ahead of the new competitors as a result.[19] The failure of Toyota's Crown in 1960 proved the point.

Detroit paid little attention when Toyota reentered the U.S. market in 1964. However something subtle but vitally important had happened in the interim. Toyota had, in 1960, begun working with the now-famous engineer, Genichi Taguchi, to design in quality. Applying and extending many of the notions first brought to Japan by the American W. Edwards Deming in 1950 (after his approach to statistical quality control was largely ignored in the U.S.), Toyota and Taguchi went on to invent KANBAN production, just-in-time inventory management, quality circles, and many other of the essentials of the quality revolution documented in the following pages. This drive crystalized into a "Total Quality Control" or TQC system of management at Toyota, given impetus by the oil crisis of 1979 and leading, in the 1980s, to dramatic advances in quality

---

[19] See "Experience Curve Concept" in Subhash C. Jain, *Marketing Planning & Strategy*, South-Western Publishing Co., 1990, pp. 351–356.

and costs and equally dramatic inroads into the U.S. market.[20] But the seeds were sown, quietly, back in 1960, and as they germinated they taught the Japanese that learning did not have to advance in a lock-step with production experience. More recently, Ford's development of the Taurus demonstrated the ability of U.S. automakers to increase their rate of learning by applying the same quality principles that have been so successful at Toyota.

Quality Improvement—A New Way to Learn

Ray Stata, chairman of Analog Devices, Inc. (a member of The Conference Board's U.S. Quality Council II), explains a new learning curve that companies experience when they enter into a quality improvement process:

> The slope of the learning curve is determined by how long it takes to identify and prioritize the causes of the problem and eliminate those causes. The skill of the people and the level of resources do have an impact, but surprisingly the time required for each cycle of improvement is largely a function of the complexity or bureaucracy of the organization. . . . Notice that this theory of learning differs from the Boston Consulting Group (BCG) "experience curve" theory that says learning occurs as a function of cumulative production volume, independent of elapsed time. The quality improvement theory says that learning, properly managed, occurs as a function of time, independent of cumulative volume. How else can we explain the success of the Japanese automobile industry, which learned faster than the U.S. industry with substantially less cumulative volume?[21]

---

[20] Masao Nemoto, *Total Quality Control for Management: Strategies and Techniques from Toyota and Toyoda Gosei*, Prentice Hall, 1987.
[21] Ray Stata, Organizational Learning—The Key to Management Innovation, *Sloan Management Review*, Spring 1989, pp. 63–73.

Here, incidentally, is a graphic illustration of the insight that quality is the opposite of the established management paradigm. Where the accepted wisdom says that learning is a function of production volume, not time, quality practitioners find that learning can be made to behave like a function of time, not volume. Conventional wisdom is turned 180 degrees. And, as Stata goes on to explain, this new insight means that, "A steeper experience curve occurring at a lower production volume can soon overcome a more shallow experience curve occurring at a higher volume."

This is a critical point, perhaps the most important point to arise out of the Japanese experience of the last three decades. For Japanese companies have proven decisively that learning can be managed, *independent of units produced*, and that companies can come from behind by learning faster than their competitors. In every industry in which the Japanese now threaten or dominate the United States, Japan has come from behind, against seemingly overwhelming odds, to overtake its entrenched U.S. competitors. Through management innovations, Japanese companies have been able to ride a far steeper experience curve. How else to explain Toyota's ability to produce its new line of luxury sedans, akin to the Mercedes in design and quality, using just a sixth of the labor Mercedes does?[22] Toyota's Lexus, positioned against the $47,200 Mercedes Benz luxury sedan, is priced 20% lower, at $38,000—not because Japanese labor is cheaper, but because Japanese manufacturing is smarter.[23] Professor Michael Porter of Harvard observes that, "The story of modern industrial history is not exploiting abundance but creating it, not enjoying advantage but coping with disadvantage." He illustrates this point by observing that "Japan and West Germany, which have had the

---

[22] Taylor, Ibid.
[23] A New Era for Auto Quality: The Very Concept is Changing, *Business Week*, October 22, 1990, pp. 82–96.

broadest success in sophisticated industries, both began the postwar period in shambles."[24]

IN SEARCH OF THE ENEMY

The reasons for Japan's success are frequently, and loudly, debated. While trade barriers, MITI and the Keiretsus may give Japanese industry an advantage over the United States, these are national policy issues. The really important issues from the *manager's* perspective are on the firm level, not the macro-economic level. How have certain Japanese companies been able to learn and innovate so much faster than their U.S. competitors? Dramatic differences in management philosophy and practice seem to hold the key—and, fortuitously, the key seems to fit the locks on our side of the Pacific as well. To many, the costs associated with opening that door seem too high. It is easier to point the finger than to look within, and easier to talk in macroeconomic or political generalities than to accept the burden that each company's individual perfor-mance drives the economic performance of its industry, and ultimately, the nation.

LOOKING WITHIN FOR A CURE

The success of Conference Board member's quality programs suggests that managers must put aside any preconceived no-tions about Japan and look deeper than East-West conflict to understand our current afflictions and seek their cure. This does not require that they deny the importance of trade policy, only that they avoid letting it blind them to the vital management-level issues raised by total quality. It is ironic that the quality revolution, holding great promise as a cure, has been nurtured on both sides of the traditional U.S.-Japan riva-lry, and has benefitted greatly by the intermingling of Japanese

---

[24] Michael Porter, Why Nations Triumph, *Fortune*, March 12, 1990, pp. 94–108.

and American culture and experience. It is truly a nonpartisan revolution, and it is important for the reader to step outside of the current partisan debate before proceeding further.

The Maturing of Global Markets

Another way to look at the context for the quality revolution is to look at how the business environment has changed over the last few decades. At one time our standards of management were admirably suited to the business environment. Now they are not. The environment must have changed. In fact, many of the problems commonly attributed to the rise of Japanese industry may actually be the result of environment-driven declines in U.S. prosperity and economic strength. Turnaround expert John Whitney has observed that:

> From 1948 through 1973, real GNP growth averaged 3.7%. Unemployment was relatively low. Inflation was high if it reached 5%, so it kept interest rates down. American business not only served a growing domestic market but also discovered Europe, Asia, and Latin America. Every year America was a net exporter, piling up at surplus of $157 billion.[25]

That has all changed. Those who are familiar with the product life cycle might see its applicability on a grand scale to this story. (The PLC model divides the life of a product into introduction, growth, maturity, and decline. Maturity is reached as all the potential customers are reached, and sales growth slows as a result. Maturity is far more competitive than growth, and poses a different set of challenges.) I think one can apply this model globally: Markets expanded rapidly during a global growth stage accompanying the rise of industrialized first-world economies, allowing companies to prosper by expanding into virgin territory, developing new

---

[25] John O. Whitney, Turnaround Management Every Day, *Harvard Business Review*, September–October 1987, pp. 49–55.

markets at home and abroad. Now we have approached a saturation point, and for companies to maintain rapid growth they must compete against similarly-endowed rivals rather than pioneer new territory. The global game changes, much as the game of marketing changes when a single product's market enters maturity. New rules apply. Yet America's management practices were appropriate to the age of ready expansion and relative stability. As Whitney puts it, "this country developed a body of business practice and literature that suited this environment." Specifically,

> The vertical organization with short spans of control made sense in a stable business environment. Executives made decisions deliberately with the concurrence of the organization's many layers. Long-term planning became a fetish . . . Then, during the early 1970s, trouble appeared. The rate of environmental change accelerated and competition intensified.[26]

THE SHIFT TO A CUSTOMER-DRIVEN ENVIRONMENT

What has changed, at least from the life cycle perspective, is the *relationship* of firms and their industries to that environment. Maturing markets lead to growing competition, and competition leads to instability. There is nothing more destabilizing in a company's environment than dozens of other companies trying their best to take its customers away. To go back to the product life cycle analogy, the competitive markets of maturity place a premium on the quality of goods and services. When a market is young and goods not yet available to everyone, the suppliers have the upper hand and consumers must buy what is available. As soon as the goods become widely available and sufficient competition exists to allow customers the power of choice, the balance shifts. Customers gain the upper hand.

---

[26] Ibid., p. 50.

Another way to see this environmental shift is as technology-driven. It is undeniable that technology is now so pervasive that "it is virtually meaningless to make distinctions between technology and nontechnology businesses and industries: there are *only* technology companies." This is what Regis McKenna argued in his instant classic *Harvard Business Review* article, "Marketing is Everything." As he observed, "Technology is transforming choice, and choice is transforming the marketplace." As a result, "The 1990s will belong to the customer."[27] Technology may indeed drive the shift, or the proliferation of high technology may simply be a response to the growing need for differentiated product lines that comes with the maturing of markets throughout the industrial world. The explanation is less important than the observation itself: The customer now dominates the company's environment.

John Whitney explains that accelerated change and intensified competition in modern markets make today's managers "look inept compared with their 1950s and 1960s counterparts. Yet today's managers are better educated, better informed, and harder working than their predecessors." The problem is, they have inherited systems that are not designed for customer-driven competition. The traditional company serves it stockholders, not its customers. And while marketers have trumpeted the value of customer-oriented management for years now, marketing departments have generally been unable to overcome the structural and cultural obstacles to customer-driven management.[28]

A useful way to look at the quality revolution is as a marketing revolution. Peter Drucker once defined marketing as, "The whole business seen from the point of view of its final result, that is, from the customer's point of view."[29] From this

---

[27] Regis McKenna, Marketing is Everything, *Harvard Business Review*, January–February 1991, pp. 65–79.

[28] This issue is documented and explored in depth in Hiam and Schewe, *The Portable MBA in Marketing*, Wiley, 1992.

[29] As quoted in Philip Kotler, *Marketing Management: Analysis, Planning, and Control*, Prentice Hall, 1984, p. 1.

perspective, it is necessary to agree with the legendary views of Leon Leonwood Bean, who in 1912 announced that, "I do not consider a sale complete until goods are worn out and customer still satisfied."[30] This is a startling statement, even today. How many managers have any idea what happens to their products after the customer buys them, and how many can honestly say customers are still satisfied, if indeed they ever were, when it comes time to throw the product away? But this is what looking at the whole company from the customer's perspective demands. It is the quality paradigm in action.

Breaking the Boundaries of Traditional Marketing

While marketing seems to most managers a discrete, and sometimes minor, staff function within the company, the marketing revolution at work here is much broader than any departmental lines can hold. In fact, it is taking place to a large degree beyond the boundaries of the traditional marketing department. The initiative is coming from manufacturing, from engineering, from human resources, from distribution, from customers, and, most important, from the CEO's office. It is driving radical changes in how products are designed, made, and delivered and in how services are structured and performed.

One might say that all the important new directions in management thought are marketing-oriented (which makes good sense, after all, in a customer-dominated environment). Flatter organization structures put managers in closer contact with their markets. Growing concern with employee training and with work and family issues can be seen as a combination of internal marketing and an investment in better service for future external customers. Corporate sensitivity to environmental issues reflects the new reality that *every* action of a

---

[30] From a 1912 L. L. Bean circular.

company impacts its customers and other constituents, and an impact is never neutral—so managers must determine whether it is positive or negative. The current excitement with improving customer service and the dramatic changes brought about by total quality programs are both driven by a view of the company from the customer's perspective. Among new management programs, the quality movement is really the catalyzing event for most companies; you might say it is the crown jewel of all the new marketing-oriented change programs at work in North American and European companies. Therefore, as we focus on the experiences of leading U.S. quality practitioners, it is helpful to keep sight of their roots in the theory of marketing.

However, we must also recognize that marketing is too narrow a term to contain all the exciting developments under way at present. It evokes images of telemarketers and point-of-purchase displays, of young interviewers laying in wait at the next turn in the mall corridor, clipboards in hand. The everyday actions of marketing, from research to advertising, are important to a firm but do not transform it. The transforming events of a total quality effort must engage the entire company, and in fact are as likely to take the marketing department by surprise as they are any other function. Ultimately, marketing, like manufacturing or accounting, is business as usual. Quality is the opposite.

That means the marketing vision underlying a quality program is very different from the banalities of routine practice in the marketing department, and, in fact, sometimes in direct opposition to them. For example, where marketers often find themselves in the position of trying to coerce customers into buying the products in current inventory—look at the incredible proliferation of advertising messages throughout our society if you don't believe there is a coercive element to marketing—a quality program aims purely to benefit customers by giving them more value than they expect or think they have paid for. That this is the ultimate key to global competitiveness, and to the quality revolution itself, seems clear enough. *How* to change the focus from seeing what we can get people to buy to seeing how far beyond their expectations we can reach is less clear, and the practical problems associated with this change of paradigm are the main concern of this book and of quality programs in general.

Incidentally, this is not a brand new paradigm. Henry Ford expressed it powerfully back in the early growth years of Ford, when he said that, "The man who will use his skill and constructive imagination to see how much he can give for a dollar, instead of how little he can give for a dollar, is bound to succeed." This sounds good in principle, but it is a difficult thought to put into practice. In practice, it is easy to shift focus from giving to the customer to worrying about the quarterly results (which can turn quickly into seeing how much you can take from the customer). One of the greatest, and simplest benefits of the new quality programs is that they turn this equation back over, establishing firmly in a company's systems and practices the simple, but easily overlooked, reality that the quarterly results are the end of a process that begins with customer satisfaction.

THE CUSTOMER AT THE HEART OF THE COMPANY

This puts customers at the heart of the company, where in many cases they once reigned supreme before the weight of corporate politics and bureaucracy displaced them with other concerns. In their early days both L. L. Bean and Ford Motor Co. had founders who championed many of the values the new quality programs are reinstating. In fact, for both of these firms, quality programs are as much a return to their roots as an adoption of Japanese principles.

However, there is an important caveat to make here. In the messy world of practical application, re-embracing a customer orientation is not simple, and not always enough. What, exactly, do we mean by the customer? How is the customer's perspective measured and represented, and how far can or should we go toward (and beyond) satisfying that customer's needs? The answers to these questions are not simple—in fact, there is nothing simple about the pursuit of quality. The process is time-consuming, costly, and emotionally wrenching for companies. And, even worse, the answers are not static. The rules of the game are evolving, even as American companies struggle to learn the rules. Listen to MIT professor Peter Senge describe the changes in the Japanese concept of quality:

> . . . Japanese firms' view of serving the customer has evolved. In the early years of total quality, the focus was on "fitness to standard," making a product reliably so that it would do what its designers intended it to do and what the firm told its customers it would do. Then came a focus on "fitness to need," understanding better what the customer wanted and then providing products that reliably met those needs. Today, the leading edge firms seek to understand and meet the "latent need" of the customer—what customers might truly value but have never experienced or would never think to ask for.[31]

Quality is a moving target, superficially because competitors move; fundamentally because customer perception continues to evolve. Quality is now moving beyond the imagination of the customers. You can't simply ask people what they want and give it to them. A competitor may have come up with a better idea in the interim, one that customers want more than whatever they told you about. This means simply bringing flesh-and-blood customers into the company's decision-making process is not good enough. Managers need to achieve greater insight into the customer's condition than even the customer has. Mazda's Miata is a simple example. No customer surveys revealed market demand for a modern, reasonably-priced throwback to the old MG-style sports cars. But one of Mazda's managers was inspired by the idea, and he was given sufficient runway to take off with his vision. According to a *Business Week* report,

> Just as U.S. carmakers are getting their quality up to par, the Japanese are redefining and expanding the term. The new concept is called miryokuteki-hinshitsu—making cars that are more than reliable, that fascinate, bewitch, and delight.[32]

Static measures of progress are dangerous as a result. It is heartening, for example, to see the gap in automobile defect rates closing. In 1980, Detroit turned out cars with *three times* as many defects (problems in the first 90 days of ownership) as the Japanese. That is an awfully big gap. But aggressive efforts to implement total quality, especially at Ford, have lowered this gap to only 25% more defects a decade later. Detroit is closing the defects gap. Meanwhile, Japanese automakers are shifting the emphasis of their quality efforts away from defect rates and toward satisfying latent demand. The thought is sobering. The work is just begun.

AND NOW FOR THE GOOD NEWS: WE'RE DOING A BAD JOB

The good news, as perverse as it may sound, is that even excellent companies are doing a bad job in an absolute sense. When companies try to close gaps such as this one, they can. They are nowhere near any ceiling on performance, if there even is one. Why? Because they were not doing a good job before. Because there is *incredible* room for improvement. What we have taken for granted as excellence, at least since 1957, is mediocre at best. The striking fact emerging from quality efforts everywhere is that companies have only been

---

[32] A New Era for Auto Quality, *Business Week*, October 22, 1990, pp. 82–94.

doing as well as they had to to get by, if that. Like their employees, many of whom are just putting in their time, entire companies have been operating without passion and enthusiasm for decades.[33] Their performance has been good enough in many cases—but good enough says absolutely nothing about ultimate potential. How good can a company be if it makes flat-out improvement its one and only priority? When a company adopts its customers' perspective, constant improvement does become the top priority. The difference is like night and day.

The results reported by some of The Conference Board's Quality Council members are illustrative. Analog Devices found that defect and failure rates in its products and components, which were typically level or rising slowly, began to fall at rates ranging from a 50% improvement in 10 months to a 50% improvement in 3.6 months upon initiation of its quality improvement process.[34] The First National Bank of Chicago made about one error in 4,000 transactions in 1982, before their quality program started. Now the rate is down to about one in 8,000 and still falling.[35] From Canada, Northern Telecom reports that the failure rate of electrical components detected on incoming inspection fell an order of magnitude in the first four years of its quality program.[36] Improvement rates like this were thought impossible—are considered impossible still—at many companies. But the evidence is undeniable. Dramatic improvements in quality can be made at every company, and they can be made *without offsetting increases in manufacturing costs.* Johnson & Johnson's Quality Institute reports a

---

[33]Behavioral scientists have coined the term 'satisficing' to describe this get-by behavior on the individual level. But it appears that organizations engage in the behavior as well.

[34]Ray Stata, Ibid.

[35]Conference Board Research Report 937, p. 60.

[36]According to Milan Kosturik, Assistant V.P., Operations, Northern Telecom Canada, at a Conference Board meeting reported in "Global Perspectives on Total Quality," 1991.

number of results that represent the wide range of improvements yielded by quality processes:

> At Chicopee [New Brunswick, NJ], the use of statistical process control to gather facts to control and ensure predictability in the manufacturing process has resulted in more than a $450,000 reduction in the price of nonconformance in less than one year.
> Using the tools of statistical process control and design of experiments, Johnson & Johnson Medical achieved improvement in two product areas. ob Tampon in-process holds/rejects for absorbency variations have been reduced to zero year-to-date 1991. Ray-Tec monofilament adherence performance was improved five fold, versus prior year, which resulted in an 82 percent reduction in customer complaints.[37]

Reduced defects, errors, and failures also translate into measurable improvements in customer and employee perceptions. American Express's customer surveys showed dramatic improvements in the first two years of its quality program. For example, the percentage of cardmembers whose expectations were met or exceeded rose in annual surveys from 82% to 94% between 1986 and 1988.[38] Employee attitudes can change dramatically through a quality process too, as Hoechst Celanese found through its annual internal survey. For example, positive responses to the employee survey question, "I will share in the business success of Hoechst Celanese," rose from 39% in 1988 to 87% in 1991."[39]

Lawrence Schein, the director of The Conference Board's Quality and Productivity Program, notes that, "As awareness has grown and as quality has improved, the margin of error in the United States has shifted from the number of defects per 10,000 or per 100,000 total units produced to the number of defects per million units."[40] Of course, results like these take a

---

[37]Company literature supplied by Sue Jacobs of the Johnson & Johnson Quality Institute, January 8, 1992.

[38]Ibid., p. 58.

[39]From comments by Dr. Drew, CEO of Hoechst Celanese Corporation, at The Conference Board 75th Anniversary Quality Symposium, Fall 1991.

huge commitment to achieve. Most Quality Council companies now track hundreds, and even thousands, of separate employee teams working on specific quality projects. Corning has put more than 28,000 employees through school at its Quality Institute—almost its entire worldwide workforce—and Group V.P. Richard Dulude of Corning Glass Works reports that, "Our commitment to training is enormous. We've built special classrooms, trained our own instructors, and translated our Quality Awareness training program into Spanish, Portuguese, German, French, and even into the Queen's English. We've established a goal of dedicating 5 percent of all time worked—that's 1.5 million worker hours a year—to quality training over the next three years."[41] When you begin to add in additional time spent in quality teams and quality circles, Corning may well be investing several million worker hours a year in quality. Costs associated with quality programs are measurable in the millions of hours and millions of dollars for most of the Quality Council members. And while the improvement process is an expensive vehicle, it does not necessarily give managers a smooth ride. As Ralph J. Rosati, Kodak's Director, Corporate Quality, puts it, "I don't want to give the impression that our quality improvement progress has been a smooth, steadily rising curve. It hasn't. Certainly there have been obstacles and setbacks, so our progress has been stair-step."[42] While the costs are high and the path crooked, the returns are enormous. Perhaps the most stunning example is provided by Xerox, which found itself at the mercy of upstart foreign competitors in the early 1980s, after its patent protection over photocopiers had expired.

[40] Conference Board Research Bulletin No. 239, p. 5.
[41] Conference Board Research Report No. 909, p. 24.
[42] Conference Board Research Report No. 909, p. 17

THE XEROX STORY: QUALITY WORKS!

James Horn, V.P. for quality at Xerox's Webster, NY copier plant, describes the problem this way: "We were targeted, just like motorcycles and VCRs."[43] Certainly the aggressive, and innovative, assault on Xerox's market share by the Japanese producer Canon had a catalyzing effect on Xerox in the early 1980s. To fully understand the Xerox case it is helpful to start back in 1970 when many of its patents expired, and in 1973 when the FTC forced it to license other patents to competing manufacturers. Donna Stoddard and James Cash of Harvard Business School have summarized the changes in Xerox's market in a recent case analysis:

> Between 1971 and 1978, 77 different plain paper copiers were introduced in the United States. Between 1978 and 1980, another 70 were placed on the domestic market. During this time, Xerox's market share, as measured in U.S. copier revenues, fell from 96 percent to 45 percent. But it was the NP-400, a compact, mid-volume, 40-copy-per minute copier introduced by Canon, Inc., a Japanese producer of inexpensive, low-volume copiers, that shocked Xerox. The Canon product, sold through office-supply dealerships, *retailed for less than the unit manufacturing cost* of competing Xerox equipment.[44]

I have added italics in this quote to emphasize a stunning illustration of the power of the new quality-driven learning curve at work. How in the world could an inexperienced Japanese manufacturer make a product that *retailed* for less than it cost Xerox to *make* a functionally identical product? (The Canon proved easier to service and more reliable in the field as well.) This is the kind of attack that lost America the VCR and motorcycle industries, and that could well have captured the photocopier industry too. However, Xerox had two

---

[43] John Holusha, Stress on Quality Lifts Xerox's Market Share, *The New York Times*, November 9, 1989, pp. D1, D11.
[44] Harvard Business School Case 9-189-022, Rev. 7/23/90, p. 2.

things going for it. Its leadership was strongly committed to recapturing market share by developing its own quality program, and, fortuitously, Xerox had a back door into the Japanese quality methods through its Fuji Xerox subsidiary. This company embraced the new quality methods early in their development (of necessity, since it had to compete against Japanese producers on their home ground), and it had actually succeeded in winning Japan's top quality prize, the Deming Award, in 1980. Xerox was able to import state-of-the-art quality methods from Fuji Xerox, and also proved resourceful at developing its own methodologies (for example, we will discuss its invention of benchmarking processes in the chapter on that topic).

The statistics tell the story. While Xerox does not like to talk about its market share, even within the sheltered confines of The Conference Board, research firms like Dataquest have tracked its share of the world photocopier market for many years. Their statistics show Xerox with a dominant 86% share of the world market in 1974 . . . and a pitiful 17% share in 1984. The company lost 80% of its market share in ten years![15] An experience like that is enough to drive many companies out of business, or, as happened at Xerox, to drive their managers to abandon conventional ideas about management excellence. The quality effort began at Xerox around the beginning of the 1980s, but really kicked in company-wide in 1983. Now eight years later, Xerox has registered a 200% increase in its world-wide market share according to Dataquest. In 1991, it held 38% of the global market for photocopiers.[16]

Paul Allaire, Xerox's new chairman and CEO, summed up the results in a recent talk at The Conference Board:

---

[15] Janice Castro, Making It Better, *Time*, Nov. 13, 1989, pp. 78–81.

[16] James Hirsch, To One Man, Selling Photocopiers is a Gambler's Game, *The Wall Street Journal*, September 24, 1991, pp. A1, A12.

We've been at it for seven years now and the results have been gratifying. Quality works! Let me give you just a few examples. Customer satisfaction has steadily increased. Our customers now rate Xerox #1 in our industry in terms of product reliability and service. Dataquest rates our products as #1 in five out of six market segments and Buyers Lab just named our product line the best in the industry. We have reduced our average manufacturing costs by over 20 percent despite inflation. We have reduced the time it takes to bring a new product to market by up to 60 percent. Our Return-on-Assets has improved from 8 percent in 1983 to 14.6 percent this year. We are the first American company in an industry targeted by the Japanese to regain market share, and we did it without closing our factories or moving our manufacturing off-shore. I could go on, but I think you get the point.[*]

The Xerox story is not about trade barriers or industry consortia. It is not about traditional East-West rivalries. It is about new challenges in the global business environment, and the development of new management techniques suited to this new environment. Like Xerox, most U.S. companies have been or will be thrown into a larger, more competitive environment driven more by customer expectations than by management and shareholder preferences.

While the transition is not always as dramatic, almost all U.S. companies are experiencing to some degree the nakedness Xerox must have felt upon losing its traditional scale and patent protections. Total quality programs are best understood as efforts to adapt the organization to the rigors of its new environment. Collectively, they also hold forth promise of macro-level adaptation and economic renewal. If individual companies can be turned around, their industries can be too, and if industries can be turned around, surely the entire economy can rediscover its lost prosperity and growth.

The message, both to individual managers and to the nation as a whole, is simple. As Allaire puts it, quality works!

[*] Based on remarks by Paul Allaire at a Conference Board meeting on October 1, 1991.

And we know that its opposite, business as usual, does not. Yet it is still a monumental task to tear down the old management paradigms and build a new one throughout the nation. Most American managers have only the foggiest notion of what quality really means, and most U.S. companies have yet to begin their own quality programs. It will take some time for managers to come to terms with the realization that quality is the opposite of everything they have believed in and practiced all along. The existence of a quality program does not necessarily mean the company has completed this turnaround. Most companies of any size have someone with "quality" in their title—but they are most likely working on quality control, which is quite the opposite of the quality concept we are talking about here. And even a serious effort to embrace the quality concept is no guarantee of success. A recent Conference Board survey found only 30 percent of 142 U.S. companies with established total quality management processes rated themselves as being 75-100 percent of the way toward meeting Baldridge Award criteria. A third rated themselves as less than half way. The median self-rating was 50 percent of the way. Only 29 percent of them reported being very satisfied with their efforts to involve employees in the process.[48] There is a long way to go, even for the leaders in the U.S. quality movement.

In 1991, the Department of Commerce mailed out 210,000 copies of the application and quality improvement guidelines for the Malcom Baldrige National Quality Award— that's two and a half copies for every one of the 80,000 companies listed in my handy directory of U.S. businesses. Only 106 applications came back, and only three companies received the prize.[49] That's good progress, but what about the other 79,894 companies? If they are still puzzling over what to

<hr>

[48]Conference Board Report Number 974.

[49]Sources: Jan Kosko, United States Department of Commerce, National Institute of Standards and Technology, Geri Hardy, General Information Inc., subsidiary of OmniGraphics. October and November 1991.

do, they may find the conclusions of M.I.T.'s Commission on Industrial Productivity helpful:

> The decline of the U.S. economy puzzles most Americans. The qualities and talents which gave rise to the dynamism of the postwar years must surely be present still in the national character, and yet American industry seems to have lost much of its vigor. In looking for ways to reverse the decline, it is only natural to turn to the methods that succeeded in the golden years of growth and innovation. Many business managers have adopted just this strategy. The results, unfortunately, are rather like those of a man who keeps striking the same match because it worked fine the first time.[50]

Quality is the new match, and many American businesses are deciding to give it a try.

---

[50]Michael Dertouzos, Richard Lester, and Robert Solow, *Made in America: Regaining the Competitive Edge*, Harper Collins, 1989, p. 46.

The Quality Imperative
A Graphical Overview
Pages 32 to 37

A. U.S. Consumers believe Japan makes the best quality products.

HOW U.S. CUSTOMERS RATE PRODUCT QUALITY

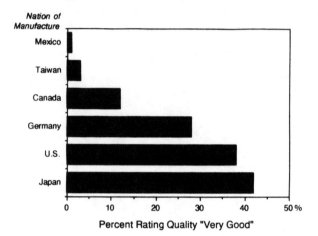

Percent Rating Quality "Very Good"

Source: Yankelovich Clancy Schulman telephone poll of 1,000 Americans, October 30–31, 1989.

B. They are disillusioned with U.S. business and political institutions.

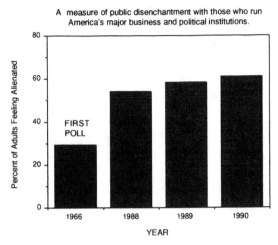

HARRIS ALIENATION INDEX

A measure of public disenchantment with those who run America's major business and political institutions.

(Source: Louis Harris and Associates)

C. U.S. industry has not kept up with the growth in Japanese industrial production.

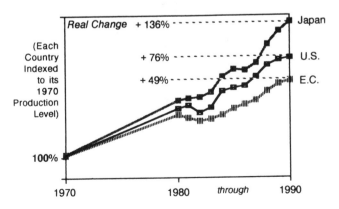

CHANGE IN INDUSTRIAL PRODUCTION

Source: Economic Report of the President, 1991

D.   U.S. spending on industrial R&D is slowing down.

REAL SPENDING ON R&D
INFLATION-ADJUSTED CHANGE, U.S. TOTALS

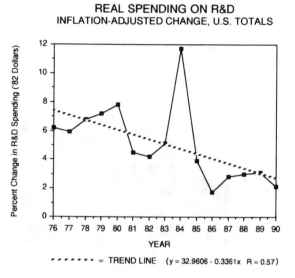

------ = TREND LINE   (y = 32.9606 - 0.3361x   R = 0.57)

(Data from Standard & Poor's Compustat Services Inc.)

E.   The American public views U.S.-Japan relations as luke-warm at best.

AMERICANS' ASSESSMENT OF U.S.-JAPAN RELATIONS

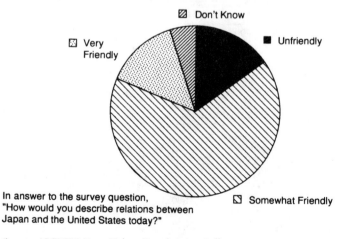

In answer to the survey question, "How would you describe relations between Japan and the United States today?"

Source: NYT/CBS News/Tokyo Broadcasting Poll

F. Both U.S. and Japanese citizens believe Japan is most likely to be the next century's leading economic power.

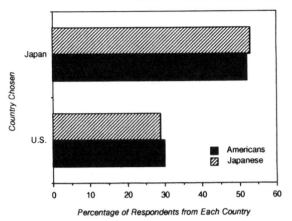

NEXT CENTURY'S LEADING ECONOMIC POWER?

Percentage of Respondents from Each Country

In answer to the survey question, "In the next century,which country will be the No. 1 economic power in the world?"

Source: Surveys, Nov. 1991, by *The New York Times*/CBS News and Tokyo Broadcasting System. NYT, 12/3/91, p. A16.

G. Some companies have turned to quality processes to recapture lost positions.

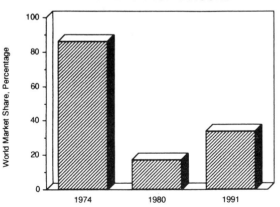

THE XEROX TURNAROUND

Source: Dataquest Estimates

H.   U.S. companies are less likely than Japanese to utilize key quality techniques.

USE OF QUALITY TECHNIQUES

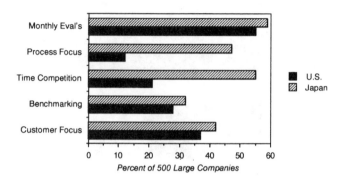

Source: Ernst & Young, Business Week/Quality 1991, p. 10

I.   Most U.S. companies have yet to undertake a full total-quality process.

U.S. FIRMS APPLYING FOR BALDRIGE AWARD

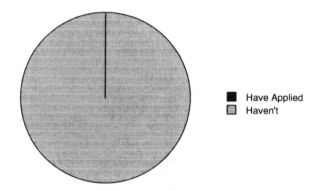

Source: U.S. Department of Commerce

J. Those who have total quality programs generally feel their work is only half-way done.

SELF-RATING OF COMPANIES WITH QUALITY PROGRAMS

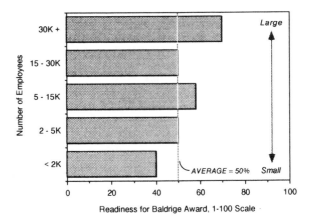

(Source: Conference Board survey, 1991; 142 companies.)

2

VISUALIZING QUALITY

> W e had been looking at the horse from the wrong end, and it was
> not a pretty sight.
> —*Marshall McDonald, Chairman and CEO,*
> *Florida Power & Light*
>
> W e all work for companies that are under attack—and I don't care
> what business or industry we're in. We all face revolutionary
> changes in customer demand, competitive threats and technology that
> are putting pressure on us like we've never felt before.
> —*Robert Bruno, Director, Marketing Resource*
> *Development, GTE*[1]

GTE, like many of the companies profiled in this book, divides
its history into pre- and post-quality periods. Like other companies, GTE now realizes that it lacked critical customer focus
and attention to quality back in the pre-quality days. As Robert
Bruno of GTE's marketing department puts it, "Pre-Baldrige—
our business's version of ancient history and definitely not
"the good old days," our telephone company was a compla-

---

[1] From remarks at a Conference Board Marketing Conference, October 29–30,
1991, New York.

cent, regulated, tradition-bound business. Strategic direction and daily operations were set by two major groups: the regulators, who set expectations and criteria for success, as well as rates and attainable profit levels; and second, the internal regulators, the technologists and operations folks, who determined what, where, when, and how new technology would be brought to customers."

That's an interesting way to plan and manage any business. While other companies have different versions of this story (especially if they were in unregulated industries), they all can say with conviction that strategic direction and daily operations were most certainly not driven by customers and the marketplace to the extent they must be today.

As Bruno puts it, "We were, at best, striving for mediocrity!" GTE's strategic plans were predicated on the fact that, "We were in a monopoly market where our competitive edge was a regulatory system that ruled out competition."[2]

What does this have to do with other companies? After all, most companies never had the kind of protection that public utilities such as telephone and electric companies have enjoyed. Is their experience relevant to others?

Yes. In fact, it is a powerful metaphor for the awakening that is bringing U.S. businesses to terms with heightened, global competition and more demanding customers. The nation was forced to turn outward by the catalyzing political and military events of World War II. And now the nation's businesses have been forced to turn outward by the catalyzing economic events of recent decades. In this ongoing economic war, U.S. businesses are losing their market protection, just as GTE lost its regulated monopoly status. First they were forced to compete nationally as evolving infrastructure eliminated many of the advantages of regional presence. Now they are forced to compete globally. In many industries the effect is as strong as if monopoly protection had just been pulled out from under them.

[2]Ibid.

This is what Bruno refers to when he says companies in any industry are under attack. His views are echoed by managers at many companies. Patrick R. Mill, V.P., Corporate Marketing, NCR Corporation said, "A decade ago, the names of NCR's principal competitors could have been easily written on a small sheet of paper . . . Today, we would need a separate list for every product area, from ATM's to software development tools. Each list might have 20 names, and each list would be different."[3]

For most companies, the traditional approaches to planning and managing change are just not sufficient. They produce incremental, don't-rock-the-boat change. They are more suited to a protected environment than to global economic warfare. Planning for a quality effort must begin with a fresh slate. The most basic management mechanisms—plans and the organizational structure to implement them—need rethinking. In fact, this is where any quality effort needs to start. Existing planning processes and organizational structure will impede the creation of a quality program.

Traditional approaches to planning and organizing are predicated on the old cost versus quality tradeoff. Capital is allocated according to the concept that cost-reduction *competes* with quality, and the company must balance cost *against* quality. Moreover, traditional approaches don't pay much attention to quality in the first place. An informal survey of planning practices supports this contention: the word *quality* does not even appear in the indexes of most of the books written on strategy and planning.

Eisenhower is often quoted as saying that, "Plans are nothing; planning is everything." The quality experience seems to bear this out. For instance, a strategic plan might report that a company will regain lost market share and improve product quality tenfold in three years. Sounds good. But how will they do it? They have no idea, since most companies have never improved anything ten-fold in three years before.

[3]Ibid.

They have been trying to stem the tide of foreign competition for years already without success. A bold new plan is useless at most companies because they will never achieve it. The only way a plan can turn the tide is if the very creation of it is a transforming event for the company. If the process of planning a quality program produces significant learning throughout the organization, if it identifies new techniques and approaches, and if it realigns the organization and focuses it more narrowly on its goals, then any goals are conceivably attainable. Planning *is* everything.

PLANNING FOR QUALITY IMPROVEMENTS

A recent Conference Board workshop on continuous quality improvement, facilitated by David Luther, Corning's quality director, concluded that commitment to a quality plan tends to flow from the underlying vision and the process whereby this vision is made tangible throughout the company. "It is necessary to set up specific plans which are renewed each year," the group concluded, as well as "to devise a vision statement, to make the process "real" at all levels, and to ensure accountability."[4] But *how* do you make the quality process real at all levels? This is a big question, and in fact the entire contents of this book focus on answering it. But right now the most important point to be made is that the underlying vision is of critical importance to the success of any program. Luther and the other managers in this workshop used the term *vision statement* to represent the core idea better than more conventional terms. Successful quality programs seem to utilize mission statements that contain and communicate a powerful quality vision as well as a more standard statement of the company's mission. This vision statement can vary in detail and focus, from the simplest example, Florida Power & Light's corporate vision[5] that "During the next decade, we want to

---

[4] Conference Board Research Report No. 958, p. 43.

[5] Company document, "Summary Description of FPL's Quality Improvement Program," provided by William J. Hensler, Vice President, Qualtec Quality Services, A FPL Group Company, December 3, 1991.

become the best managed electric utility in the United States and an excellent company overall and be recognized as such," to more elaborate visions as expressed in some of the statements of principles that we will review shortly.

In recent years, planners have come to realize that the old mission—strategy—plan sequence needs to be extended. Where does the mission come from, and what makes it compelling enough to translate into powerful strategies and plans? In many cases, nothing. But when there is a compelling vision to shape the organization's mission, the strategies and plans have a great deal more strength to them. And every successful quality plan seems to be built upon some variant of the quality vision. The most successful planning sequence is therefore as follows:

Quality Vision
↓
Quality Mission
↓
Specific Quality Processes[6]
↓
Specific Quality Plans and Programs
↓
Impact on Daily Work

While the who, what, where, and hows of specific plans seem critical to the success of quality efforts, the considerable variation in planning experiences at different companies suggests that there are many ways to accomplish them. Different companies implement in different ways. Every successful quality program does seem to have at its base a powerful vision of what quality means to the company and its customers. This, the starting point of the strategies and plans, is the closest thing to

[6] Strategies have been replaced by processes in this quality planning sequence. This reflects the successful practice of guiding managers and employees toward development of their own strategies, focused on the vision and goals of the organization, via strategic processes, as seen at many Quality Council member companies.

a common ground in the area of planning, and therefore seems especially worthy of our attention. A focused planning effort, informed by this underlying vision, is likely to succeed regardless of the details of its pursuit. The inverse is even more likely to be true—any quality plan, whether by the book or not, has little chance of success without this underlying vision.

The Starting Point: Quality Vision and Principles

Vision and principles—this is where a quality plan must start. And the vision must start with senior management and end with everyone—all the employees, suppliers, and even the external customers need to understand the company's mission and be included in some way in its fulfillment. So right away it is obvious that a quality plan differs from a conventional strategic plan. The traditional approach to planning often segregated the planning activities in a specialized department and produced a confidential document. Senior management did not write it, although they had to approve it. And most of the company never saw it. Even where this mold has already been broken, it is common to find mission statements as dusty as last decade's financials and uncommon to find any agreement, let alone conviction, over what the company's real purpose is.

In contrast, successful quality programs are often based on a set of principles that is drafted directly by senior management, typically in a team effort, and the principles are disseminated widely. To be disseminated widely, they need to be relevant and valid. A hollow commitment to quality in principle, not followed through in every aspect of management, will produce just one more framed mission statement for the bathroom wall. So senior management needs to dig deep into what makes quality work and needs to think hard about the practicalities of implementing it before drafting anything. A management learning process is necessary first, and in fact the effort to develop a quality vision for the company, and a new statement of principles that express it, is an excellent vehicle for management learning. Companies often bring in outsiders, both consultants and the managers of companies with existing quality programs, for help at this stage. But it does not work to adopt Deming's principles, or Juran's principles, or Crosby's principles of quality, or even Xerox's, Corning's, or HP's—this is where the managers need to define *their* company's individual approach to quality.

With this in mind, let's look at how different companies have tackled the vision statement. While each has its own approach and emphasis, there are some strong common themes as well.

MAYTAG'S APPROACH: GO ON THE OFFENSIVE

Maytag's vision of quality is considerably deeper than the lonely repairman ads might indicate. As chairman and CEO Daniel J. Krumm puts it, "Good advertisement is fine, but all the lonely repairman ads in the world will not sell a poorly made product."[7] At Maytag, the quality effort is described as a move from "a defensive to an offensive position," again according to Krumm, who believes that about a quarter of the typical factory's costs are associated with finding and fixing mistakes. This is a costly approach, and it is from this approach that the idea of a tradeoff between cost and quality arose. To catch more mistakes, you have to spend more time and money on quality control. In contrast, the offensive approach builds quality into products and processes by design, and in general cost goes down, instead of up, as quality is improved via offensive work. As Daniel Krumm puts it, "Taking the offensive

[7]Conference Board Research Report No. 937.

posture with quality means providing a continual, upfront, company-wide commitment from the design phase to purchasing, and from manufacturing to servicing."[8]

Note that this is not a set of principles or a formal statement of purpose. It is an image—offensive to defensive—and a statement of vision from the most senior manager in the company. It is an essential vision, without which Maytag's formal principles of quality cannot function. It seems very simple, and it is. Yet it is a critical conceptual underpinning for *any* quality program, not just Maytag's. Some companies express the idea with different imagery, as we will see when we review other statements of principles. But in some way, shape, or form, each company must make a distinct turnaround, from the old ways in which quality is viewed "as a minimum standard to be met in the manufacturing process," as Krumm puts it, to a new vision of quality in which it is built into products and processes through design, procurement, production and all the other functions of the firm. When this happens, quality suddenly goes from being a cost center to a profit center, and quality guru Philip Crosby's famous adage that quality is free[9] suddenly begins to make sense.

That is the vision underlying Maytag's quality principles, and indeed the fundamental vision with which any successful quality program must start. Here are Maytag's principles, with explanatory commentary from CEO Krumm:

1. **Keep it simple.** If you took off the front of a Maytag washer, for example, you would be astounded at how

---

[8]This and the following quoted remarks from a Conference Board presentation by Daniel J. Krumm, highlights of which are presented in Research Report No. 937, pp. 51–54.

[9]Crosby argued in his book, *Quality is Free* (McGraw-Hill, 1979) that "Quality is free. It's not a gift, but it is free. What costs money are the unquality things—all the actions that involve not doing jobs right the first time . . . If you concentrate on making quality certain, you can probably increase your profit by an amount equal to 5 to 10 percent of your sales. That is a lot of money for free." This argument and Crosby's book catalyzed quite a few of the early U.S. quality efforts (although it is now clear that the cost of poor quality is close to 20 or 30 percent rather than 5 or 10 percent).

simple the machine is and how few components there are. The concept of design simplicity contributes a great deal to the overall dependability of our final product. The fewer parts there are, the fewer parts there are to malfunction.

2. **Respect and listen to your people.** We use the team approach in making quality products. This is the area with the greatest need for improvement in American business . . . Americans are realizing that the minds of workers are just as important as their hands.

3. **Hire only the best workers possible and actively involve them in the manufacturing and decision-making process of your products.** It is common at Maytag to see two and three generations of one family on our production lines. We believe we have as skilled and highly motivated a workforce as any that exists in U.S. manufacturing. We aim to keep it that way.

4. **Manufacture your own component parts.** This ensures product quality and keeps costs in line. But whether you manufacture or buy, the point is that excellent component parts and material play a vital role in the quality of the finished product.

5. **Effective capital spending is critical to achieving and maintaining quality.** Appliance manufacturing is always entering new eras, and wise capital investment is paramount to keeping a company's quality product at the forefront of a changing marketplace.

6. **Use common sense.** Our whole business is based on whether or not our customers feel we have succeeded or failed. We know that our only real business is continuing consumer satisfaction. One-time buyers contribute to short-term gains; repeat buyers generate long-term success. Too many American corporations have forgotten this simple rule.

These principles are not as abstract as many that one sees in more traditional company mission statements. They get down to specifics right away. They link capital budgeting with quality, specify a number of policies concerning employee hiring and treatment, define a conceptual approach to product design, and specify a make-rather-than-buy components policy. They help the company see how to realize the offensive approach to quality visualized by its senior managers. This is a hallmark of many successful quality programs: principles that go the distance, providing not only inspiration but also clear signposts to help apply that inspiration in actual practice.

FORD'S CONCEPT:
CUSTOMER-DEFINED VALUE

Like Maytag, Ford needed to make a clean break with the traditional approach to quality control in manufacturing. James Bakken, Ford's Vice President of Corporate Quality during the development of its quality program, explains; "The inspection departments of the auto companies were staffed by receiving inspectors, production inspectors, gauge and layout inspectors, and chief inspectors," an impressive defensive line-up, but nothing like the offensive approach Ford, like Maytag, is now implementing.

Also reflecting the manufacturing tradition, little attention was paid to variation in component parts. Reducing variation is a strong central theme of all quality programs, but Bakken argues that it was traditionally overlooked in U.S. industry. "Looking back at the U.S. and European industrial revolutions, we see the profound effect of producing interchangeable parts. It was a keystone to mass production. Once the industrial revolution got underway in Europe and America, it was propelled by rapidly changing technology and resulted in major productivity improvements. But these productivity increases were almost assured by the expanding economies of scale. Once these dramatic increases came about, there was no reason to challenge whether interchangeable parts were really identical. Subtle part-to-part variation, which can have significant influence on system quality, was neither observed nor understood."[10]

Thus Ford's quality vision is founded on these two themes; prevention rather than detection of errors, and reduction of variability in parts. It also picked up three more fundamental elements in recent years: that quality must be defined in *customer* terms, that *continuous* quality improvement is required, and that continuous improvement required a change in Ford's organizational *culture*. Here is Bakken on these three topics:

> A major milestone in Ford's changing quality culture took place in the late 1970s when the chairman addressed the quality control managers worldwide. He said, "From this day forward quality in its broadest context will be the number one priority in the Ford Motor Company." This led to some introspection about our definition of quality . . . It was clear that we did not define, or recognize the need to define, quality in customer terms. We saw it in terms understandable only to ourselves. The product being generated was either accepted or rejected. Quality was achieved when products were made within engineering design tolerances and specifications. All products within specifications and tolerances were quality products and those that did not meet specifications were subject to repair, rework, or scrap.
> Born from this reassessment, a new philosophy was established called Ford Total Quality Excellence. This policy focuses on continuously improving customer quality by providing products and services that meet customers' needs and expectations throughout their lives at costs that represent value.

To implement this new concept, "customer quality" as it is termed at Ford, requires a commitment to moving standards, not the static standards of the old, defensive tolerances and specifications. *Customer* standards are never static, at least not as long as there is a global competition to come up with

[10]Remarks by James K. Bakken are reported in Conference Board Report No. 937, pp. 15–18.

newer and better ways of pleasing the customer. The customer-defined value in Ford's new definition of quality is constantly moving. What was a good value a few years ago might now be viewed as too little quality for too high a price. In fact, that is the real significance of innovation—it moves the customer's value curve[11] outward, either by increasing quality, reducing cost, or doing both at once.

James Bakken explains the idea of continuous improvement and its relationship to Ford's culture and mission:

> We feel total quality means realizing that the only way to ultimately satisfy customers is to have everyone continuously improve processes and systems, and to make suppliers and dealers partners in our movement . . . Continuously improving quality systems requires more than learning about quality tools and methods. It requires a change in the culture of the organization . . . A changed quality culture has not been instituted or installed at Ford; it has simply evolved from defect detection to defect prevention and finally to continuous improvement . . . To be truly effective we needed to change the culture of the enterprise—in Ford's case, from rugged individualism and functional autonomy to a quality culture based on people working together in the pursuit of continuous improvement of product and services.

And, as Bakken concludes, "This can only be brought about by a management that establishes an environment in which all employees work to create, nurture, and sustain change." Thus Ford's guiding principles not only reflect management's underlying vision of quality, as elaborated above, but also focus sharply on some of the key elements of this new culture. The

[11]A value curve represents the various combinations of price and quality that consumers find to be of equal value. It is drawn on a graph in which cost rises on the vertical axis and quality rises along the horizontal axis. An upward-sloping line on this chart links low-cost, low-quality alternatives on the lower left with high cost and quality alternatives on the upper right. To compete at all, a company must be on the line. But to win, or gain share, a company must place its product or service *to the right of the current line*—which redefines customer expectations and makes the value curve jump outward to bisect the new point.

culture serves customers, collaborates with suppliers and dealers, involves employees beyond their traditionally narrow functions, and does not allow compromise in the pursuit of quality. Here are Ford's principles.

1. Quality is our number one priority.

2. Customers are the focus of everything we do.

3. Continuous improvement is essential to our success.

4. Suppliers and dealers are our partners.

5. Integrity is never compromised.

As with Maytag, Ford's principles are deceptively simple. Five short sentences. But once one sees how they flow from Ford's supporting vision, and understands the need to move Ford from a traditional manufacturing culture to a new culture dedicated to adding value for customers, they become three-dimensional.

As with Maytag, Ford's principles translate fairly easily into concrete programs and actions. For example, statements like "employee involvement is our way of life" and "suppliers and dealers are our partners" are clear signposts when it comes to dealing with employees, suppliers and dealers. Certain policies and actions will be consistent with these principles, and others will not. In many cases Ford's traditional policies and practices are *not* consistent with the principles, and have had to be replaced. The quality process usually leaves a trail of discarded policy manuals in its wake.

PUTTING FORD'S PRINCIPLES TO WORK

Several years ago Ford's Casting Division undertook a major study of quality in its casting operations. This hands-on quality effort flows directly from the quality vision and principles defined by the corporate headquarters, and it is interesting to see the principles in action in this case. Thomas P. Enright, Manager of the Quality Control Office of the Casting Division, explains:

> A primary indicator of quality at the Casting Division is first-time capability, or FTC—the percent of our castings or forgings that are processed through our customer plants without rejection or rework. It is the goal of all production casters and forgers to attain consistent 100 percent FTC levels on all products they supply to their customers.[12]

Where does a goal like this come from? It is obviously not a typical "defensive" quality goal. Nor is FTC a traditional defensive measure, since it is designed to measure quality based on whether the product can be used *by the customer* the first time around—the customer in this case being Ford's automobile plants. The standard approach would have been to establish an arbitrary acceptable defect rate and inspect sufficiently to achieve it. But the FTC measure makes this approach impossible, since anything less than 100 percent FTC means customer plants are running into quality problems with the Casting Division's products. The goal obviously flows from the basic vision that says quality must be defined by the customer, and from the principle, the third in Ford's list, that says "continuous improvement is essential to our success."

The Casting Division had raised its FTC rate from 92.3 percent in 1982 to 98.8 percent in the beginning of 1987, which Thomas Enright terms "excellent by industry standards." But the principle that "continuous improvement is essential to our success" suggests that "excellent by industry standards" is not good enough. One can assume industry standards will improve, and it is better to lead the trend than follow it. But going beyond defect rates as low as 1.2 percent required a new approach to problem-solving in the Casting

---

[12]Thomas Enright's remarks are reported in Conference Board Research Report No. 909, pp. 70–74.

Division. As Enright explains, "In the past, we used the traditional detection method of controlling quality with 100 percent inspection—sorting the "OKs" from the "not-OKs" for scrap or rework. This after-the-fact detection system was both too costly and too late for effective process control. So achieving the 100 FTC goal by inspecting every casting is out of the question for cost reasons. Instead, the Casting Division now focuses its effort on understanding where the unwanted variations come from, and modifying the production process to eliminate these root causes. Enright explains:

> We have replaced our traditional method of problem solving with the experimental design technique developed in the 1920s by an English mathematician, R. A. Fisher, and adapted and introduced in the Japanese automotive industry in the 1960s. We adopted this technique in 1984, and it has been very valuable in resolving chronic problems that had eluded our efforts. Whereas the traditional problem-solving techniques usually allow for the evaluation of only one characteristic at a time, experimental design provides for the full evaluation of all major process variables and their interaction, which is very important in the casting process. Over 100 experimental design studies have been completed throughout the division, and we have achieved major quality improvements in every case.
>
> In December 1986, we decided to apply experimental design thinking to FTC . . . Initially, we worked on the problem using the standard "one-at-a-time experimentation" approach to determine root cause. For example, a process variable such as the temperature of the molten metal was adjusted based on past experience, with the results then evaluated and applied. Using this method, our FTC increased to 99.4 percent by year end.
>
> That was quite good. However, as metal casting processes have a wide variety of process variables, we found this problem-solving method slow. So, in December 1986, we applied experimental design to the problem and involved all persons in the plant who could provide input for the experiment. These were the steps:[13]

---

[13]Details of each step available in Conference Board Report No. 909, pp. 73–74.

1. **Brainstorming.**
2. **Designing the experiment.**
3. **Organizing [running] the experiment.**
4. **Determining the "best" operating pattern.**
5. **Confirming the results of the experiment.**

The following week we completed the necessary revisions to the casting models and arranged our processes to accommodate our new operating parameters, which were based on the experiment's results. Our performance for the balance of 1987 showed an increase in FTC to a consistent level of just under 100 percent—a quantum improvement in performance by the plant team.

The principles at work in the Casting Division's efforts are a good example of continuous improvement aimed at giving greater value to customers. The Casting Division followed its own well-defined quality process in pursuit of continuous improvement, and this process derives from Ford's vision and principles. The quality process is defined at the Casting Division as follows:

- Focuses on customer requirements and continuous improvement for all products and services.

- Involves the entire workforce in team-oriented improvement efforts.

- Uses problem solving and statistical techniques.

- Measures progress made in each area against a baseline.

- Works toward the overall vision of the division.

These are a sort of working person's version of Ford's principles, the majority of them specifying what tools and techniques will be used to achieve the continuous improvement which Ford's over-arching principles demand. The Casting Division uses these tools in the case described above—problem-solving techniques, base-line measures, and teams—

to apply the vision and principles via continuous improvement for the customer. The principles really do translate into coordinated, planned improvements, even far from corporate headquarters, and that is a triumph of planning.

CORNING'S "SHORT LIST" OF QUALITY VALUES

Corning defines four guiding principles upon which its quality program is based. You might call this the "short list" of quality values. For some reason, Corning has managed to define its vision of quality in extremely simple terms. Corning's principles are common to virtually every statement of vision, and are perhaps the closest thing to a formal definition of what constitutes a quality program. You aren't doing quality, in the new sense of the word, unless you incorporate these core concepts into the process in some manner:

I. Meet the Customer's Requirements

First, **understand** and **agree** on the requirements; then meet them. People often confuse beauty, price, or luxury with quality. For example, a Steuben vase meets the requirement for a memorable gift, while a Pyrex beaker meets the requirements for an experiment in a science lab. The vase is costly. The beaker is not. Yet each is a quality item; each meets the requirements.

II. Error-Free Work

This defines the standard for meeting the requirements; the first time, every time. It does not mean that errors will not happen. It does mean **an attitude that errors are not acceptable**. There's no more "Acceptable Quality Level" with its allowable percentage of defects. This new attitude leads to asking "why?" when an error occurs, tracking down the root cause and taking action to keep it from happening again.

III. Manage by Prevention

Quality must be built into the work. It cannot be "inspected in," "improvised in," or "repaired in." This means anticipating problems, and making permanent changes to prevent errors. The more emphasis that is placed on preventing errors, the more often the customer's requirements will be met the first time, every time.

IV. Measure by the Cost of Quality

The cost of quality is made up of three parts: error cost, detection cost, and prevention cost. Error cost includes the cost of doing work over. Detection cost is the cost of inspecting for errors. Prevention cost is the cost of building quality into the work. The goal is to cut the cost of quality by reducing error and detection costs. Measuring by the cost of quality accomplishes three things: it focuses people's attention on problems; it helps to set priorities for error correction; and it marks progress toward eliminating problems.[14]

The emphasis on meeting customer requirements is a constant, and critical, theme in quality improvement efforts. The idea of error-free work, or building quality into the design and the production process, is also a constant theme. That this involves tracking down root causes of problems, rather than assigning causality to the individual who is immediately responsible, is not always clearly articulated—but this principle is also of primary importance. Similarly, Corning's emphasis on measuring the cost of quality is not always paralleled in other company's statements of principle, but it is a critical element of successful quality programs nonetheless.

MARS INCORPORATED:
THE CONSUMER IS BOSS

Mars' mission statement defines five principles: Quality, Responsibility, Mutuality, Efficiency, and Freedom. Because I just promised a succinct presentation, I will not reproduce the

[14]Conference Board Report No. 239, p. 6.

statement in its entirety, but it is important to reproduce the explanation of the first, and most relevant principle, Quality[15].

The consumer is our boss, quality is our work and value for money is our goal.   Mars began to prosper in the depths of a depression, thrived against strong competition and grew to its present size all as the result of countless purchases made each year by the consumers of our products. These purchases are typically among the smallest monetary decisions a consumer ever makes, yet their cumulative impact has paid our wages, built our plants and fueled our growth. Why has this happened? How are we to continue this success?[16]

The consumer is our boss.   First, we must remember that we cannot influence millions of consumer choices until we have convinced first one, then a second and a third consumer that our product is worthy of purchase. Each individual sale must be regarded as our most important sale. Without an understanding of this truth, we could grow content with our past and ignore our future.

Second, we must regard the consumer as our boss; the consumer's needs and desires are the reasons why our product is chosen or rejected. By every means available, we must seek to discover what these needs are, so that we can shape our products to satisfy them.

Quality products with unique benefits.   Our experience has proven that there are certain things consumers will always prefer. Quality products, perceived as having fine in-

---

[15]Andrew Campbell and Sally Young, *Do You Need a Mission Statement?* The Economist Publications, Management Guides, July 1990, pp. 110–111. Mars' mission statement is wonderful, and I recommend it for background reading if you are composing one yourself. If you cannot obtain this publication, try contacting the company directly (in McLean, Virginia), but don't tell them I sent you!

[16]I am really taken by this paragraph. Think about the value of focusing your company's attention on the *purchase transaction* and why it occurs—or doesn't. Also, note the use of questions, the only ones I have ever seen in a mission statement. This mission statement is intended to make readers think.

gredients and consistently meeting standards of excellence, will attract consumers, confirm their right decision, and attract them again. Others also claim quality, but we believe few will match our commitment not to compromise or offer the consumer less than our best.

However, in our competitive markets even a product of superior quality must still satisfy specific consumer wants. For this reason, we strive to create products with unique benefits—a combination of characteristics that will make our product distinctive, preferred and the better alternative—and thereby capture the consumer's attention.

Value for money. To our belief in quality must be added the challenge of achieving value for money. The consumer will weigh value for money—the balance between our product's perceived benefits and its price, relative to all other choices. When we combine the best quality with the best value, we will be able to offer consumers the best buy.

Federal Express: "People-Service-Profit"

Mars' statement gives readers insight into the nature of the business and the importance of each individual customer transaction. In contrast, Federal Express's mission statement is more about how to run the company's operations than how to understand them. To fully appreciate this mission statement, you must understand what is meant by the "People-Service-Profit philosophy" it mentions, and it will be helpful to start with Federal Express's definition of it.

People/Service/Profit: Our Corporate Philosophy

Our company always balances the needs of employees, our customers, and our shareholders, considering each in making plans or policies. We always consider the effects on our people first in making decisions, recognizing that if we take care of our employees, they will deliver a superior service which our customer will, in turn, utilize. Only by making a surplus or profit we can ensure our Company's continued existence, future opportunities, and our employment.

Our Mission Statement

Federal Express is committed to our People-Service-Profit philosophy. We will produce outstanding financial returns by providing totally reliable, competitively superior global air-ground transportation of high priority goods and documents that require rapid, time-certain delivery. Equally important, positive control of each package will be maintained, utilizing real time electronic tracking and tracing systems. A complete record of each shipment and delivery will be presented with our request for payment. We will be helpful, courteous, and professional to each other and the public. We will strive to have a satisfied customer at the end of each transaction.

Hoechst Celanese: Mixing the Old with the New

Conference Board member Hoechst Celanese Corp. traces its origins to the November 1986 sale of Celanese Corp. to the West German (now German) company, Hoechst A. G. Arthur Nichols, the first director of quality management for the combined entity, reports that "Nothing has been the same since. Aside from combining two unpronounceable names into one impossible mouthful, it was—and is—a good deal for all parties."[17] The synergies between these two chemical companies have led to significant growth in U.S. markets, but in one respect the two were quite incompatible. As Nichols explains, "At Celanese, quality was a total mind-set translated into action by means of processes we developed and applied to make the

[17]Conference Board Research Report No. 909, pp. 9–13.

whole company run more smoothly and efficiently. We saw quality as a way of doing business, conducting relationships, dealing with customers, and practicing management." In contrast, Hoechst's quality philosophy "was quite different. In Hoechst, with some exceptions, quality was not viewed as a cultural issue requiring top management leadership and participation." And, while "Hoechst had good, traditional, product-oriented quality programs operated by Quality Control and Quality Assurance staff," the total quality concept had not really taken root. The two organizations represented the old and new management, and they had to be combined into one and given one all-encompassing vision. The problems this entailed will be touched upon later, but for now it is interesting to note that, in this clash of old and new management paradigms, the new triumphed. Although Hoechst was an order of magnitude larger than Celanese, the quality vision and values of Celanese Corp. are now transforming the larger company as well. Here is the latest statement of this vision from Hoechst Celanese,[18] as presented at a recent Conference Board conference on quality:

Quality Policy

Quality leadership is vital
to the long-term success of Hoechst Celanese
in an increasingly competitive marketplace.

Building quality into our
workplace, products and services is
essential to a successful future
for our customers, employees, suppliers,
communities and shareholders.

Hoechst Celanese will work with customers
to provide products and services
that always meet or exceed their expectations.

[18]From Conference Board Quality Program files.

*Management will commit the resources
and create an environment in which each employee
can contribute skills, talents and ideas
to a never-ending process of improvement and
innovation in all aspects of our business.*

HEWLETT-PACKARD CO.:
RETURN TO ROOTS

HP is unusual in that its principles predate its quality program, and have not changed significantly with the introduction of full-scale quality improvement. Apparently it is not always necessary to overthrow the old values with new ones—sometimes a reinterpretation or return to roots is possible. As John Young of HP explains, "The principles of the HP way are still the basis for how we operate." Here are HP's organizational values as they appear in the company's mission statement:[19]

We have trust and respect for individuals. We approach each situation with the understanding that people want to do a good job and will do so, given the proper tools and support. We attract highly capable, innovative people and recognize their efforts and contributions to the company. HP people contribute enthusiastically and share in the success that they make possible.

We focus on a high level of achievement and contribution. Our customers expect HP to be of the highest quality and to provide lasting value. To achieve this, all HP people, but especially managers, must be leaders who generate enthusiasm and respond with extra effort to meet customer needs. Techniques and management practices which are effective today may be outdated in the future. For us to remain at the forefront in all our activities, people should always be looking for new and better ways to do work.

[19]Andrew Campbell and Sally Young, *Do You Need a Mission Statement?* The Economist Publications, Management Guides, July 1990, p. 93.

We conduct our business with uncompromising integrity. We expect HP people to be open and honest in their dealings to earn the trust and loyalty of others. People at every level are expected to adhere to the highest standards of business ethics and must understand that anything less is totally unacceptable. As a practical matter, ethical conduct cannot be assured by written HP policies and codes; it must be an integral part of the organization, a deeply ingrained tradition that is passed from one generation of employees to another.

We achieve our common objectives through teamwork. We recognize that it is only through effective cooperation within and among organizations that we can achieve our goals. Our commitment is to work as a worldwide team to fulfill the expectations of our customers, shareholders and others who depend upon us. The benefits and obligations of doing business are shared among all HP people.

We encourage flexibility and innovation. We create a work environment which supports the diversity of our people and their ideas. We strive for overall objectives which are clearly stated and agreed upon, and allow people flexibility in working toward goals in ways which they help determine are best for the organization. HP people should personally accept responsibility and be encouraged to upgrade their skills and capabilities through ongoing training and development. This is especially important in a technical business where the rate of progress is rapid and where people are expected to adapt to change.

Union Pacific Railroad Company: The "Chain" Image

W. Kent Sterett served as Union Pacific's vice president-quality (he is now EVP, Distribution Systems—Quality, Southern Pacific) and he introduces the company's principles with a little history: "In the 1970s, rail earned a significant percent of traffic revenues for freight transportation in the United States. A decade later, the competitive issues had changed and the rail industry was rapidly losing market share. To address this continuing issue, Mike Walsh, the chairman of Union Pacific, has stated that our fundamental business strategy is "understanding and meeting customer needs on time and in a quality manner."[20] This is the underlying vision upon which Union Pacific's principles are based, and it bears noting that they entail an about-face for the company. As Sterett puts it, "When we talk about meeting the needs of a customer at an individual location, we are discussing a fundamental shift in the rail industry's operations." Here are the principles that Union Pacific is following in its effort to make this fundamental shift.

1. We focus on external and internal customers. We focus on internal customers because there is a series of processes that add up to meeting the external customers' needs; this chain is only as good as its weakest link.

2. We meet or exceed the customer's expectations. For example, when a customer phones the customer service center, the call is answered within three rings; the customer's history with us is available immediately to the representative.

3. We are committed to continuous improvement in everything we do. To move rapidly, the entire company—accounting, line operations, marketing—must share this commitment since all areas together add up to the service and quality of products we provide.

4. We manage by objective measures. Data must be available to determine where the improvement opportunities are, where the focus should be, and where the high-leverage items are.

[20] Based on remarks at The Conference Board's Third Annual Quality Conference, April 2–3, 1990, Grand Hyatt, New York.

5. We involve our employees, customers, and suppliers in our teams. Because over one-third of our money is spent through suppliers, they have a great deal to do with the quality of our outputs. Our employees are the channel through which we provide quality. We cannot decide what our customers want; they must be involved.

The image of a 'chain that is only as strong as its weakest link' is a powerful way to visualize the relationship of internal to external customers. Many companies place high value on the principle that internal customers are as important as external customers, but it can be difficult to see why this is so. Union Pacific's principles start with this "chain" image and the idea that the company performs a sequence of services, starting with services to internal customers and culminating in the services for which external customers pay. This makes clear the contribution of every process and task to customer quality, much as does the "value-added" concept from Federal Express.

IBM: EVOLVING VISION

The vision of the various companies that have pioneered the U.S. quality movement is not static. One might think that ringing statements such as those appearing above would provide sufficient inspiration for many years of quality improvement. While that is true to some extent, it is also true that companies tend to refine and strengthen their vision as they go along. The quality improvement process is a learning process, and learning drives change throughout the organization, even in an area as seminal as the organization's vision and principles. IBM illustrates this point best. Its official position is that "the dedication to quality at IBM began in the earliest days of the corporation," as a spokesperson from the company's Corporate Information office puts it. But nonetheless, IBM's management systems and approach were also rooted in the traditions of business management, and the company has gone through as dramatic changes as any along the path toward winning a Baldrige in 1990 (awarded to IBM Rochester). When IBM began its formal quality improvement program in the 1980s, it focused heavily on process improvement, and in fact pioneered a number of valuable techniques that we will look at in the chapter on this topic. However, it initially considered customer service issues separately from its quality initiative, which was more oriented toward performance improvement through process management. But over time it became increasingly clear that the two initiatives were two sides of the same coin, and last year IBM merged the two and redefined its quality effort. As the spokesperson describes it, "IBM formally merged market-driven and quality into a single business strategy."[21] This entailed a restatement of the fundamental principles guiding IBM and its entire quality initiative. The new principles are:

- Make the customer the final arbiter

- Understand our markets

- Commit to leadership in the markets we choose to serve

- Execute with excellence across the enterprise

This evolution toward a stronger customer focus may also be occurring in the quality visions of other companies, and it certainly is no surprise to see it happening at IBM. Most managers learn from the quality process that "total customer satisfaction," as IBM chairman John Akers puts it, is the ultimate objective of every company. As this vision is explored more fully, some of the principles that seem primary at first come to be seen as secondary, supporting the primary goal of making the company more customer-driven. For example, at IBM now a number of the elements one sees in the principles

---

[21]These quotes from company press releases titled "Quality at IBM: A Perspective" and "Market-Driven Quality," provided to the author by Paul Bergevin, Corporate Media Relations, IBM, December 6, 1991.

of other companies have been "bumped" by the new principles above, and are now considered "initiatives" that describe how the company will put its new principles into practice. Here are the five initiatives IBM now pursues:

- Define the needs of the market

- Eliminate defects

- Reduce the total cycle time

- Increase employee participation

- Measure progress

These echo themes heard in most of the vision statements from companies with quality programs, yet by treating them, in an active voice, as specific initiatives the company will pursue, IBM has pushed them into the realm of specific strategies. This is a natural evolution, and in fact every statement of principles implies change in practices as well. Which raises a whole new set of implementation issues, some of them more difficult than any examined so far.

PUTTING TEETH INTO YOUR PLAN

These statements of vision and principle are inspiring, but inspiration alone will not transform a company. Every manager has a healthy serving of skepticism about such statements of principle, having seen a good many "best laid plans" go awry. It is easy to give lip service to quality through a statement of principles but it can be hard for a company to sink its teeth into the quality process. As Kent Sterett of Union Pacific observes, "Today, most companies are on the quality journey. We have all learned the techniques and tools of quality in our training courses. But the journey is not easy. Why is the implementation difficult? The answer is not in the techniques, tools, or principles. The answer lies in changing the culture so we can create change in the way a company operates and uses these tools and principles."[22] While changing a company's culture certainly takes a powerful new vision, it goes far beyond the inspirational vision statements we have reviewed above. Planning and management processes, and the organization that supports them, must be redesigned to support the new vision. That is the subject of Chapter 3.

[22] Ibid.

PLANNING
FOR QUALITY

I n most businesses, Quality was being done separately from business planning; they were not integrated. As a result, conflict sometimes occurred, and many customer-satisfaction issues were not addressed in business plans.

—Peter F. Volanakis, director, corporate
marketing, Corning, Inc.[1]

Q uality must be viewed as the all-encompassing process that
guides and drives the entire enterprise.

—Jeffrey S. Siebenaller, Director of Quality
Management, Chemical Group, Hoechst
Celanese Corp[2]

Jeffrey Siebenaller argues that quality is an all-encompassing
process, guiding the entire enterprise. "Vision—the heart,
mission—the head, and strategy—the hands, must come together as one. Quality, in effect, becomes part of the very

[1]From remarks by Perter F. Volanakis at The Conference Board's 1991 Marketing Conference, October 29–30, New York.
[2]From remarks by Jeffrey S. Siebenaller, Director of Quality Management,
Chemical Group, Hoechst Celanese Corp., at The Conference Board's 1990 Marketing
Conference, October 30–31, New York.

fabric by which business strategy or planning is woven, whether it be market planning, financial planning or capital planning. It applies to everything."[3] How is this accomplished? It is not always easy.

Too Much Hype, Not Enough Action

David George, an ex-quality director for Johnson Matthey, surveyed 20 quality program managers across Europe and reports that "Many felt there was too much hype, a lack of action, and a feeling that all the good news in the quality newsletters did not coincide with the perceptions of the individual employees." Furthermore, "There were too many meetings, too many committees disguised as teams, and not enough ownership by the businesses. Quality improvement teams were coming up with many trivial suggestions, and missing the crucial few that are really important."[4] At Johnson Matthey (the U.K. precious metals company), in a three-year effort to implement a quality vision and plan, "There had been some important improvements; however, the overall program was not having profound effects in the organization's profits."

This is a common complaint; witness the Conference Board survey described in Chapter 1 in which managers reported their companies are, on average, only halfway toward Baldrige quality levels in their programs. And the Ernst & Young study also discussed in Chapter 1 found that most U.S. companies have yet to adopt key quality practices in the areas of employee involvement, customer focus, and quality measurement. The vision quickly founders when it comes time to translate it into daily activities. David George of Johnson Matthey refers to this issue as, "Moving from 'conscious competence' to 'instinctive quality behavior.' "

George believes that it is essential to avoid creating a "quality bureaucracy." He argues that instinctive quality behav-

---

[3]Ibid.
[4]A summary of his remarks is available in Conference Board Report No. 958.

ior develops only when quality "becomes an attitude that permeates the whole organization, especially management, rather than a special activity supervised by a highly ranked quality director . . . quality should not be led by a non-line manager." At Johnson Matthey, the line managers now run the quality program, and "quality has returned to the sharp end of the business."

While other companies continue to centralize the quality management function under a single director of quality, all, at least all of our success models, do seem to agree that the line managers must be the ones to *implement* quality within their spans of control. A dual or matrix reporting process does not work as well because it can set up competing demands. The quality office pulls one way, the traditional line of command pulls the other, and usually the line managers win the tug of war. This is in part an organization issue, and the relationship between organizational structure and quality plans is an interesting and important one. But it is also very much a process issue. If senior management declares a new vision and set of principles, but fails to guide line managers in how to undertake the transformation that this vision requires, then line managers will be unable to implement this vision.

PLAN AS PROCESS:
LOOK AT THE BIG PICTURE

The case history from Ford's Casting Division hinted at the critical next step in planning and organizing for quality: the creation of a quality *process*. The concept of work as process is central to total quality programs. The view of business as made up of many interconnecting processes is critical to quality improvement, and stands in opposition to the conventional viewpoints. Normally managers see the company as composed of a series of black boxes, the inner workings of which are too obscure and small for managers to discern the details of the processes within these boxes. If the black box analogy seems farfetched, think of the standard organization chart and what it shows—boxes! The view from the front lines is different, but also fails to appreciate the processes. Normally workers fail to see the process at all, since their work focuses them so narrowly on just one disconnected function within a process. The views are either too distant or too close; nobody is in a position to see the details and understand how they fit in the big picture. Without this insight, it is impossible to roll up your sleeves and start experimenting and problem-solving in pursuit of continuous improvement in each system. Thus the process viewpoint is something that comes in with a quality program and is essential to its implementation.

More than that, the process approach seems essential even for a quality program's initiation. Planning is the process whereby people *implement* the plan, not just the process of creating it. This is especially true of quality programs, perhaps because the vision and principles represent such a break with the organization's past that no one would have any idea how to pursue them without some kind of a process to guide them. In fact, one reason that the development of specific strategies and tactics is pushed down into the organization in quality improvement processes may be that senior management often has no idea how to define specific problems and strategies. It usually takes intense digging and brainstorming by interdisciplinary groups of line managers and employees to pinpoint specific causes and effects and suggest specific improvements in line with management's goals. The days of simple prescriptive strategies like 'invest, harvest, or divest' are gone forever!

UNION PACIFIC: FOCUS ON THE CUSTOMER'S PRIORITIES

At Union Pacific, management has defined a total quality management system consisting of three elements: planning and control; employee involvement; and business processes. Kent Sterett explains:

The Union Pacific total quality management system is the vehicle for realizing our quality commitment. First is planning and
control. We begin with a strategic plan that states where we are
headed. Our goals and objectives are communicated through a
mission statement. Employee involvement—everyone from the
chairman to the worker on the track—is the second aspect. This
is how we will actually make the changes and achieve our plan.
The third aspect is the business processes we use to maintain
our gains. This is the way we do the work in our company.[5]

The first element of this system, planning and control,
sounds in this brief description much like any company's
planning process. However, the details of the planning process
are not ordinary at all. According to Sterett, "The chairman and
the entire top-officer staff meet one day each month to review
the monthly customer satisfaction survey and to discuss improvement projects." Out of this customer-oriented process
comes plans and controls that "direct the company's resources
and energies to critical issues." Then the company focuses its
improvement efforts on these critical issues using benchmarking against "the best—not just other railroads," and they "use
measurements to track our results." A simple example: customer surveys indicate that late deliveries are a major issue, so
the planning process has focused the company's energies on
improving on-time performance. In 1989 it was only 62 percent; it is now over 85 percent.

One of the distinctive features of Union Pacific's planning
process is its emphasis on focus. Management looks at the
company from the customer's perspective a dozen times every
year, focusing the efforts and resources of the organization on
the customer's highest priorities every time. The process
seems designed to prevent the organization from wandering
from the planners' goals or losing its new customer orientation. This focusing role seems to be important in other companies' processes as well, perhaps reflecting the complaints of

[5]Based on remarks at the Conference Board's Third Annual Quality Conference, April 2–3, 1990, Grand Hyatt, New York.

quality managers, as reported above by David George of Johnson Matthey, that their employees "were coming up with many trivial suggestions and missing the crucial few that are really important."

Chasing the Right Number of Rabbits at FPL

At Florida Power and Light, one of the three components of the quality improvement program is concerned mainly with this issue of focus:

1. **Policy deployment.** A management process to focus the company resources on a few high-priority issues in order to achieve breakthrough.

2. **Quality improvement teams.** To provide a structured environment to improve the quality of products and service, develop employee skills and enhance the quality of work life.

3. **Quality in daily work.** A process to systematically control and improve daily or repetitive work processes.[6]

Within this company, one often hears talk of "too many rabbits," in reference to the Japanese saying, "If you chase too many rabbits, you won't catch any." Focus is clearly a priority for FPL.

FPL's Quality Improvement Program (QIP) is in many ways a model when it comes to the processes used to create, implement, and manage quality plans. FPL was the first non-Japanese company to win the Deming Award, in 1989. Run by the Japanese Union of Scientists and Engineers, this prize is most commonly referred to as the Japanese version of the Baldrige Award, but it differs in its greater emphasis on pro-

[6]Conference Board Report No. 958.

cess. William Hensler, previously FPL's director of quality improvement and now with FPL's Qualtec Quality Services, says, "The award, unlike the Malcolm Baldrige National Quality Award, places more emphasis on the management process supporting total quality, rather than on the end results."[7] Perhaps this explains FPL's focus on process, but whatever the reason, this company's quality process is considered the best in the country by some of the other leading quality practitioners. Xerox, for example, used FPL to benchmark their QIP process against, and an executive from Hewlett-Packard once boasted the HP's quality improvement process was the *second* best in the country—next to FPL's.[8]

FPL's quality journey began in 1981, just two years after the Three Mile Island accident had attracted the nation's attention to quality issues at electric utilities. It reflected a recognition that, "The company's internal and external environments were changing faster than the organization could adapt and that corporate goals needed to be established and achieved using new management techniques."[9] FPL chairman Marshall McDonald puts it more colorfully:

> I made the observation that we had been looking at the horse from the wrong end, and it was not a pretty sight. We had been concerned with keeping rejects down, instead of quality up. We had been busy keeping imperfection under control, rather than trying for perfection. We had sometimes burnt the toast and then scraped it clear, instead of fixing the toaster. Some of us had even learned to like burnt toast.[10]

It started, quite modestly, with the introduction of Japan-inspired quality improvement teams (like many companies, FPL was struck by the quality circle craze of the early 1980s). However, as the company's own published history of its quali-

[7]No. 958, p. 27.
[8]Harvard Business School Case No. 9-689-041.
[9]*Summary Description of FPL's Quality Improvement Program*, FPL, p. 8.
[10]As quoted in Harvard Business School Case No. 9-689-041.

ty program puts it, "Management soon realized that QI teams alone would not achieve the results needed to change the company." In the mid-1980s FPL went on to create a full-blown quality improvement process, one that included but expanded greatly upon the quality improvement teams. It's three components, policy deployment, quality in daily work, and quality improvement teams, were mentioned briefly above. The QIP is best understood by looking in greater depth at its three components.

POLICY DEPLOYMENT: DECISION BY CONSENSUS

Policy Deployment "is a management process for achieving breakthroughs on major corporate problems and focuses on customer needs by deploying resources on a few, high priority issues," according to FPL's published documentation on the topic. What exactly does that mean? Policy Deployment is a cyclical process for setting long-term, short-term, and mid-term plans via a series of committees using consensus-based decision making. The FPL Management System diagram (Exhibit 3-1) shows how this is done. It starts, in the upper left corner, with an analysis of the environment and identification of customer needs—this involves survey research and other efforts to actually find out what the *customers* say their needs are. According to professor Christopher Hart of Harvard Business School, this analysis takes the form of a "problem diagnosis based on a new program of regular Executive Visitations to all areas of the company, a Presidential Review (ideas for improvement submitted by each manager—but developed through consensus among the manager's employees), and consumer surveys".[12] The results of this analysis feed directly into the executive committee's long-term plans. Long-term plans, plus the first draft of the annual business plan, provide

[11]*Summary Description of FPL's Quality Improvement Program*, FPL, pp. 12–20, in part.
[12]Harvard Business School Case No. 9-688-043, p. 7.

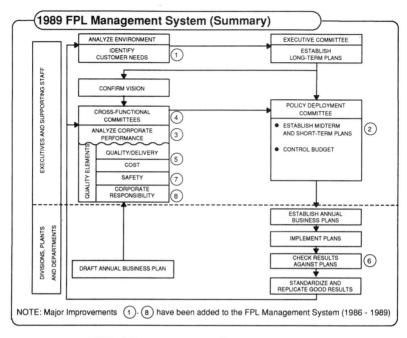

1989 FPL Management System (Summary)

NOTE: Major Improvements ①-⑧ have been added to the FPL Management System (1986 - 1989)

Exhibit 3-1 FPL Management System

the two inputs for a series of cross-functional committees that dig into the details of corporate performance, especially as regards the four quality elements, quality/delivery, cost, safety, and corporate responsibility. Senior management can no longer define the specific strategies that will accomplish corporate goals—the hands-on analysis of individual processes by the people who know them best is required. These committees perform this function for FP&L. The work of these cross-functional committees is turned over to a policy deployment committee (including executive representation) that establishes the mid-term and short-term goals for FPL. (The PD committee evolved out of the old budgeting committee, and still is responsible for budgeting.[13]) This process, shown in full above the dashed line in Exhibit 3-1, produces a firm set of

[13]Harvard Business School Case No. 9-688-043, p. 7.

customer-focused goals, ranging from long-term to short-term at the corporate level. It relies heavily on input from functional managers, not just senior management, in the translation of long-term goals into mid-term and short-term goals.

The resulting corporate plan provides the input for the divisions, plants, and departments as they establish and implement their annual business plans. This second phase of planning is a four-step process, rather than the traditional three steps of creating a plan, implementing it, and then reviewing performance next year when it comes time to rewrite it. The steps include two on-going, formal control processes, in which results are checked routinely against the plans, and then good results are standardized and *replicated*. Without conscious recognition of this latter step, no management process can consistently produce continuous improvement.

There are three emphases to the policy deployment process:

1. Establish policies focused on achieving customer satisfaction,

2. Develop consistent policies and targets, and

3. Strengthen review of implementation activities.[14]

These emphases reflect shortcomings of the traditional management process on which policy deployment was constructed. FPL's management processes have evolved gradually from a traditional top-down system to a quality-oriented system that incorporates customer and line-manager input. In fact, FPL's management systems continue to evolve; there have been significant changes with each planning cycle. For example, "In 1988 cross-functional committees were introduced to help the executives coordinate the major activities of the company from a corporate perspective."[15] Right now it is both a

[14]*Summary Description*, ibid., p. 12.
[15]Ibid., p. 12.

bottom-up and top-down planning process, with ideas for improvement coming from employees and customers, and support and long-range planning coming from the executive suite. Mechanisms exist to ensure extensive participation and to keep it focused both on customer perception and on factual analysis of problems:

> The PD process entailed setting short-term, mid-term, and long-term objectives, through consensus, at every level of the organization . . . By 1987, managers were allowed to select only a few areas for emphasis in the PD process. These areas were identified through a two-pronged research effort. Customer surveys were conducted by an outside market research firm. In addition, in-house surveys were administered to employees to ascertain their thoughts about the company's needs. Once this information was collected and tabulated, top management used it as an important source of input for setting the company's mid-term strategic agenda.
>
> Departments were expected to develop their QIP projects based on PD objectives. The company's mid-term plan of achieving customer satisfaction, for example, would be supported by a short-term plan to improve reliability and carried out at the departmental level by projects designed to reduce power outages . . .
>
> The PD Committee and the Executive Committee . . . drafted mid-term and short-term plans and presented them for review at a biannual Situation conference (Sitcon) that all managers and executives attended. After these goals were formalized, each department and division was asked to develop an action plan (the short-term plans and their associated projects) that spelled out the support these plans would receive. This process too was based on management by fact: comprehensive data collection, proposed performance improvements (including performance measures to be used), and schedules.

To the outsider this might seem like a lot of work. Is it worth the added effort to involve so many managers and employees in the planning process? Perhaps not, at least if the involvement is achieved by delegating work. This is the most common approach. Tasks like creating sales forecasts, writing endless reports for the senior executives, and the like tend to generate more heat than light when they are pushed down in the organization. However, in the FPL process, the *thinking* is pushed down along with the work. This seems to be the most outstanding feature of the planning process. The raw materials for thinking about improvement strategies are made available: data on customer attitudes and company performance; long-term plans and corporate mission. Dozens of managers must wrestle these raw materials into a consensus of practical, focused proposals using formal analytical methods. It contradicts the traditions of strategic planning—and it works.

QUALITY IN DAILY WORK

The second component of FPL's QIP process is known as quality in daily or repetitive work, and bears the tongue-tieing acronym QIDW. McDonald, FPL's chairman, set out in establishing the quality program "to create dissatisfaction with the status quo, to recognize that there is always a better way of doing things," and he observes that, "this means we must encourage continuous improvement in every job."[16] Before QIDW was introduced in 1987, a variety of other techniques were tried, but they were essentially top-down in character. According to company documents, "the primary methods for standardizing and replicating activities were through corporate and local procedures and on-the-job training." However, "as FPL focused on meeting its customers' needs, the need to identify out of control situations and more frequently monitor improvement efforts became apparent."[17] In other words, the old systems did not work—they failed to follow through with PD initiatives at the level of the individual job.

According to FPL training material, QIDW's characteristics are that it:

---

[16]Harvard Business School Case No. 9-688-043, p. 7.
[17]*Summary Description*, ibid., p. 16.

1. Focuses on managers' and supervisors' key accountabilities.

2. Develops control systems for the "Top Priority Jobs."

3. Provides control systems to standardize, replicate and improve daily operations.

4. Focuses on the customers' needs.

5. Identifies areas for the development of computer systems that free many line employees from repetitive tasks.

One of the major initiatives has been to create software systems that help employees do routine, repetitive work. A Trouble Call Management System (TCMS) now analyzes a half-million calls from customers every year, determines the location of the service interruption, and helps employees in responding to the problems by creating and prioritizing "trouble tickets" for the dispatchers, providing analysis to support repair efforts, and tracking all activities from the initial reports on through restoration of service. A great many repetitive tasks, and sources of errors and delays, were eliminated or redesigned with the introduction of this system.[18] However, not all the QIDW efforts are on this large a scale. Professor Livingston reports that "Some QIDW projects were . . . simpler. One secretary, for instance, followed the process in analyzing her job. She easily identified both her customer (her boss) and her top-priority job (typing his letters accurately). She tracked and graphed her error rate in typing documents and identified the root causes of the errors (documents that had to be retyped). One root cause was her boss's poor handwriting. By identifying this problem and conveying it to her customer, she cut her error rate significantly."[19] This sounds like a trivial example. What secretary wouldn't tell her boss that his handwriting was too messy to read? However, in

[18]Summary Description, ibid., p. 17.
[19]Harvard Business School Case No. 9-688-043.

many, perhaps most, traditional corporate cultures, this kind of analysis and communication does *not* take place naturally. It takes a formal process, supported by training and subscribed to by management, for individual employees to step forward with their suggestions—or even to turn their complaints into constructive suggestions in the first place.

The "process" referred to in the secretary's story is a self-administered quality improvement process, one that boils down the entire QIP effort to its skeleton so that it may be applied by the individual to his or her own job. It encapsulates many of the important points about quality processes in a simple, robust form that other companies may find equally applicable.

Although this process was created midway through FPL's quality program, it has much to recommend it as a starting point for other programs. It implements the core process at the simplest level: the individual or department. The use of this QIDW process to diagnose, analyze, and eliminate causes of problems at the individual and department levels is the basic building block upon which an entire company's quality improvement process can be built. When quality improvement processes are developed at the firm level (such as the management and planning process described above), they still follow this basic flowchart, only with additional bells and whistles. Any quality improvement process must have, as a bare minimum, these core components:

- Identifying top priority tasks or problems

- Identifying the customers

- Measuring process from customer's perspective

- Creating limits and controls

- Implementing controls

- Checking, standardizing, and improving controls

EXHIBIT 3-2 QUALITY-IN-DAILY-WORK PROCESS

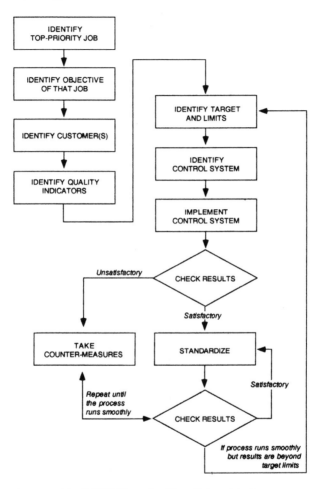

(This version copyright © 1992 Alexander Hiam & Associates)

These are what the QIDW process does, and the use of it on simple one-person or localized work processes is a wonderful way to teach employees how to use quality tools. QIDW helps make the use of quality tools automatic instead of conscious.

FPL's TEAMS: BUILDING EMPLOYEE INVOLVEMENT

One clear indicator of whether a company is striving for mediocrity (to use Robert Bruno's phrase) is the level of employee participation. In general, one can count on the majority of employees showing up and performing their work with sufficient care to earn their salaries and an occasional bonus. So when participation is used in reference to quality programs, it does not refer to participation in the ongoing, routine work of the company. It refers to participation in the learning and improvement of the company's operations. In our traditional management paradigm, employees perform the tasks assigned, but do not participate in the design of those tasks. This lack of participation in task design closes off the main avenue for learning (both personal and organizational) and for improving the ways in which tasks are performed. If only management can redesign tasks and processes, then management, with its inevitably limited understanding of all the complex tasks and processes in the firm, becomes the main bottleneck to change and improvement.

This failure to participate is not the fault of employees, even though it often seems that way to management. How many times have you heard managers complain that employees won't participate in a new program, or don't come forward with ideas and suggestions? Managers want employees to participate in positive change, but don't always know how to make it happen. So one could say that it is management's fault, but this misses the point as well. Traditional management systems actively discourage participation, making it dangerous in many cases, or at best just plain unrewarding, for employees to participate actively in organizational change. This is probably the key reason why organizations themselves seem to have so much trouble changing in response to environmental challenges and opportunities, and it is a point to which we will return in the chapter on participation.

Like GTE, FPL can point to a considerable history of mediocrity in areas like participation.

> Before the introduction of QI teams, FPL's employees were not systematically involved in the incremental improvement of their work functions. Teams were used before this time, but they consisted of only a few exempt personnel working on priority problems and issues and did not use systematic methods or statistical tools to solve problems. An employee suggestion program existed, but only about two percent of employees participated.[20]

Two percent! That's not participation. However, it is typical of companies without quality improvement processes. Since the suggestion program was redesigned, participation has skyrocketed. For example, in 1987, about 600 suggestions were received, and less than half were implemented. In 1988, with a new program in place, the number jumped to about 8,500, and now tens of thousands of suggestions are received each year. The main differences are that the new program makes it far simpler to submit suggestions, reduces the time and complexity of evaluation by decentralizing it, and increases the implementation rate. When it is easy to make suggestions, when the response to suggestions is rapid, and when the likelihood of implementation is high, employees are suddenly full of bright ideas. In fact, that is what FPL decided to call the new program—Bright Ideas.

The primary vehicle for participation, however, is QI teams. FPL uses two kinds. Functional Teams are groups of line employees who decide, on a volunteer basis, to tackle problems in their workplace. They use the QIDW procedures, and typically meet once a week. Task Teams, in contrast, are made up of employees selected because of their backgrounds and positions, and appointed to the team for the purpose of addressing specific problems. According to the company, "Task

[20]*Summary Description*, ibid., p. 20.

teams typically are formed to support Policy Deployment or locally identified high priority issues."[21]

Teams are supported by managers and supervisors, who themselves form the lead teams, and who provide the necessary resources and advice to teams and also are responsible for recognizing and rewarding the achievements of each team. FPL also employs some facilitators to help teams manage their group problem-solving processes.

The teams have their own specific process for problem-solving and presentation of suggestions, called the QI story format. This is a standardized approach to "storyboarding" an analysis and resulting suggestions, and every team must use it. It actually involves drawing pictures—charts and diagrams—to tell the story of the quality improvement. The history of this unusual technique provides an amusing metaphor for the history of the entire quality revolution, because the original innovation came from the U.S., was applied and refined in Japan, and then brought back to the U.S. with further refinements by FPL in the 1980s. It actually originated with the invention of storyboarding by illustrators at Disney Studios, in order to have quick visual plans so that script-writers and animators could better coordinate their efforts. The storyboard concept was picked up by Komatsu and used to tell quality control stories, as they called them. Years later, an FPL task team observed a presentation at a Japanese company that used this technique. They were impressed that they could understand the presentation completely, even though they spoke no Japanese. The method was soon adapted to the seven-step storyboard now in use at FPL:

1. Reason for Improvement

2. Current Situation

3. Analysis

[21]Ibid.

4. Countermeasures

5. Results

6. Standardization

7. Future Plans

The technique gives teams a powerful, common language with which to visualize and communicate quality problems and improvements—and for this reason contributes significantly to the success of FPL's quality process.

FEDERAL EXPRESS'S FIVE-POINT STRATEGY

Chairman Frederick Smith has defined five specific strategies to guide the company's pursuit of providing "totally reliable" transportation:

1. Use the Quality Improvement process to improve service levels to 100 percent and lower our costs at the same time—in short, Q = P (Quality Equals Productivity) management;

2. Use information and information systems as strategic weapons to achieve Q = P goals;

3. Recognize that Federal Express must become a truly global company;

4. Get closer to our customers; and,

5. Continue to emphasize our people-first philosophy by "investing" in our employees.[22]

The quality improvement process of FedEx emphasizes measurement. A cornerstone of it is a new system that replaces the

---

[22]This and following quotes are from "Federal Express Corporation Information Book" and other company documents.

old service measure, percent of packages delivered on time, with a new measure that is made up of "12 components weighted to reflect the customers' view of our performance" (it is survey-driven). We will look at this measurement system in detail in a later chapter, but the key point is that it links evaluation of daily performance with concrete measures of customer satisfaction, thus putting real teeth into the verbiage about serving customers. FedEx also relies heavily on employee participation through teams—they are called Quality Action Teams—and as at FPL, they are used to "get employees involved in designing the work process." The concept of internal customers is important at FedEx, as it was in the FPL model, and FedEx has a simple analytical process that parallels FPL's QIDW process. Here is how FedEx's process is presented in company documents:

> To make the work process flow smoothly and deliver a Quality product to our external customers, we need to build positive working relationships with our internal customers. We can accomplish this by asking them three questions:
>
> • What do you need from me?
>
> • What do you do with what I give you?
>
> • Are there any gaps between what I give you and what you need?[23]

In addition, Frederick Smith has identified five criteria that are considered key to the quality improvement process:

1. Establish clear Quality goals;

2. Measure accurately what we are doing;

3. Identify the critical points in the value chain—such as final sort points—and manage flawlessly;

4. Demonstrate discipline in our operations; and,

[23]Ibid., p. 17.

5. Provide immediate and accurate feedback to our employees.

These criteria pop up in various forms in almost all quality improvement processes. For example, FPL's process was designed to focus attention on key issues, and not chasing too many rabbits is also important at Federal Express. The way in which this is expressed by Smith is interesting; he uses the value chain model and speaks of "critical points" in the chain. The concept underlying this is that companies add value to the raw materials they take in through the production processes or services they perform—and that while value may be added in a great many ways and places, only a small number of the value-adding functions account for the greatest amount of value-added. Or subtracted, in the case of errors and problems that detract from quality. Value is a customer-defined measure of the firm's activities, and by visualizing the firm's activities in this way, Smith insures the customer viewpoint will guide the improvement process. Often something as simple as a visual image or model can play a critical role in the quality improvement process. Following are two simple visual representations of the quality improvement process, one in the form of a triangle and the other a circle.

The Quality Management Triangle

Kodak's Eastman Chemicals Division has had a total quality management system in place in its chemical plants since 1984. Like most quality programs, this one was a response to increasing competition from lower priced, higher quality products from Europe and Japan—no industry is immune. Eastman Chemicals' quality program is based on what they call the quality management triangle, illustrated in Exhibit 3-3.

The triangle represents the quality process as resting on three legs: performance management, teamwork, and statisti-

Exhibit 3-3 The Quality Management Triangle

Source: Eastman Kodak Company

cal process control. Performance management, like many of the management processes we have reviewed, provides focus and direction for the quality improvement efforts of employees. The process starts with the establishment of what the company calls Key Result Areas, or KRAs. A set of quality measures is developed for each, controls are established, and then planning and resource allocation occurs to improve performance in the KRA.[24]

Teamwork is used in the KRA process, and in fact everyone in the entire organization serves on one or more quality management teams. These teams were added onto a traditional, top-down hierarchical authority structure, so while there is full and open participation within each team, the results of team decisions must still struggle upward in the organization for approval, and (in many cases) downward or outward for

---

[24]Company documents.

implementation. This means the teams overcome the normal organizational impediments to identifying problems and generating ideas—but not to implementing them. To eliminate this potential bottleneck, some members from each team serve on other teams that are higher or lower in the organization, creating a new, more open channel of communication outside the normal reporting channels.[25]

The third leg of Eastman Chemicals' quality process is statistical process control (SPC). SPC is one of the formal methodologies for analyzing, tracking, and controlling process variables and outputs. A considerable variety of consulting firms now sell SPC methodology and training to companies. Incidentally, quality programs that are based entirely on these quantitative techniques don't do very well; it takes more than good measurements to change an organization's culture. However, measurement is an essential cornerstone for any quality process, and every one of the quality processes described so far has relied on improved measurement and control techniques to a considerable extent.

The T.Q.C. Wheel

If you don't like sharp corners, Weyerhaeuser's model (Exhibit 3-4) may be more appealing to you. It visualizes the quality process as a wheel whose axle is a customer-driven master plan, with a hubcap made up of management processes: these include daily control, management-by-planning, and cross-functional management at Weyerhaeuser. Finally, the wheel has a series of spokes consisting of hands-on tools and techniques, including various types of teams and QC circles, statistical methods, and information systems. This is a helpful image, as it shows the important relationships between these three elements.

[25]Harvard Business School Case No. 9-190-039, p. 2.

Exhibit 3-4 Weyerhaeuser's Quality Wheel

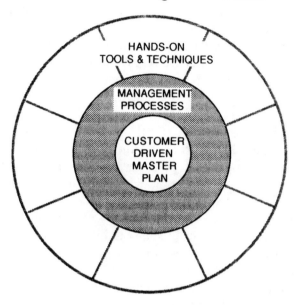

Source: Adapted from Weyerhaeuser Paper Company materials

The plan at the center of the wheel consists of:

- a mission statement,
- goals,
- how total quality control will be used to achieve goals,
- beliefs ("a guide to expected daily behaviors"),
- a definition of quality,
- a set of "Quality in Action" principles, and
- a set of implementation strategies.

This master plan is one way to integrate a number of the key elements of quality that we have seen in other company's visions, principles, and processes. It provides a context for the company's vision and principles and shows how they relate and how they translate into goals, strategies, and beliefs. This is still not enough to bring the vision all the way into daily work throughout the company. It is just the center of the wheel.

The plan, informed by the vision of customer-driven quality, is translated into the daily work of the organization through management processes, and then by hands-on quality tools and techniques. The wheel focuses attention on all three of these elements and represents their relationship along a sequence from planning, at the center, to the impact on the work of the organization, at the rim.[26]

Mike Cordry, Weyerhaeuser's vice president, quality, observes that the critical issue in implementation is, "The improvement in how you manage day-to-day business. The rest will follow." This observation echoes the sentiments from other managers and companies concerning the necessity of making the use of quality tools instinctive, and of moving from conscious to instinctive quality behavior. Quality can start as a simple, centralized vision and plan, as in the wheel diagram used at Weyerhaeuser, but it must be expanded through dozens of spokes until this instinctiveness is achieved throughout the organization. As Cordry puts it, "People make quality happen, if it's going to happen."[27] This is why the planning efforts must reach all the way into daily tasks. What starts as a simple vision and set of principles must end by transforming the organization's daily management system. According to Cordry,

A daily management system is quite simply all the things all of us do, each day, to produce a product, service, whatever. It is

[26]Presentation by Mike Cordry at the Conference Board's Second Annual West Coast Conference on Key Issues in Human Resources Management, May 9, 1989, Los Angeles. See Conference Board Report No. 937.
[27]Ibid., p. 44.

the sum total of our accumulated practices, habits, responses, mandates, beliefs, etc. Many of these have been appropriate and successful, as measured by our progress in historical terms. What total quality does is bring all these accumulated behaviors and beliefs into question, along with the systems and processes of the business. Not once or twice, but all the time, forever. That's the business of continuous improvement, a basic tenet of total quality.

The interesting thing about this idea of bringing the organization's accumulated beliefs into question is that it is not some big event that happens and then is over. You don't just throw tea into the harbor, write up a declaration, and settle down to some new order. Instead, it is a quiet, controlled revolutionary process that percolates along continuously, and is fomented by the same people at which it is directed. Everyone is expected to call their *own* actions into question, and force changes in them whenever positive change can be envisioned. For this remarkable process to happen, the focus of planning and change processes must be on the individual's daily work. Hence the constant emphasis on techniques and methodologies to enlist individuals and teams in the redesign of their own processes and tasks. This is the critical outer rim of the Weyerhauser wheel, and it is also the subject of Corning's "Ten Total Quality Actions," a set of specific, hands-on processes that Corning combines with its four quality principles (see Chapter 2) as a way to make the principles take root.

Turning Principles Into Results

CORNING'S TEN TOTAL QUALITY ACTIONS

Commitment: A continuing personal action in support of Total Quality.

Teams: The organization of people to manage Total Quality at each location.

Education: Programs to create awareness and teach the skills and techniques needed for Total Quality.

Measure/Display: Using charts and other displays of error rates to focus on the need for corrective action.

Cost of Quality: Use of procedures to measure error, detection, and prevention costs, so problems can be prioritized and solved.

Communication: Keeping everyone informed of company and unit progress, and the ways employees can become involved.

Corrective Action: Establishment of a system in which the individual and the organization can identify and eliminate problems. An essential element of the system is that it is able to respond to individual employee suggestions.

Recognition: Recognizing individual and group participation in, and contributions to, Total Quality.

Event: A gathering of employees to celebrate and rededicate themselves to Total Quality.

Goals: Establishment of error reduction goals by everyone.[28]

Each of these 10 items is something that *individuals* can do, by themselves or in groups, in their daily work. They are the principle ways that Corning's quality program reaches out and involves all the employees. Actually, there is one item missing from this list, one that is so central to Corning's quality plans and programs that it does not even have to be included, except for outsiders such as us: Training. Most quality programs elevate one of these various principles or techniques

---

[28]Conference Board Research Report No. 239, p. 7.

and make it the keystone of their quality plans and programs. For example, at American Express it is customer focus; and customer research and the measurement of customer attitudes informs every aspect of the company's quality program. At IBM it is the process paradigm, and the analysis and management of processes is the keystone of IBM's programs. Perhaps there is a lesson in this for all companies. While all the elements we have seen so far are essential to a successful quality effort, it may work best to emphasize one of them above the others and use it as the main lever for all quality efforts. This is the case with Corning, certainly, and there is no doubt that the majority of Corning's investment in quality has been in the area of training, and that the organization and its employees are more capable and learn more rapidly as a result.

According to David Luther, a Conference Board Quality Council member and Corning's corporate director of quality, "Training is a major driver of quality. We elected to make it a big piece of our quality program. Our requirement is that every employee spend 5 percent of their time on training every year, and we're almost there."[29] This requirement was established in 1986, and it formed the first five-year goal for Corning's quality program. (A five-year goal is often an excellent planning tool when a major, costly and difficult change is envisioned.) Now that every employee at Corning spends 5 percent of his or her time on their own learning, the company has set a new, and equally ambitious goal: to double the measured effectiveness of training (in other words, to produce twice as much learning and performance improvement from the same investment in training). David Luther explains that, "This is an ambitious goal. It's going to take some innovation. We don't know how to do that yet."[30] But a consistent focus on it, over a five-year span of time, is in all likelihood going to produce the kind of innovation needed.

[29]Personal communication with author, January 7, 1992.
[30]Ibid.

Revealing Hidden Decisions

Traditional planning involves a centralized effort by senior management or staff to translate a company's mission into a handful of specific strategies that are then 'handed down' for middle management and employees to implement. In contrast, planning for quality programs pushes much of this process down and out within the organization, and of course this means much greater involvement and participation in the planning process—that is why the daily management process must be redesigned at the same time the quality plan is prepared. What is less obvious is that pushing strategy formation down in the company changes the nature of the resulting strategies, both producing many more strategies and producing strategies that are more targeted and narrow (and thus far easier to implement at the local level). The typical quality program generates hundreds of initiatives and strategies, each conceived of and implemented by an individual or group in the spirit of the corporate vision and principles. (At first this proliferation of strategy is difficult to control—too many rabbits—but organizations soon develop mechanisms to prioritize and focus their new rabbits.)

Quality planning sheds light on many decisions that were not articulated in the old management paradigm. It does this by pushing the identification of problems and opportunities, and the analysis and strategizing that follows, downward into working groups and teams that are focused on specific processes. You might say these decisions are hidden in the conventionally managed organization, and that one of the most important tasks of the quality planner is to reveal them—to look inside the black boxes of processes and systems that are traditionally taken for granted. (A hidden decision is one that people do not realize they are making. They think they are following standard operating procedure, or that they are doing their work the way it has always been done, and do not see the hidden assumptions and choices underlying their actions.)

Planning traditionally focused on the most visible decisions and progress was primarily the result of the occasional adoption of a big idea. Only the highly visible issues make it all the way to the top of a vertically-organized company where assumptions can be questioned and decisions made. In quality planning, however, many smaller, incremental improvements are also made. Newt Hardie, vice president, quality for Milliken & Company, explains that "The Japanese have taught us that a thousand small steps add up to a giant leap. It is important to get all ideas, not just big ideas."[31] This requires the conscious evaluation of hundreds of day-to-day actions and decisions, which only becomes possible when employees are given greater control over the design of their own jobs and work processes. In many quality programs the revelation of previously-concealed decisions, many of them suboptimal, is visualized as bottom-up management. For example, James C. Cline, quality manager of Baldrige Award-winner Globe Metallurgical, Inc., believes that "Information flows both top down and bottom up. Top down, we bring in new ideas and concepts and approval for projects. The foundation is the people working in the plants who bring ideas up to us."[32]

The problem of hidden decisions has been recognized by academics in the social sciences for years, but has not really been pursued in the field of business planning. Here, for example, is how one of the classics on research methodology in the social sciences describes this problem:

> A particularly important difficulty is that decisions are often not isolable as such, so that there is no well-marked phase in the process of decision making where planning can intervene . . . Yet virtual decisions can be made ever more explicit, and as their grounds are set out they may be subjected to inquiry.[33]

[31]Conference Board Report No. 990, p. 30.
[32]Conference Board Report No. 990, p. 20.
[33]Abraham Kaplan, *The Conduct of Inquiry: Methodology for Behavioral Science*, Chandler Publishing, 1964, p. 404.

The term *virtual decision* is probably unfamiliar, as it is not in common use in business, or in any field for that matter. My copy of Webster's defines *virtual* as, "being such in essence or effect though not formally recognized or admitted," and in this context it refers to actions that constitute decisions, but are not recognized as such. If you think about it, virtual decision is a good description of much that a manager does, or does not, do in a typical work day. Whenever something is not changed, for instance, there is a virtual decision to keep it as it is. And whenever an opportunity or problem is overlooked, there is a virtual decision not to pursue the opportunity or solve the problem. Finally, whenever a decision is made in a routine manner, according to convention, policy or tradition, then a virtual decision has been made not to examine other possible approaches to the decision or to look hard at the assumptions underlying it.

Are virtual decisions a problem? Yes. I think the failure to question and reexamine assumptions and routines explains why we saw such high failure rates when we looked at the *Manual of Excellent Managements 1957*, and why the researchers who study organization behavior find that "There are strong inertial forces at work in organizations, and . . . individual organizations rarely change form. Most changes in diversity at the aggregate or population level come about not through transformation of existing organizations, but instead through turnover in units: the creation of new organizations and the dissolution of old ones," as a recent review of the literature reports.[34]

When a major decision *is* articulated and change is planned by senior management, dozens of related but hidden decisions, ones that have not been articulated, may serve to

[34]Howard E. Aldrich and Peter U. Marsden, Chapter 11, "Environments and Organizations," p. 368, Neil J. Smelser, Ed., *Handbook of Sociology*, Sage, 1988, reviewing research by Michael T. Hannan and John Freeman; for details consult "Population Ecology of Organizations" by these authors in *American Journal of Sociology* 82, 1977, pp. 929–964.

reinforce the old ways and keep the planned change from occurring. Management consultant Eileen Shapiro recently postulated the existence of a hidden equation that explains the difficulty organizations have in actually implementing any major change, even when the decision has risen above the virtual and management has decided change is necessary. In her recent book, she says, "Despite the combination of smart managers, clear incentives and large investments in internal reports and consultants' recommendations, the effort to improve performance often results in little or no change."[35] The hidden equation may be the counterweight of virtual decisions working against the articulated decision to change.

Another recent study of this phenomenon concluded that corporate traditions come to be taken for granted, and it is these traditions that stand in the way of change. And in an insight that touches upon the topic of this book, the author of this study notes that "tradition is both a mode of knowing and the content of what is known."[36]

By 'mode of knowing' I think he means that corporate traditions shape the way employees, including managers, think and learn. They do this, in all likelihood, by allowing people to take many actions for granted, and therefore to make virtual decisions without realizing they have. Through this influence on the individual's mode of knowing, traditions limit and direct the rate of organizational learning and change.

FROM VIRTUAL TO ACTUAL

What is it about the quality-focused company that allows it to break the rule that says organizations are not able to change dramatically or rapidly? The planning and management processes seem to accomplish this in part by moving many decisions from the virtual to the actual. This is done, first, by

[35]Eileen C. Shapiro, *How Corporate Truths Become Competitive Traps*, Wiley, 1991, front material.

[36]Alan M. Kantrow, *The Constraints of Corporate Tradition*, Harper & Row, 1987, p. 62.

providing a change-oriented philosophy and a vision that gives clear direction to this change. Next, the quality programs set dozens, hundreds, and even thousands of employees to work digging around for problems and opportunities, examining how their systems and processes work and asking how to improve them. This means that, where a handful of planners used to articulate a handful of strategic issues every year, hundreds of planners are now articulating thousands of issues every year. A great many assumptions are questioned, a great many traditions reexamined, and as a result, decisions are made in a more conscious manner. The quality plans work because they shift many decisions from the virtual to the actual.

To do this, the program must also give employees the tools and resources needed to do planning in the trenches. (Obviously a small circle of specialized planners cannot handle this far larger scale of analysis and planing.) To borrow an analogy, often used at Xerox, the kinds of tools that employees used to keep in their intellectual toolboxes are not always appropriate, and in addition many new ones must be added. This is why so much training is involved in every quality program, and no doubt why a program such as Corning's that stars training can be so successful.

While this thesis seems to explain much of what we discover when examining quality plans and programs, it does present one possible objection. Conventional wisdom holds that "organizations develop the capacity to adapt at the cost of lowered performance in stable environments,"[37] as some of the researchers cited earlier put it. In other words, there ought to be a *tradeoff* between flexibility and efficiency. The idea is, has always been, that traditions, assumptions, and other things taken for granted are efficient; they allow people to act quickly and decisively without having to ponder every action. Assump-

---

[37]Michael T. Hannan and John Freeman "Population Ecology of Organizations," *American Journal of Sociology* 82, 1977, p. 937.

tions are efficient, questions are not. In theory, the organization that questions everything will find it difficult to match the productivity and focus of less philosophical organizations in any relatively stable environment. The more flexible organization runs the risk of paralysis by analysis.

This does not seem to be true of quality-driven organizations. They have somehow overcome this tradeoff, just as they have overcome the old notion of a tradeoff between cost and quality. They are able to change fast, and they certainly must be doing a lot more thinking to achieve this fast rate of change, but somehow they also are able to *think* fast. I suspect the secret is that they are using more of their employees to make decisions. It would certainly be inefficient to ask senior managers to tackle hundreds and thousands of decisions that used to be virtual, made unthinkingly according to convention, tradition, or policy. However, that is not what these quality programs do. Instead, they ask employees to start making important decisions for the first time. The plans and programs push the identification of strategic issues downward, and they push the making of strategic decisions downward as well.

It is said that humans do not use the majority of the brain's processing power. Many brain cells are simply idle. This is true by analogy in the traditional corporation as well. Most of the employees are expected to work. Only a few are expected to think. One of the hallmarks of the quality programs is that they ask lots of employees to begin thinking. They start to utilize those idle brain cells for the first time. And this may explain how they violate the principle that adaptability ought to come at the expense of efficiency.

If this is so, employee participation ought to hold one of the keys to successful quality implementation, and we will examine it with care in a future chapter. How companies and their employees learn, think, analyze, and generate ideas— also seems to be of prime importance. The processes that guide this new brain work throughout the company, and that underly the programs of companies like FPL, depend upon a process approach that we will take up later in the book as well. But first and foremost, we must look at the customer and how management can insure that the heightened thinking and activity throughout the organization is focused on pleasing this customer.

Customer orientation is probably the strongest and clearest of all the themes that run through the quality plans and programs we have examined. It is this fundamental orientation that keeps hundreds and even thousands of planners focused productively and efficiently on the principles and goals of their company's quality program. By making the customer and his or her needs more visible and tangible throughout the organization, management not only keeps the entire effort focused on those rabbits that are of greatest relevance to the customer, it also keeps all the rabbits hopping in the same direction.

Chapter 4

REDISCOVERING THE CUSTOMER

Our industry had been shifting from a hardware emphasis to one of software and services, developing thousands of new competitors in every niche. Competition had become tougher than ever. We were heavy with resources, with structure and not responsive enough to customer needs. We decided the way to get straight answers was from the source—the customer.

—S. B. Schwartz, senior vice president— Market-Driven Quality, IBM[1]

We all fell on the floor. We couldn't believe it. The customer was right.

—Edwin Coate, v.p. for finance and administration, Oregon State University[2]

---

[1]From remarks at a Goal/QPC conference, Boston, MA, November 12, 1991, as provided to the author by Mr. Schwartz.

[2]Liz McMillen, "To Boost Quality and Cut Costs, Oregon State U. Adopts a Customer-Oriented Approach to Campus Services," *The Chronicle of Higher Education*, February 6, 1991, p. A27.

For years, Oregon State University's physical plant office had received complaints that it took "forever" to finish even the simplest construction projects. For years, administrators assumed the complaints were the result of misapprehensions on the part of a small number of people. Then the university began to implement a new quality program, modeled on the quality programs of the companies covered in this book. One of the first things the administration did was to follow up on all those customer complaints about construction delays.

To their great surprise, the customer was right—the average remodeling job took a semester-eating 195 days. As administrator Edwin Coate put it, "We all fell on the floor. We couldn't believe it. The customer was right." (George Fisher, chairman and CEO of Motorola, Inc., observes that even "the simple question, "Who is my customer?" can lead to total upheaval."[3] The customer perspective can have considerable shock value, as Coate also discovered.) Now the processes involved are being redesigned to shorten project length, and the quality lessons learned in the physical-plant office are also being extended to other functions at the university—even teaching. More surprises are sure to follow, because management and employees no doubt forgot long ago that the customer is *always* right. This wisdom is given lip service in the traditional management paradigm, but to walk the talk, managers usually have to initiate substantial organizational change via a quality or customer service program. They have to rediscover the customer, or, as Steven Schwartz of IBM puts it, they have to realize that "the way to get straight answers [is] from the source—the customer."

What is quality? As consumers, we all know what quality is not, since we encounter a great deal of what quality isn't every day. So much, perhaps, that we become jaded to it, worn down, and no longer expect quality. As professor Peter Senge

---

[3]George M. C. Fisher, "Measuring the Unmeasurable," *World: The Magazine for Decision Makers* (published by KPMG Peat Marwick), No. 2, 1990, p. 4.

of MIT's Sloan School of Management has found, "Most Americans don't know good service. They haven't had it."[4] A brief personal anecdote illustrates this point.

Hello . . . Is Anybody There?

I received a telephone call last Halloween from an old friend and occasional co-author, Professor Charles Schewe of U. Mass. Amherst, "Alex, do you get *Business Week?*" I said, I didn't. "Well, you better go out and buy this week's issue, because it's on quality. There's a special report called 'The Quality Imperative.'" We laughed over the fact that the early drafts of this book (which I was working on at the time of this conversation) used that same phrase as its working title. That evening I stopped by the newsstand downstairs from my office to pick up a copy. But the next issue was already out, and I had missed the issue on quality. Undaunted, I made a note of the telephone number listed in the magazine for the circulation department, and the next morning I called *Business Week* to have a copy of the quality issue sent to me—and was treated to a marvelous example of the principle that is a lot easier to talk, and write, about the quality imperative than to actually achieve it. Here is how the telephone conversation went:

Ring. Ring.

Operator: McGraw-Hill.

Me: I need a copy of last week's *Business Week*.

Operator: Please hold.

Click. Pause.

Second Operator: McGraw-Hill.

[4]As quoted in Howard Schlossberg, "Author: Consumers Just Can't Wait to be Satisfied," *Marketing News*, Feb. 4, 1991, p. 13.

Me:	How do I get last week's *Business Week*?
Second Operator:	That's Back Copies. I'll connect you.

Click. Pause.

Computer:	Your call has been forwarded to an automated voice message system. The *Business Week* single copies sales desk is full. To disconnect, press 1. To enter another number, press 2.
Me:	Hello? Anybody there?

Pause while I try to figure out what to do, since I don't know anybody's extension at McGraw-Hill, but I don't want to hang up without placing my order.

Computer:	Are you still there? Please dial the number of the person you are calling.

I try dialing "0" for operator.

Computer:	If you have a mail box on this system, please press pound.

I get mad and dial "0" several times in a row.

Computer:	Are you still there? Sorry you are having trouble. Please call again. Goodbye.

Click. Dial tone.

The normal caller, when hung up on in this manner, would no doubt go away forever. The excessively persistent caller, such as myself, might try to reach the *Business Week* single copies sales desk repeatedly, only to be rebuffed by variants of these messages from the automated voice answering system. From the customer's point of view, this is the very antithesis of quality customer service.

How Does Bad Service Happen?

Let us imagine a company's perspective on such an incident. In my imagination, a new quality initiative has just set tight standards on the servicing of requests for back issues. Let's just say, since it is so commonplace in this sort of customer service function, that the single copies sales desk is tracked on how fast it turns around each order for back copies. Now, let's say that whoever manages the desk must cut turnaround time on orders, and perhaps they also must cut the length of time the employees spend talking with each customer on the phone, and the time customers are kept on hold waiting to talk to someone, and the number of incorrectly-addressed back issues sent out, and so forth.

But how? Let's also say that these directives are not accompanied by bigger budgets, extended authority, or special training—at least in my fantasy they are not, because in reality they seldom are either. So the picture is pretty hopeless for the poor manager of the single copies sales desk—until a new Automated Voice Answering System is installed.

Suddenly the solution to all these problems is delivered from above. Here is a system that, under the pretense of improving customer access and reducing hold time, confusion and other problems at the reception desks, actually gives managers the power to *avoid customers* altogether. How wonderfully the statistics improve when the new computerized answering system turns most of the customers away! Hold time is completely eliminated, since customers cannot get far enough in the system to even be put on hold in the first place. Nobody complains about the service anymore either, since they cannot reach a human being with whom to lodge their complaints. Finally the sales desk can get on top of its paperwork, since it now has the power to control the inflow of orders.

What, one might ask, is the cost of this wonderful progress? None, at least by the most common measures employed in companies. Payroll is not up. No special order-handling equipment was purchased. Nothing has changed—except that the number of orders falls far short of market potential. Let's imagine that is a different department—it's the problem of marketing or sales. By the kind of internal measures often used to track quality, my imaginary manager of the single copies sales desk is a hero.

These ruminations are simply what popped into my head as I wrestled with the telephone computer that morning. (I suppose I should have called up McGraw-Hill to find out what the real story was, but, in truth, I was a little afraid of what I might encounter elsewhere in that computerized telephone answering system.) However, the case in question is not dissimilar to many negative customer transactions that occur across the United States daily, and it illustrates the difficulty of controlling, or even monitoring, customer contacts throughout a large organization—a difficulty that does not go away with the initiation of a quality program.

Perhaps the greatest challenge for quality programs is the detection and elimination of negative customer experiences in the many far-flung points of customer contact. Standard approaches to measurement may entirely overlook negative customer experiences, and even if their impact is detected indirectly in negative customer attitudes, the root causes of these attitudes are rarely identifiable. Something as minor as an order for back issues of a magazine is too far from the executive suite to receive direct attention, even from the most fastidious and committed of quality-driven managers. But, to the customer in question, it dominates the perception of the firm, making it essential that firms somehow manage to track and control such events.

Wearing my customer's hat again for a moment, I can tell you that my dead-end calls to *Business Week* made a lasting negative impression—probably an unjust impression, shaped as it was by just one negative transaction. Wearing my author's hat again, I have to say that this kind of service blunder is amazingly hard to control; most managers will secretly admit that their company could just as easily have provided a bad service case-history for this book. *Any* company that interacts with the customer through hundreds or thousands of different individuals, each delivering a customized service, faces a far greater quality challenge than the company that produces a relatively small number of standardized, and thus readily controllable, products for customer consumption. Further, this service challenge is no longer confined to the service sector, for most manufacturers now realize that their delivered product is actually a bundle of goods *and* services. Any company, whether service- or product-oriented, will find it very hard to track and control all the points of customer contact.

Thus, while it is important to avoid bad service, it is also vital to become good at *recovering* when problems do occur. When I called McGraw-Hill a week later to make a final attempt at ordering that special issue on quality, the phone system was reconfigured to be more customer-friendly and I obtained my copy with ease. Since then, the special issue on quality has gone on to outsell all previous issues. We can therefore assume that the problem was diagnosed and corrected; an important component of service recovery. (Another component, compensating or otherwise satisfying the individuals who experienced the problem, was presumably not as easily done because the company has no way of knowing who they were.)

THE MISSING INGREDIENT: CUSTOMERS

What can possibly account for dead-end phone systems, poor customer service, products that break or do not do the customer's work as well as desired, and all the other frustrations we face as consumers? Why is it that "Most Americans don't know good service," as MIT's Senge puts it—or good quality in general, whether in services or products? (Contrary to popular perception, customer service improvement programs are simply the other side of the quality coin—management needs to address service and product quality in the same breath.) Why do management decisions that are supposed to be improvements sometimes result in far worse service or products from the customer's perspective? The most common cause is that a key ingredient is missing—the customers.

In too many companies, the customer's viewpoint is not represented accurately when decisions affecting quality are made. Companies are unable to focus their efforts on customer value largely because they simply do not understand what the real costs and benefits are from the customer's point of view.

Two fundamental problems stand in the way of customer-based quality management. First, managers often fail to appreciate that they are making quality decisions because they do not see how most of their decisions affect the customer. Sales and marketing departments see the obvious relevance of customer perception in developing marketing strategies and tactics, and product designers are increasingly likely to see the importance of customer input as well. However, other decisions throughout the firm are seldom examined from the customer's perspective, because, at first glance, most decisions do not appear to affect the customer.

To return to our opening example, companies may not look at the purchase of a new telephone system as a customer service issue, but rather as a capital expenditure to be justified internally on a cost-benefit basis. The computerized system that dead-ended my call to McGraw-Hill was probably purchased because it was able to handle more calls with fewer operators, providing a return on investment in wages saved. However, in its application to the single copies sales desk, and probably to many other departments, the new system is capable of incurring far higher costs in customer ill will and lost sales than it could possibly save in reduced payroll—making customer considerations the central issue in both the purchase decision and (if bought) in all subsequent decisions concerning how to manage the system. Unfortunately, the most important dimension, the customer impact, is easily overlooked.

The ease with which the customer dimension of management decisions is overlooked is an added twist on the notion of latent decisions raised in Chapter 3. Even when decisions are recognized and tackled in a formal manner, their customer dimension may remain latent. These are *latent quality decisions.*

Even when management takes stock of customer perceptions through a standard customer survey, the survey rarely represents the customer viewpoint in a useful manner. The current research paradigm is not suited to the task of supporting customer-driven quality improvement, at least not at a rapid rate, and this paradigm must be replaced with more aggressive and personalized ways of representing the customer's perspective. In an example of what many managers might consider extremely aggressive customer research, Steven Schwartz of IBM describes how his company "invited customers from around the world to join us at IBM's top level strategic planning conference." Nobody likes to be criticized, and I think there is a general tendency in customer research to avoid methodologies that 'look for trouble' by inviting customers to air strong criticisms. But in this case, Schwartz reports, "We asked them [the customers] to tell us what we were doing right but—more important—what we were doing wrong or not doing at all."[5] That constitutes looking for trouble in a big way; the company better be willing and able to change before it invites customers to critique it in front of senior management!

American companies spend considerably more than $3

---

[5]From remarks at a Goal/QPC conference, Boston, MA, November 12, 1991, as provided to the author by Mr. Schwartz.

billion a year on market research purchased from specialized vendors[6] (and their internal research expenses are not even tallied). Thousands and thousands of customer surveys are performed every month, and probably a million or so reports are delivered yearly. The market research industry, and certainly the purchasers of its reports, will no doubt take great offense at the statement that managers do not understand their customers' perspective. But they do not.

ROOT CAUSES OF CUSTOMER PERCEPTION

Why don't all those surveys reveal problems such as negative customer transactions? Don't surveys provide an effective checks-and-balances system for McGraw-Hill and other companies? The problem is that surveys are not designed to perform that function. In the old management paradigm, a fistfull of statistically significant customer surveys was considered sufficient representation of the customer viewpoint. In the new paradigm, it is not. According to Sheri Mitchell, director of Humana's quality program, "We use a survey *only* as a measure of a trend." Year-to-year improvement in customer ratings on a standardized survey means this large health-care provider is improving. But it does *not* say what should be done to achieve further improvements. It does not say what the existing problems are and which should be given highest priority. To answer these questions requires more detailed, personal, and aggressive research. At Humana this kind of research is called *root cause analysis*, and it has been refined

---

[6]An American Marketing Association survey of the top fifty U.S. market research firms, plus 105 others, reported total revenues of $3,132.3 million in 1990. A 1988 AMA survey of marketing directors at U.S. companies found that the respondents spent, on average, about $1.3 million a year on external vendors of marketing information. The European Society for Opinion Research (ESOMER), located in the Netherlands, estimates that world expenditures on marketing research totalled 5,358 ECU in 1990 (the ECU is worth about $1.30 at time of writing), however, their figure for the U.S., 1.916 ECU or about $2.5 billion, is considerably short of the AMA's figure, and considering that the AMA sample did not include many smaller firms, it is likely that both the U.S. and the world markets are substantially underestimated.

to such a degree that it is now used to drive the entire quality effort. As Mitchell explains it, "Our whole department [the quality department] is focused on root cause analysis."[7] Humana's quality improvement process starts by identifying a root cause of customer dissatisfaction. The quality office coordinates efforts by all relevant groups to examine and eliminate this root cause. Then standardized surveys are used to see whether the quality improvement has altered Humana's overall ratings—the trend analysis Mitchell says surveys *are* good for. Note also that Humana's quality improvement process both starts and ends with customer research. To start the process, root cause research identifies a customer problem. After the organization has responded, surveys track trends in customer perception to measure the impact of the response.

Marriott has evolved a similar approach to customer research. The company relies not on its surveys but on direct comments and complaints from its customers to identify problems for improvement. John Herold, a vice president of Marriott Hotels-Resorts, explains that, "The most difficult part of our business is managing these employee/customer interactions." To find out how customers feel about their interactions with the company, Herold says that, "The fundamental system we use is the Guest Service Index (GSI)—the little form in hotel rooms that says, 'We care. Please fill out this form.' " While there might be more aggressive ways to solicit customer complaints, this system certainly meets the minimum requirement of asking customers what they *don't*, as well as do, like. It looks for trouble, so to say, so that the company can prevent that kind of trouble in the future. Then, like Humana, Marriott uses a periodic survey to track trends in customer ratings. Herold explains: "Once a year we perform a division-wide consumer survey that we've been developing for 15 years. It

---

[7]Telephone interview with the author, January 8, 1992 (Incidentally, Humana, along with HCA and a few other companies, is leading a new movement among health care providers to utilize quality improvement concepts.)

asks a series of standard questions to compare our services and is conducted by an outside agency that asks a group of consumers how they perceive Marriott, in relation to its competitors, in different aspects of our operation . . . Because the survey is repeated annually, we get a good sense of where we're gaining or losing and what we need to emphasize."[8]

But why are surveys relegated to the end of the quality improvement process at Humana and Marriott? What is the matter with the venerable customer survey? To understand their shortcomings, imagine you wanted to write a survey to find out how customers rated the quality of a company's services or products. What would you ask the respondents? How about,

> On a 1 to 10 scale (where 1 =
> poorest quality and 10 = highest
> quality), rate the quality of Company
> X's services and products: 1 2 3 4 5 6 7 8 9 10

That is a pretty straightforward way to do it, and in fact, not much different in concept from thousands of survey questions asked every day. We all know the standard survey techniques, since we have ourselves been buttonholed by interviewers at least a few times over the years. The rating scale type of question, if asked to dozens or hundreds of randomly selected consumers, produces a robust estimate of how consumers judge quality on a 1 to 10 scale. What does management do with this information? If customers give the company a 7 or 8, management will make an effort to tweak quality up a bit (as management defines quality, of course). If customers give the company a nine or ten—or if customers rate the company a little higher than competitors—managers will deposit their next bonus checks with pride. But what does the result really say about quality? It only tells us how customers judge overall quality, *based on what they expect.*

[8]Conference Board Research Report No. 909, p. 80–81.

The initiative must be taken by the *company*, not the customer, and no one-to-ten customer rating of a company will tell managers what the major existing problems are, or what the potential for quality is. It takes a much more intimate examination of customer experiences, and much more imagination on the part of management, to begin to see how to improve customer-defined quality. The company must begin to see itself as responsible for solving customer problems, and must perform research designed to identify and diagnose the causes of customer problems.

At American Express, a new kind of customer research has been developed to identify and diagnose customer problems. Maryanne Rasmussen, previously senior vice president of quality with American Express Travel Related Services (and now with Amex's Shearson subsidiary), explains:

> We consider a transaction every contact a customer has with us—telephone calls, billing inquiries, a charge authorization question, etc. This is a most difficult element to measure. Companies can determine customer expectations, measure transaction time, analyze error rates. But we go beyond that: through unique transaction-based surveys we focus on how customers perceive a particular single contact with us. For instance, we analyze how their perception affects our card: Will they renew it, increase or decrease usage, and will they recommend it to others.[9]

The key to Amex's new approach is its focus on "how customers perceive a single contact," or a transaction with the company. My entanglement with the computerized telephone system at *Business Week* was one such single contact—a highly visible and negative one from the customer's perspective, even though it was invisible to the company. Individual transactions do not have to be negative or neutral; they can also be highly *positive* from the customer's perspective. Management consultant Ken Blanchard uses the term "legendary customer ser-

[9]Conference Board Research Report 937, p. 58.

vice" to describe the strongly positive impact a good transaction can have on customer perception. In addition, many actions within the firm can have a less visible, but nonetheless important, impact on individual customer transactions. These are the latent quality decisions we described above. Ralph Rosati, until recently Kodak's director, corporate quality, tells an anecdote about a production manager "who stopped an emulsion coating machine to bring the process to a higher standard." Rosati explains that "Shutting down one of these gigantic machines is not a casual act. They run 24 hours a day, 365 days a year. So this manager's decision meant significant production losses."[10] But it also meant that individual customers would not have a negative experience the next time they developed Kodak film; perhaps even that they would be surprised at how *well* their pictures came out. Every quality decision can be seen as shaping individual customer transactions with the company, and this is as true of decisions on the front lines of a service organization as it is of decisions in the production facilities of a manufacturer.

Transaction Analysis at Amex

At American Express, transaction surveys ask individual customers about their most recent transaction with the company. The surveys are designed to measure any change in attitude toward the company as a result of that transaction. For example, a customer who held a low opinion of American Express might report a greater likelihood of using his or her card after a very positive transaction. Rasmussen explains this approach to transaction research as follows:

> A model is useful to describe and quantify the business impact of service delivery. We know that prior to contacting American Express, every card member has perceptions about our company based on expectations or even prior experience with us.

[10]Conference Board Report 909, p. 17.

Each service contact, we feel, results in a level of satisfaction that in turn creates new attitudes and new behaviors. For example, in a current survey, of all our highly satisfied customers, 75 percent said that our handling of their situation raised their opinion of the company, while 25 percent said their opinion was unchanged; of the highly satisfied customers, 43 percent said they would use the card more often based on their positive experience.[11]

What about other groups of customers, such as the ones who went into the transaction with a low prior opinion of Amex? The company has not released the full results of the survey, perhaps because one might expect that the less satisfied customers will be harder to please in a transaction (and, incidentally, represent an important opportunity for the quality effort). But the important point is that, whatever the effect of recent transactions on customer opinion, Amex is *aware* of it. And awareness is the first and biggest step toward improvement. (At IBM, as we will see shortly, the continuous improvement process starts and ends with an awareness-building process assessment, one that requires the company "talk to customers."[12])

Amex incorporates this awareness into formal yearly goals for every manager. As Rasmussen's model indicates, one can think of every customer as starting with some preconceived notions about one's company. These perceptions form the basis of customer expectations. How well does Amex meet and exceed its customers' expectations? This is the kind of question that lends itself to trend analysis through repeated surveys over time, and thus can be used as a measure of how well managers respond to specific problems identified in the root cause analysis used at Humana or transaction analysis of the type Rasmussen describes. At Amex, Rasmussen tells us

---

[11]Conference Board Report No. 937.

[12]Steven Schwartz, Senior Vice President—Market-Driven Quality, IBM. From remarks at a Goal/QPC conference. Boston, MA. November 12, 1991, as provided to the author by Mr. Schwartz.

that the transaction research led to development of "a world-wide service tracking index whereby each market's performance is continually followed. Specifically, we will track how we met customer expectations. Each general manager is expected to set a yearly goal for improving this service." In other words, the loop is closed by tracking management performance against customer perception, just as in Humana's quality program. At Amex, the emphasis is on how service quality effects the customer's usage of the company's service. According to Rasmussen, "We track service and performance against two key measures: the customer's intention to renew and to use our card."[13]

An interesting outgrowth of Amex's customer research is the finding, again according to Rasmussen, "that satisfying a customer costs about one-tenth or one-fifteenth the amount of money it takes to get a new customer. So, losing a customer hurts."[14] This is a theme echoed everywhere one finds a health quality program, and it has led many companies to realize that the investment needed to recover from a service blunder and make an angry customer happy is minor in comparison with the cost of developing a new customer to replace the old one. But the realization that customer retention is the right way to go is only a first step. To keep dissatisfied customers means surprising them with excellent service. In fact, this is true of satisfied customers as well—witness, in Amex's survey of already-satisfied customers, the correlation between a transaction which further raised their opinion of the company and their increased intention to use Amex in the future. And to provide better-than-expected service *or* product quality comes down to listening harder to what customers say and watching more closely what they experience—the kind of aggressive, root cause research that goes deeper than conventional surveys of customer opinion.

---

[13]Conference Board Report 937, pp. 58–59.
[14]Ibid., p. 59.

INNOVATIONS IN CUSTOMER RESEARCH

To listen harder and watch more closely often requires innovations in the field of customer research. But innovations in this area are not on most managers' agendas. Most managers pay little attention to details of research methodology. In fact, few companies have much in the way of in-house expertise in the field; they have ceded core competency in customer research to the thousands of specialized survey research firms and statisticians that perform studies under contract, and many managers consider it improper to dirty their hands with surveys and the like.

I remember one experience, early in my own career, that brought this point home in an amusing manner. I had just been hired to do strategic planning and analysis at the headquarters of a large company, and was given the task of finding out why a competitor's salespeople seemed to be selling more productively. In my naivete, I simply started calling up salespeople, both from my company and from several of our leading competitors. (I viewed our sales people as internal customers, and figured that in-depth interviews with these 'customers' was the obvious first step.) Many of them were quite happy to tell me just what *they* thought the answer to my question was. After 30 or 40 of these conversations, I had a pretty good idea as to how attitudes and practices differed—and how to begin closing the gap between our sales performance and our competitor's. But when the rest of my department learned I had been doing interviews from my office, all hell broke loose. "You can't just call people up and ask them questions!" "Who gave you authority to talk to our salespeople?" "If the Chairman hears about this from our competitors' Chairmen, you're outta here!" "Well, it could have been worse; thank goodness you didn't talk to any of our customers!" And so forth.

I am not sure where this aversion to primary research comes from, but it is a hallmark of old management thinking, and it is refreshing to see it set aside in many companies with quality programs. The customer research at Humana, Marriott, and American Express has required a more active management role in the design of research methodology. Managers have come to see themselves not just as passive consumers of reports, but as active designers of research methodology, and this has helped them take control over information that used to control them. Dr. Paul Batalden, vice president for medical care at Hospital Corporation of America, tells a story that illustrates this point:

> Over the past two years, my colleagues at HCA, along with experts at the Rand Corporation, and at the Harvard School of Public Health, have been at work developing a method to regularly and reliably measure patient views of hospital performance. We developed this system with the assumption . . . that many patients were capable of giving us feedback about much more than we had traditionally sought. It became clear to us that patients could judge whether their care was personalized and seemed technically competent. If they've been on orange pills and suddenly get a green one, they know that something has changed. They realize that if the IVs routinely run dry, there's something wrong; patients can judge technical competence. They know whether their questions were answered and if services were readily accessible and available, when the call light was answered and when it wasn't. They can tell you whether they were comfortable and secure in the hospital environment, whether the food was palatable, warm, or cold. They can assess whether the outcomes of care met with their expectations. If you tally up that list and compare it to what we've customarily asked patients, you realize how trivially we've treated them in the past. In short, we realize that patients are in a position to give us low-cost, reliable feedback about hospital care that we can't get from any other source.[15]

This kind of story is very exciting, because it represents a rediscovery of the customer. Rediscovering the customer de-

---

[15]Conference Board Report No. 909, p. 77.

mands more of management than the writing of a customer-oriented vision statement and principles. It requires developing competency and stimulating innovation in the field of customer research. At HCA, these goals were pursued through collaborations with a think tank and a university. In addition, management learning in the field of customer research is also required. Batalden explains that "CEOs must know how to use this information. If they're illiterate in this respect, it won't help."[16] I did not want to be the one to say it, but in fact many managers are illiterate in the area of customer research, and one of the first steps management needs to take in any quality effort is to learn more about the topic.

Do-It-Yourself Research

A good way to learn more about customer research in general, and specifically about one's own customers, is to perform or observe closely an actual customer research project. The surprising thing is that so many managers have *not* had this experience. Further, I think the research experience is the easiest way to see for oneself the power of the new, more aggressive root-cause style of customer research, and to witness the kind of surprises and insights it can produce.

In short, the best way to see how much one can learn from this research approach is to try it for oneself. American Express, HCA, and other Conference Board members have, and they report having considerable success with transaction-oriented research. But, quite understandably, they are hesitant to share their raw data on customer complaints in a public forum such as this. I was not able to obtain permission to print a full and detailed description of a research project of this type. Therefore to demonstrate the power of transaction analysis to the reader—and to learn more about it myself—I performed

---

[16]Ibid., p. 77.

an independent service-transaction study through my consulting firm. We sent an interviewer out to a nearby mall to perform open-ended, in-depth interviews with passersby. The topic we chose was the quality of the health care services provided by their doctors and insurer. And, to make sure we got a peak into the real, emotional impact of the service provided, we used Amex's methodology of having the interviews focus narrowly on each respondent's last transaction.[17] (In a product-oriented business, this would be like asking respondents to describe in detail the last time they used the product; transaction-based studies can be applied to products as well as services.)

Why health care? First, of course, every reader has experience in this industry as a consumer. And second, health care services are high-touch, important, and emotionally laden for the consumer, making it likely (we figured) that consumers would have strong enough opinions to produce interesting results from a modest sample size. Further, it is striking that in most published surveys Americans are more worried about health care than about any other issues in their lives, and it is also relevant that our health care system is an object of national concern at present.[18] Yet when one talks to managers in this industry, they generally believe that they are providing high quality care (quality programs such as those at HCA and Humana are still rare in the industry). Most people do not recognize a quality problem in the industry. There is general agreement that the health care industry has a *cost* problem, of

---

[17]The results of this study are reported in *Health Care Transaction Analysis: What's Wrong with our Health Care System? Ask the Customers*, January 1, 1992, Peggy Tagliarino Public Relations, Inc., New York.

[18]See for example the New York Times/CBS poll of August 1991, in which 20% of respondents are dissatisfied with the quality of health care and 62% dissatisfied with the cost, as reported in Erik Eckholm, "Health Benefits Found to Deter Job Switching," *The New York Times*, Sept. 26, 1991, pp. A1 and B12. See "For Better or Worse?" *Newsweek* Special Issue: The 21st Century Family, Winter–Spring 1990, p. 18, for information on consumer concerns (21% of respondents worry about healthcare most).

course, but in fact I suspect it would be more productive to look at it as a quality problem.

For these reasons it makes an interesting demonstration to use transaction analysis to probe the personal feelings of a sampling of customers of the health care system. It is not an especially difficult experiment to perform, since most everyone uses health care services. For this example, the interviewer approached 38 people, 31 of whom participated, and spoke to each for five or ten minutes. The total cost of the study, including interviewer's time and a day of analysis, was under $2,000. The results were quite illuminating.

RESULTS OF THE DEMONSTRATION TRANSACTION STUDY

Most surprising was the finding that 23 of the respondents reported aspects of their most recent interactions with their health care provider had made them upset or angry: Three-fourths of the people in the sample! And they were not just a little upset; many of them were red faced and emphatic—the poor interviewer had never seen such strong reactions before. Only 5 of the respondents were reasonably happy with their last transaction (and 3 had no recent transactions).

When the complaints about recent transactions were broken down by type (a somewhat questionable practice given the use of a convenience sample of small size—but we'll let it slip for the sake of the demonstration), it turned out that most of the satisfied customers had been to see their dentists for routine care. Of those whose most recent transaction was with a doctor, not a dental hygienist, 82% reported some negative feelings as a result. (The results are summarized in two pie charts, although it is important to remember that this is a qualitative study and the exact proportions are therefore less important than the substance of specific interviews. See Exhibit 4-1.)

Would the average hospital, insurance company, or HMO obtain this kind of information from a typical survey? No. In

Exhibit 4-1 Nature of Recent Transactions

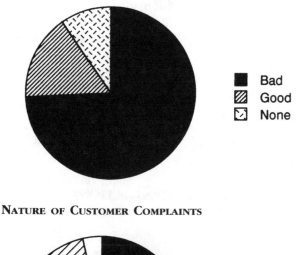

■ Bad
▨ Good
◨ None

Nature of Customer Complaints

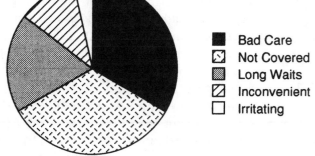

■ Bad Care
◨ Not Covered
▨ Long Waits
◪ Inconvenient
☐ Irritating

Source: In-depth intercept interviews, Alexander Hiam & Associates, Amherst, Mass., 1992.

fact, these problems do not show up in the routine customer surveys of the largest health care provider in the area where this study was performed.[19] It takes standing quietly and listening to each customer's individual story to bring out these feelings and begin to understand what causes them. In some

[19]The results of the demonstration study were compared with recent survey results from the local HMO, as described in their member newsletter, and were also discussed with one of the people responsible for their customer surveys. This

cases, the customer did not even recall the problems or complications until the interviewer probed for details of the transaction. Even if a standard survey revealed some dissatisfaction, it would not be of much use in tracing the cause. In the transaction study we conducted, customers were very clear and vocal concerning what made them upset—with the result that each interview generated a full page of interviewer's notes. Naturally it took more time to analyze the text of each interview than it would have to compile results from a formal quantitative study, but the results from a transaction analysis are worth the extra effort since they can reveal what the common complaints are and illuminate root causes of customer attitudes. A brief look at the results of this demonstration survey provides a good illustration of this point.

While each respondent's story was detailed and unique, it was possible to group their complaints into a small number of general categories. One third of the complaints centered on conflict or dissatisfaction over medical costs which the insurer would not pay, either in full or in part. These consumers did not have a clear understanding of what is and is not covered by their medical insurance, and were frequently surprised to learn that care they had obtained, or felt they needed to obtain, was not fully covered. Part of this problem must be attributable to the fact that insurers and employers are probably making efforts to control their costs by limiting treatment and by pushing costs onto the patient. But much of the problem boils down to poor communications and confusingly structured plans. If these consumers, and their insurers, were clear on what coverage has and has not been purchased, the customers would not have experienced post-purchase dissonance of the kind found in this study.

As an example of the kind of dissonance we found, one respondent described a routine physical in which the doctor

(continued from page 126)
example is not intended as a critique of any company's practices, so it is not appropriate to give the name of the company mentioned. The study was performed in an area where neither Humana or HCA operate.

diagnosed an irregular heartbeat and referred her for an EKG. She went in for the test and eventually was told she was fine. But her insurer refused to pay for the EKG on the grounds that it was a preexisting condition. She was infuriated by this, since it had never been diagnosed previously, and indeed had turned out not to be a condition at all. The insurer told her she needed a letter from a doctor to prove her case. By her account, she called the hospital "ten or twenty times" over a two-week period, leaving a message each time, without response. When she finally reached a doctor he chewed her out for bothering him after hours—it was 6:00 p.m. Although this transaction occurred three months before the interview, the interviewer characterized her as still "really mad." In this case, confusion over what ought to be covered was coupled with a terrible service response; the service recovery after the initial error occurred was even worse than the error. The insurer and doctor's office probably ought to have handled this matter themselves, or at the very least have answered the customer's call and acted with alacrity. This customer will hold a grudge for years. As Sheri Mitchell of Humana (whose customers do not show up in our demonstration study) puts it, "I think the real differentiating factor is how companies resolve problems." The customer whose case is described above would no doubt agree with Mitchell's assessment.

About a fifth of complaints focused on delays in treatment—again a common problem in many service industries. Some respondents were kept waiting too long when they arrived for appointments. Others felt they were kept from seeing necessary specialists for months because of the red tape and cost-consciousness of their HMOs. Some people were frustrated by long delays in filling prescriptions. These problems are, I suspect, eminently manageable; but not until timing and scheduling issues are identified as a root cause of customer complaints. While a doctor may think of quality in terms of the percentage of correct diagnoses or successful surgeries, the customer often measures it by how long he or she must wait to see the doctor or receive diagnosis and treatment. Also important in the demonstration study were inconveniences associated with hours of operation and location of facilities. About a tenth of complaints focused on these distribution, or time-and-place, issues. For example, one HMO's policy of closing some local facilities on weekends and substituting an 800 number seemed to cause considerable stress and inconvenience for respondents. While the HMO's doctors may feel a registered nurse can make accurate determinations over the phone, patients did not (a solution to this problem might be to inform customers of the specialized training and support provided to the nurse on call).

However, the most troubling of the complaints are those that focus on the quality of the medical care provided. A third of all complaints involved concerns that substandard diagnosis or treatment has been provided! The health care providers would probably disagree with their customers' perception that the health care provided was of dubious quality. The important opinion here is the customers', not the managers'. The transaction study suggests that there may be a major, unrecognized lack of trust. Here is a quality gap of immense proportions that can only be defined and addressed from the customer's perspective. Specific incidents from the interview notes provide some interesting insights into the nature of this trust gap:

A 65-year-old HMO member had hernia surgery at 6 A.M., and when he was discharged at 10:00 A.M. the same day, "They didn't even ask me if I had help at home." He experienced "a severe, painful complication" the next weekend. His local HMO facility was closed, and his wife "couldn't find one single doctor to assist us" by telephone. "All she could get was some phone number with a 24-hour nurse" who suggested buying an over-the-counter pain remedy. He did not believe the nurse was competent to diagnose the problem over the phone, so went to the emergency ward. In his opinion, "The system should have easy access to a surgeon who can cover for the original surgeon instead of me going around the USA trying to get help." (Would his doctor say he was in danger? Probably not, but the important issue is that he *felt* he was.)

A middle-aged woman and mother of five complained that she had a chronic foot problem but does not like the approach to treatment suggested by the doctor at her HMO. She felt a specialist was needed, but the HMO would not give her a referral. To obtain the quality of care she required, she had to pay for the specialist herself.

A college student complained about the low percentage her university-sponsored insurance plan paid, and believes that it is a disincentive to proper health care. She says that, despite the insurance, "We can't afford to get good health care."

A woman went to the doctor with a urinary tract infection. She had to wait a week for medication because of delays in obtaining test results from the lab. The doctor did not diagnose and treat the condition in a timely manner, and she felt that she was not trusted. "Women know when they have urinary tract infections, but the doctors don't believe them and have to do a zillion tests before giving medication."

A woman in her fifties saw a doctor at her HMO because of back pain. A few weeks later she was called by a nurse, who told her, "You have some kind of disease in your spine," but that she should not worry about it. She was extremely concerned, and tried to call the doctor to learn more about this disease. The nurse impatiently insisted it was "nothing serious" and prevented her from talking to the doctor. Finally she set up an appointment with another doctor, since the one who made the diagnosis was unavailable. The new doctor did not know about the disease, "did not look at the X-rays," and apparently was unable to tell her anything about the original diagnosis.

THE VOICE OF THE CUSTOMER

What we hear in these interview summaries is the voice of the customer, and it raises many challenges and issues. The customers speaking in these quotes certainly view their transactions in a different light than do the employees and managers on the other side of the transactions. And it is only through research that makes the customer's voice audible to managers, and indeed to all employees, that companies can hope to make substantial and ongoing quality improvements. As Batalden of HCA puts it, a total quality system that is designed "to listen and use the voice of the patient/customer has helped our leaders focus on and manage the process of quality improvement."[20] Incorporating this voice into a company's change process is a critical management issue, perhaps the critical management issue.

I find the results of this transaction study fascinating, not so much because of anything they might say about the health care business as because they represent the customer's voice in *any* industry. There is something very powerful about the voice of the customer, at least when it is not attenuated beyond recognition by the filtering effect of closed-ended surveys. Amplifying the customer's voice is, on a day-to-day level, the job of researchers in the quality and marketing departments. But ultimately the job of *championing* the customer's perspective falls to senior management. Steven Schwartz opened this chapter with a brief description of IBM's recognition that "the way to get straight answers was from the source—the customer." IBM's top-down effort to refocus the company and its quality processes on the customer demonstrates the importance of senior management leadership in this area.

TOP-DOWN CUSTOMER FOCUS

Stephen Vehslage, a senior manager in education for IBM, teaches employees that "IBM's major challenge is to learn to become more market driven."[21] This is, if not a new thought, certainly a rediscovery of an old idea for the company. IBM's quality program began with a bottom-up orientation, and its emphasis was on process-management tools. As we saw in

---

[20]Conference Board Report No. 909, p. 78.

[21]From an interview appearing in *Newslink*, Fall 1990, IBM International Education & Management Development, publishers, p. 8.

Chapter 2, IBM redefined its quality program in 1990, integrating into it a top-down, customer-driven approach, and renaming it Market Driven Quality (MDQ). This effort to instill a customer orientation to the quality program, and the entire company, tackles the aspects of IBM's culture that are most resistant to the new quality paradigm. In 1991, IBM announced its first quarterly loss ever—a sobering event for "the company that started off the 1980s by declaring itself America's best defense against a surging Japanese computer and electronics industry," as a recent *Business Week* cover story put it.[22] Despite its optimism, IBM has not been immune to the impact of competition, and its share of the world computer market dropped from 36 percent to 23 percent during the decade.[23]

The loss at IBM reflects write-downs associated with a huge restructuring of the company (and investment analysts calculated that IBM actually earned a small profit in the fourth quarter of 1991 before the write-downs).[24] This restructuring is the latest (and largest) in a series of efforts by management to force change on the organization. A company the size of IBM does not change easily—traditions are strong and corporate culture resistant to realignments. Yet IBM has long recognized the need to become faster on its feet and closer to its customers. MDQ appears to be a stronger-armed approach to breaking down what remains of the old corporate culture and allowing the benefits of the quality program to ripple through the organization with greater speed. Ironically, this top-down initiative is in part aimed at breaking up the top-down decision-making that characterized the old IBM.

A corporate reorganization, announced at the end of 1991, pushes through a variety of structural changes that will

---

[22]"The New IBM: Is it Enough?," *Business Week*, December 16, 1991, p. 114.

[23]Ibid., citing the Yardstick Service of Garnter Group.

[24]IBM reported a fourth-quarter 1991 loss of $1.38 billion, but analysts calculated an operating profit for the quarter of between $2.25 and $2.50 share after the write-downs were subtracted, according to Paul B. Carroll, "IBM's Outlook for '92 Remains Cloudy After 4th-Quarter loss of $1.38 Billion," *The Wall Street Journal*, January 20, 1992, p. A3.

help decentralize decision making, moving many strategic decisions from the executive committee to individual units. Here is how *Business Week* describes the challenges and opportunities involved:

> If IBM really can dispense decision making from Armonk, it stands a chance of unleashing enormous resources. Hidden with the troubled $67 billion Goliath are the world's largest personal computer company, a software organization five times the size of Microsoft Corp., and a disk-drive maker that dwarfs industry "leaders" such as Seagate Corp. But many of these units have been held back by headquarters-mandated policies that stopped them from competing flat-out with nimble young upstarts. More significant, because so many important decisions have been left to headquarters, managers haven't been motivated to take risks.[25]

IBM's reorganization decentralizes authority and cuts layers of management. MDQ imposes a new, more centralized influence over the quality process as it is implemented in each of the far-flung business units. Apparently management is determined that greater autonomy be accompanied by a stronger customer focus. According to Chairman John Akers, this need to rediscover the customer may be the key lesson learned from IBM Rochester's successful bid for the Baldrige Award; "IBM Rochester learned it primarily needed to close the loop between the laboratory, manufacturing, and the customer. We thought we had a pretty closed-loop system, but we didn't. The work that IBM Rochester did to facilitate communication between the site and the customer really made the difference."[26]

Decentralized decision making plays well in the current climate, since employee empowerment looks to be a contender for biggest management fad of the decade. Empowerment on its own does not mean much—the concept is too amorphous for most managers even to know how one might

[25]Ibid., p. 113.
[26]Karen Bemowski, "Big Q at Big Blue," *Quality Progress*, May 1991, p. 18.

go about implementing it. However, in the context of a quality program, empowerment seems to have a more clearly defined role. It refers, or should refer, to the combination of decentralized authority along with the creation of a higher authority—the customer. This is the formula emerging from the combination of MDQ and restructuring at IBM, and the desired end result is expressed nicely in this quote from one of IBM's employees, senior secretary specialist Paulette Caroleo: "My customers are my managers, my reps, and my SEs [Service Engineers]. We're taking on more ownership to support them. I've found that when you can take things into your own hands, you get a lot done quicker."[27]

In this simple example, a secretary is taking on more authority in order to perform better and faster for her internal customers, the people at IBM who consume her services. Autonomy alone would not help IBM's turnaround, and nor would customer orientation without the autonomy to act on it. Together, they add up to greater care and responsibility for customers at each of the thousands of points of customer contact where transaction quality, and customer perception, is shaped.

There is a lesson to be learned from IBM's experience. It is not enough to create values and processes that have a customer focus, leaving it to the rest of the company to implement this focus. Management must actually take up the customer baton and run with it, and when the company pursues any quality improvements, it helps if management slaps the customer baton firmly in the hand of each business unit and employee. Only then should they be given the authority to run with it. The customer relationship is the very core of the company, and must not be left to the lower levels of the organization. It is, or ought to be, a central management concern in any quality initiative.

[27]As quoted in the company publication "Market-Driven Quality": As Basic As Our Beliefs," IBM Corp., 1991, p. 11.

And that is, or ought to be, the concluding point for a chapter on customer focus. However, it is important to ground every observation in practical advice, and in this case, the abstract notion that management must focus on the customer can certainly stand additional grounding. When management focuses (and focuses the company) on the customer relationship, what exactly should it be looking for? Is going out for lunch with major buyers enough? Does management have to get on the phone and conduct surveys? How one actually adopts a customer focus is not always very clear. In fact, quality-based management requires active participation in the customer research process, but not in a hands-on manner. Rather it is management's role to ask the right questions about customers.

The best way to illustrate this point is to share the advice offered by Edward Kane, vice president of quality and management systems for Dun & Bradstreet Software (and previously director of IBM's quality program): "The first step toward improvement was to ask, Where is the pain for our customers? The customers were asked and the people who serve the customers were asked."[28]

Kane's question, "Where is the pain for our customers?" cuts to the heart of the quality improvement process. This question, posed throughout the organization, necessitates aggressive efforts to listen to the voice of the customer through transaction research and root cause analysis. And this question drives the company to look at what might once have been considered threatening or negative viewpoints (such as "it takes forever to finish a construction project at this university") and see in them opportunities to please and ease the pain of customers.

Aggressive inquiry into the customer condition is the starting point for the improvement cycle, and, in a way, also

---

[28]From a draft article by Edward Kane, intended for publication in 1992, entitled "The Ascent of Quality in a Software Company," DBS, Atlanta, 1991.

the ending point. At Dun & Bradstreet Software, Kane ends the improvement process by asking what benefits the quality effort delivered to the customer. The company answers the question as follows:

> Leadership Through Excellence [DBS' quality program] delivers tangible benefits to our customers. It continually
>
> - Improves product and service quality
> - Makes it easier to do business with Dun & Bradstreet Software
> - Increases our ability to be proactive and responsive to customer needs
> - Provides value for Dun & Bradstreet Software deliverables, helping customers achieve a competitive advantage, maximize ROI, and increase productivity.[29]

While other companies may wish to deliver different benefits to their customers, they too must make sure that the quality initiative does produce real, tangible customer benefits. The ultimate measure of the success of a quality program is whether it adds value for the *customer*. Since the customer does not run the company, it falls to management to make sure this question is both asked and answered, daily and weekly, as a backdrop to every management decision and as a driver of every quality improvement effort.

---

[29]Quoted from brochure, "D&B Software Quality," Dun & Bradstreet Software Services, Inc., 1990.

Chapter 5

THE PROCESS PERSPECTIVE

> Traditional organizations frequently conduct their business through a vertical structure of distinct functions, each with narrowly-defined responsibilities and roles, divorced from the paying customer. Work, in reality though, is accomplished through a series of horizontal, cross-functional processes.
>
> —*Johnson & Johnson Quality Institute*[1]

When managers attack the whole subject of quality improvement, an emphasis on processes provides a new and valuable foundation. The quality revolution brings with it a fundamental shift toward a process-oriented view of the firm—a new perspective. This process perspective is an intangible but essential component of quality, and one of the reasons that total quality stands in opposition even to the most excellent of standard management practices.

---

[1]From a description of Johnson & Johnson's Business Process Quality Management Program, provided by Sue Jacobs, Johnson & Johnson Quality Institute, January 8, 1992.

WHO'S RESPONSIBLE FOR THIS MESS?

There are two essential aspects of the new process perspective. First, it says that *problems arise because of processes, not people*. Masao Nemoto, a director of Toyota and one of the architects of its just-in-time and quality programs, puts it this way:

> I believe that people are not gods and they are bound to make mistakes no matter how hard they may try. There is no benefit in assessing responsibility for committing errors. It is better to clarify the facts and work toward prevention of recurrence."[2]

In Japan, fear of shame and penalties are natural impediments to innovation and risk taking. In America, a more internalized sense of guilt replaces shame as a motivator, but the effect is similar: the individual who will be held accountable for a mistake behaves so as to avoid making one, and this often means avoiding taking risks. How the organization assigns causality, especially when things go wrong, has a tremendous impact on how fast the organization can learn and adapt. The fact that our conventional management thinking holds the individual accountable for mistakes goes far toward explaining why we do not routinely see every individual learning and innovating at a high rate.

Conventional wisdom says that when people are held accountable for their work they will do better work. But that quickly degenerates into nothing more than the old "kick in the ass" theory, so eloquently dismissed by Frederick Herzberg in 1959,[3] just two years after the American Institute of

---

[2]Masao Nemoto, Total Quality Control for Management: Strategies and Techniques from Toyota and Toyoda Gosei, Prentice Hall, 1987, p. 9.

[3]F. Herxberg, B. Mausner, and B. Snyderman, *The Motivation to Work*, John Wiley and Sons, Inc., 1959. Or, for a more accessible description of his theories, see Herzberg, "One More Time: How do you Motivate Employees?", *Harvard Business Review*, Sept–Oct. 1987, pp. 109–120. Herzberg coined the terms "hygiene" versus "motivator" factors, and found that factors offering the highest employee motivation

Management's ill-fated list of excellently managed corporations was published. The problem was that management needed something else to kick, and the process provides a more constructive target. In the process perspective, the individual is *not* held accountable in the conventional manner (there is no guilt or shame, and no penalties are imposed). This frees the individual to concentrate on how to improve the process without fear. (To implement this concept, management must ask, "What is wrong with the process?" rather than "Who is responsible for this?" when something goes wrong.)

BUSINESS AS A PROCESS

The second essential element of the new process perspective is the view that *business is nothing but a collection of processes*, each of which can be modified and improved at will. There are two advantages to this view. First, it sees the firm as a fluid, changing thing. The forces that traditionally work to prevent constructive change[4] are swept away by this viewpoint. (Why? Because the process perspective makes everything visible in the firm. It is only when processes operate out of sight— in black boxes, for example—that they are able to become inflexible.) Second, it gives the individual a useful handle by which to grip the firm and pull it in desirable directions. Because when you look at any individual function and model it as a process, you at once begin to see how to *improve* it. Just as a balance sheet gives the accountant a powerful view of the firm for accounting purposes, a process model gives managers a powerful view of the firm for the purpose of making quality improvements. The process perspective allows us to peak beneath the lids of many boxes that we used to paint black and hide in a corner.

(continued from page 138)
are achievement, recognition, the work itself, responsibility, advancement, growth, and salary, in descending order of impact.

    [4]'Isomorphism' to the scholar of organization behavior.

The insights offered by the process perspective explain away something that puzzled me for a year or more as I followed the progress of Analog Devices' quality program. Ray Stata, its president and chairman, has collaborated for a number of years with a group at MIT that applies systems dynamics to organizations. System's dynamics is a pretty obscure field—most managers don't even know what the term means! I figured, hey, the guy's an engineer by training, so he gets into that sort of technical stuff. But it couldn't have much of anything to do with Analog Device's quality program. After all, you don't hear quality practitioners talking about systems dynamics.

I was wrong. The systems dynamics approach is fundamental to Analog Device's quality program. As Stata explains, "One of the early lessons learned from system dynamics is that organizations are like giant networks of interconnected nodes."[5] He observes that tools are now available to "simulate organizational behavior and show how the structure and policies of companies may generate undesirable performance that is often blamed on the external environment." The language of systems dynamics provides the tools needed for Analog Devices to peek inside those black boxes. Their black boxes are filled with diagrams of organizational systems, with their nodes and interconnections. Systems dynamics is one way to analyze and manage the processes of an organization, and it is through systems dynamics that Stata shifted his organization to the process perspective.

THE WESTINGHOUSE COST-TIME PROFILE

One of the best ways to understand the process perspective is to study process tools, and it will be helpful to look briefly at several higher-level conceptual tools in this chapter.

---

[5]Ray Stata, "Organizational Learning—The Key to Management Innovation," *Sloan Management Review*, Spring 1989, pp. 63–73.

Like any tool, a quality method can tell much about the work that is performed with it, at least to the trained eye. Archaeologists have constructed profiles of entire civilizations largely from the tools left behind (although admittedly they are at an advantage since no one is still alive to refute their theories!).

Westinghouse makes extensive use of two general-purpose tools in its quality program: The cost-time profile and business process management. No quality project would be undertaken at that company without these tools close at hand, and as a result they offer considerable insight into both the details of Westinghouse's approach and, more important to managers, the broader question of how to analyze and manage quality from a process perspective.

The cost-time profile is used to analyze a process, whether on the factory floor or in the office. It might be used to look at the cost and time gains from installing a just-in-time inventory system, for example, or to analyze an order-entry system in a sales office.

It is based on the idea that a company's investment in any process is a factor of both the money spent on it and the *time* spent on it. For example, a factory has cash investments such as inventories and labor, which are spent over the production cycle as a product is made.

As time passes during the completion of a process, the company's investment in that process increases. Therefore a profile of investments over time is cumulative. For example, the company spends money on raw materials, then labor and energy, then, if unfinished goods are held in the factory, on work-in-process inventory. The longer each step in the production process takes, the more time and money are spent. Total manufacturing costs (or any other process costs) can be reduced either by reducing specific costs, such as the cost of a raw material, or by reducing process time. Yet analysis traditionally focuses on materials costs rather than cycle time. In the quality concept the emphasis is reversed, and Westinghouse uses the cost-time profile to make sure people focus on time factors at least as much as cost factors when trying to improve processes.

REDUCING MANUFACTURING CYCLE TIMES

According to George Dorman, V.P., Human Resources at Westinghouse Electric Corp. (and a former member of The Conference Board's U.S. Quality Council), "Every process has a unique profile that illustrates the aggregation of costs over time." Exhibit 5-1 is an example of the kind of diagram Westinghouse uses.

Dorman explains that,

> . . . the shaded area represents investment in the business—it's cash! In the factory, this takes the form of inventory we can count—either raw materials, works-in-process, or finished-goods inventory. In the office, it's less tangible—it's knowledge, data, paper, and information—but it still represents cash spent on the business. The goal of process improvement is to shrink this profile. Obtaining significantly less cash investment is a

Exhibit 5-1 Cost-Time Profile

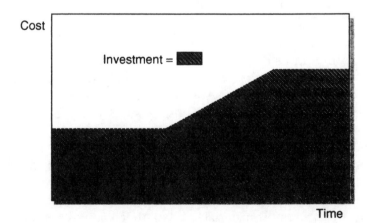

Source: Adapted from Westinghouse company documents.

powerful way to build value and gain competitive advantage. And by far the most effective improvement lever we have found is cycle time.[6]

Westinghouse first applied the cost-time profile in its analysis of manufacturing operations, especially in the application of just-in-time inventory management to reduce manufacturing cycle times. Again according to Dorman, the cost-time profile "was initially developed for use in the factory as a way to reduce inventories dramatically. It involves cutting process cycle time by an average of 60 to 70 percent, with resultant cost reductions of 25 percent or more." (Other companies have found a similar relationship between process time and production costs.) At Westinghouse this effort was estimated to have cut factory inventories by more than $700 million over a three year period[7]—quite a bit of work for such a simple tool!

FOCUSING ON WHITE-COLLAR PRODUCTIVITY

Now the Westinghouse quality effort is focusing more on white-collar productivity. This reflects, in part, the likelihood that many of the most dramatic gains in manufacturing have already been made, while the processes of information workers are still virgin territory for quality improvement at most companies. At Westinghouse, Dorman estimates that "information workers now represent two-thirds of our workforce," and that "nearly two-thirds of our costs-of-quality failures are due to white-collar issues—not factory problems."[8] In this regard, Westinghouse typifies a trend felt all through U.S. industry. Thus the process perspective, traditionally applied at the factory, may ultimately prove even more valuable when applied

[6]Conference Board Research Report No. 909, p. 30.
[7]Ibid., p. 30.
[8]Ibid., p. 29.

to white-collar and information workers than to factory workers and their work.

But back to the tool. Dorman observes that "quality and cycle-time reduction are directly related." This point is shown graphically in a diagram used at Westinghouse that pictures quality increasing as cycle time declines (Exhibit 5-2). Incidentally, this generic diagram can be customized to track the results of any specific process analysis and improvement, and the diagram shown here generalizes on Westinghouse's specific experience. (A customer-driven measure of quality is of course preferable if you decide to actually plot this chart for one of your company's processes.)

Why should quality improve as cycle time is shortened? Dorman explains:

> When quality of product and performance improves, cycle time comes down—because you're eliminating rework and false starts, as well as reducing organizational redundancy. Looking at it another way, working to reduce cycle time forces you to

Exhibit 5-2 Quality Versus Cycle Time

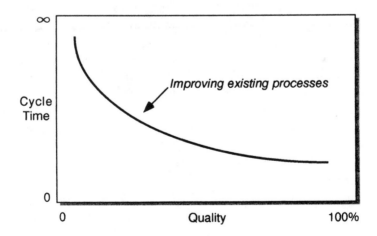

Source: Adapted from Westinghouse company documents.

improve your quality performance. In either case, working on the existing process will eventually get you to the zero defects stage, with an associated minimum cycle time.[9]

This is a striking point, stated forcefully by a manager with personal experience to back up in the assertion. The relationship between cycle time and quality holds up in all Westinghouse's quality improvement efforts, and it is also generally true that just-in-time inventory systems develop arm-in-arm with improved product quality in many industries. It may be that processes exist in time and, in fact, that this is the single most important aspect of them. Their time profile is their skeleton, and to change their outcome significantly the entire body must be modified, from the skeleton out. Yet any process, when analyzed and dissected in the effort to find out how to improve it, ends up as a diagram or flow chart on a single piece of paper—seemingly existing outside of time. A more realistic, though more difficult, way to study processes would be to make animated models of them.

When I first started studying U.S. quality programs, I was puzzled by the insistence of some practitioners that competing on time and competing on quality were one and the same. (This puzzlement seems widely shared; the business press consistently treats competing on time as a *separate* strategy from competing on quality.) These strategies do seem on the face of it to be different; for example, why couldn't one company make a superior-quality product slowly by hand without infringing on the market of another that mass-produced a lower-quality product very quickly? This certainly used to be the case, and in fact 'quality' was reserved for custom-crafted, expensive products such as the Rolls Royce, in contrast to rapidly-made, mass-produced items. Thus speed of manufacture was associated with cheapness, not quality. Here is yet another example of the axiom that quality is the opposite of standard management practice, as if another was needed!

[9]Conference Board Report 909, p. 31.

REDUCING TIME WITHOUT SACRIFICING QUALITY

Westinghouse is not the only company to have discovered the parallels between cycle time reduction and quality improvement efforts. At IBM, employees are trained in cycle time reduction and told that,

> Since everything we do can be measured in cycle time, and customers consider this an important gauge of responsiveness, everything possible must be done to reduce it—without sacrificing quality. This is best accomplished by eliminating the causes of defects and simplifying processes. Shortening cycle time has been shown to reduce defects. Cycle time is a critical indicator of the health of any business.[10]

From a process perspective, when you start looking at the causes of poor quality and the causes of lengthy cycle times you are generally dealing with the same problems, not different ones. And this is an insight that the cost-time profile, as a management tool, hammers home to its user—just as a hammer makes clear to its user the relationship between fastener and material to be fastened.

Westinghouse has found that every process has a unique cost-time profile, its finger print, you might say. For example, Exhibit 5-3 is a cost-time profile for customer order processing. It starts with a telephone call from the customer to place an electrical parts order. Costs rise rapidly as personnel first record the order and create the necessary paper-work to get the order in the cue. As you can see from the diagram, the order only waits a couple days (time is measured here in hours) before the right parts are pulled out of inventory, packed up and shipped (these activities account for the additional cost increase at the end of the process). The process has

---

[10]From p. 14 of company document, "Market-Driven Quality: The Framework," provided by Andrew C. Russell, MDQ Communications Advisor, Market-Driven Quality, IBM, January 1992.

Exhibit 5-3 Westinghouse Customer Order Processing

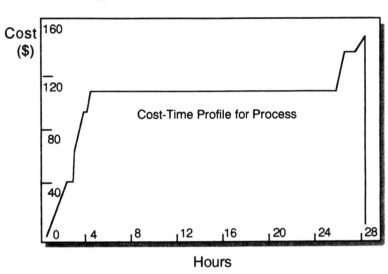

Source: Westinghouse

a characteristic profile, with step-wise cost increases in the first four hours of the process, a static period of about 22 hours, and a second step-wise increase of costs in the last two hours of the process.

If you examine it closely, you might conclude that this cost-time profile is not too bad from a quality perspective. After all, many pick-and-pack warehousing or parts-supply operations turn customer orders around in a week or more, rather than in a couple of days. But what if customers need the electrical components Westinghouse makes in a hurry—the next day, if possible? Since research suggested this might be the case, management was faced with one of those classic quality decisions: Would it be worthwhile to incur the extra cost associated with cutting the cycle time in half?

That is a trick question designed to test your faith in the quality philosophy. The traditional approach to providing faster delivery would require a cost-time tradeoff. It would probably involve hiring more staff to move the paperwork and parts through the existing process faster, and to expand inventories and warehouse space as needed to support the fever pitch of this new, larger operation. Should this course be followed, a 50 percent reduction in cycle time might double the costs of order-processing. Assuming these incremental costs must be passed on to the customers, it might be a high price to pay for a little added convenience. A tradeoff analysis via customer survey or focus groups might well show that customers would rather not pay the higher price just for the convenience of faster delivery times, and so the project would be shelved.

DELIVERING PRODUCTS FASTER, FOR *LESS*

However, a careful analysis of the process might instead lead to a series of insights into how to improve the efficiency of the existing process, and ultimately perhaps to innovations that modify the process dramatically, in order to deliver products faster, *for less*. In other words, a willingness to work on the process itself, rather than taking it as a given, makes it possible to reduce the area under the curve on the cost-time profile (rather than to just change its shape without reducing its area). And this is just what Westinghouse did. Dorman reports that, "A cycle-time program helped restructure and then automate order-entry procedures, cutting the time needed to handle an electrical parts order from 28 hours to just 10 minutes and at the same time slashing cost per order by two-thirds" (see Exhibit 5-4). Wow. Unlike finger prints, cost-time profiles can be modified.

The numbers are real—Westinghouse really achieved these cost and time reductions. Sometimes it is difficult to believe that charts like this are not some pie-in-the-sky diagram on a chalkboard—or that companies can realistically cut process time by 96 percent and process costs by 66 percent, as

EXHIBIT 5-4 WESTINGHOUSE CUSTOMER ORDER
PROCESSING

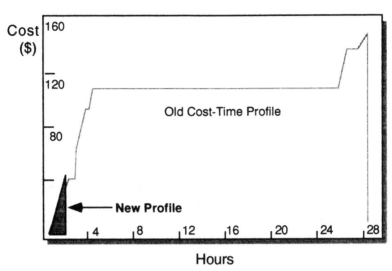

Source: Westinghouse

in this example. How can there possibly be that much ineffi-ciency and waste left on the table? It seems impossible until you peak under the skin of individual processes. And the evidence suggests that performance gaps exist in every pro-cess within a business, and thus within an organization's over-all process of serving its customers. Here is another tool that helps managers peak under the skin of the business as a whole, not just one specific process at a time.

PROCESS IMPROVEMENT MANAGEMENT

If you want to drive a single nail, the hand-held hammer is just the right tool. What if you want to drive thousands of nails in a single day? You are in for a sore elbow. Better to reach into the carpenter's toolbox for an air compressor and pressurized-air nail driver. It does the same job, but on a much larger scale.

When companies want to step back from specific processes to look at the company as a whole, they need a different tool too. Westinghouse uses a method they call process improvement management for this larger-scale problem. George Dorman of Westinghouse explains the problem that process improvement management is designed to solve:

> What business is really all about is performing a series of interlocked processes, starting with sales and going through order entry, resource planning, production, distribution, and payment collection. Not one of these basic business processes is performed within the walls of one single functional department. All of them are, almost by definition, multifunctional. Now what happens as we pursue a customer and then move to satisfy his need for performing these processes every day? Do we get a smoothly flowing integrated operation, with a minimum cost-time profile and 100 percent quality performance?[11]

No. According to Dorman, "Too often we operate with a less than truly efficient process in which, for example, the customer's order bounces back and forth between functions, before it finally moves on to the next step in the overall process." Ambiguous information is passed on to another department, which must then come back to the first department to clarify the information. Errors are passed on and must be corrected. And so on . . . the possibilities for confusion at departmental or functional interfaces are enormous. The natural boundaries between various departments are bottlenecks for the over-all process of serving a customer. Like large work-in-process inventories or out-of-adjustment manufacturing machines, they add time and money costs to the company's overall business process. And improving particular processes within each department does not do anything about these interdepartmental bottlenecks. As Dorman puts it,

[11]Conference Board report 909, p. 35–36.

Total quality requires process innovation in this overall business process just as much as it does in individual, day-to-day processes. We want to achieve a smoothly integrated flow, where every activity performs its part of the process to optimize total performance. That's how we can eliminate traditional interface problems between functions and slash the extra organizational costs they produce.[12]

The tool Westinghouse uses is a simple one, a diagram (see Exhibit 5-5). It starts with the company's organization chart, which generally shows a series of separate functional areas side-by-side across the top of a page. This organizational structure defines the bottlenecks as well—they are the gaps between functional areas. Using this organizational structure as a scaffolding or frame, the diagram shows customer needs on one side, the various processes the company performs across the middle (each under the functional areas responsible for it), and customer satisfaction at the other end.

In this diagram, each of the more specific functions is shown in sequence (it helps to reorganize your chart if necessary to make the flow go from left to right). This seems almost absurdly simple—of course the company performs a process designed to satisfy customer needs. Of course, each department plays a role by doing its own specialized part, just as a factory produces a product by giving responsibility for sub-processes to a sequence of workstations along the production line. Yet, management seldom thinks this way, and companies are seldom managed this way. What would happen if you were to analyze total costs and time through the entire process of satisfying the customer? What would the company's total cost-time profile look like? You can imagine both costs and time accumulating at the transitions between each department. You could measure them, if you wanted—perhaps a good project to put a quality team to work on.

[12]Ibid., p. 36.

Exhibit 5-5 The Business Process Model

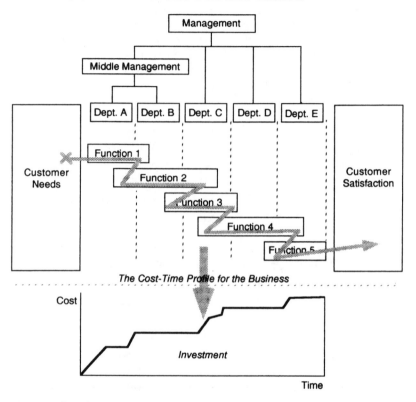

Source: Adapted from Westinghouse company documents.

THE OUTCOME IS WHAT COUNTS

IBM flowcharts the business process of designing, making and delivering a product or process. It is a variant on the Westinghouse model (although I do not know which was developed first) and it expresses the same underlying concept. Here is how it is drawn at IBM:

Design-Development Cycle

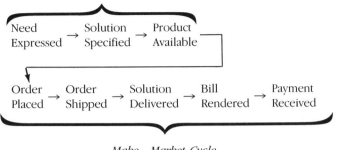

Make—Market Cycle

At IBM, this diagram is helpful in relating the work of individual functions to the broader process of serving customers. As company training materials explain, "Although different parts of IBM play a role in different segments of this cycle, the customer does not see that distinction. It is the total effort—and the outcome—that counts with our customer. Therefore, it is the total cycle that must be executed with excellence."[13] A great advantage of the business-process view of a firm is that it helps every component of that process focus on the customer.

Just as you can innovate at the level of a specific, narrowly-defined process like order processing, so too can you innovate at the business process level. Redefining the nature and relationship of component processes can alter the business process dramatically. What if you just eliminated all the bottlenecks between functional areas? This is analogous to making work-in-process flow smoothly through a factory, with each subcomponent made and delivered just as it is needed by the next process in the line and the whole thing controlled by the pull of customer demand at the end. That is, in essence,

---

[13]From p. 14–15 of company document, "Market-Driven Quality: The Framework," provided by Andrew C. Russell, MDQ Communications Advisor, Market-Driven Quality, IBM, January 1992.

how a just-in-time inventory system works in a factory. However, there is no reason, except tradition, not to look at the entire business process in a similar fashion.

SOUNDS GOOD . . . BUT WILL THE CUSTOMER LIKE IT?

Another subtle, but vital, point—the business process determines the effectiveness of innovations in individual functional processes, *from the customer's point of view*. A department may cut order processing time dramatically, but will this improve the quality of the products and services the business delivers to its customers? Not if some other functional process is, or becomes, the critical path that determines time or costs in the overall business process. There has to be a coordinated effort to improve each functional process more or less in unison, and to do it with an eye to the overall business process. Some functional efforts will have greater leverage on the overall business process than others at any one time. So management can use business process management to coordinate and manage the more narrowly-defined process improvements of individual departments.

Finally there is another, more obvious point: Process innovations can be applied to the business process itself, with the result that new ways of doing business may be discovered. This will have an impact on individual functional processes, just as work on individual processes has an impact on the business process. The two tools, and the two levels of process management they represent, are interactive in a beneficial and powerful way, and when both are applied the business process improves in quality and/or its cost-time profile shrinks. The company's organizational chart is the starting point for the charts used in business process management, but it can also be the ending point, as innovations suggest new ways to conceive of the firm's work, and new ways to organize and perform it. Here, for example, is an improved business process diagram from Westinghouse, the result of a series of process innovations (Exhibit 5-6).

George Dorman of Westinghouse explains that this chart represents a new organization "that can rapidly identify customer needs and move efficiently to satisfy them . . . We want to achieve a smoothly integrated flow, where every activity performs its part of the process to optimize total performance. That's how we can eliminate traditional interface problems between functions and slash the extraorganizational costs they produce."[14] In Exhibit 5-6, all the various functional groups are coordinated and focused on customer needs, and through this

EXHIBIT 5-6 CUSTOMER-ORIENTED TOTAL QUALITY PROCESS

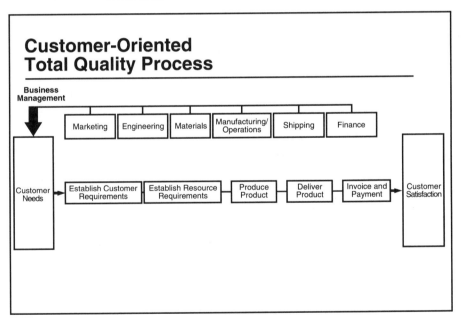

Source: Westinghouse

[14]Conference Board Report No. 909, pp. 36–37.

focus they all take responsibility for a smooth flow of processes designed to provide customer satisfaction. And in this new view of the business, senior management is moved from its traditional spot, above all the business functions, and placed at the interface between the functional areas and customer needs. The role of management is to provide coordination and focus for all the functions, and it takes responsibility for (or *owns*, in quality-speak), the entire business process. This is the process perspective in action, and it is substantially different from the traditional management paradigm. The cross-functional coordination is no doubt a big change for middle management, but the biggest change is the new role that senior management must play—a role that is predominantly concerned with managing the business process so as to provide customer satisfaction.

CREATING A
QUALITY CULTURE

The culture of an organization is not always apparent—until it becomes an obstacle to progress. Listen, for example, to the story of Hoechst Celanese Corp.'s quality journey, as told by its CEO, Ernest Drew:

> We began with Crosby's 14 steps on a company-wide basis. Significant improvements were made in the early 1980s but by 1984 we began to plateau and we had seen only limited success moving beyond manufacturing. We still had the old culture. Recognizing that a change in our basic culture was needed, we introduced our Quality Values which defined the desired culture and the need for broad participation.[1]

Culture became an issue when the company found it could make no further quality progress without changing its culture.

[1]Speech at The Conference Board's 75th Anniversary Quality Symposium, October 1, 1991, New York.

Corporate culture is often described with terms like philosophy, values, attitudes, and ethics. Culture is reflected in the relationships among employees, the mores and taboos within a company, the legends and stories told, even the language and imagery used when discussing business decisions. It can be transmitted through subtle messages such as the way parking spaces or offices are allocated or the nicknames applied to managers when they are not listening. It can also be manifested in more obvious ways, such as in the criteria by which advancements and raises are awarded. Culture is a subtle but tremendously powerful influence over everything people do. It can influence not only employees but also suppliers, distributors and others within its reach.

Managers are not accustomed to managing culture. Indeed, most managers are not conscious of how their corporate culture shapes their actions and beliefs, and especially, of how *they* reinforce and direct their corporate culture. In a stable organization, one that is already well adapted to its present and future environments, there is no particular need to manage corporate culture. (Indeed, if such an organization really exists, there would be little need for management of any kind!) But in organizations whose competitiveness is determined by how rapidly they can learn and change, corporate culture must be managed. If it is not put to active use as a lever for changing the company, it will by default become an obstacle to change. For the first time since the industrial revolution, large numbers of companies are finding it necessary to undertake conscious management of their corporate cultures.

The tools available for managing corporate culture include innovation, participation, competition, leadership and training. These tools help translate the new values of an organization, as expressed in a vision statement or quality plan, into a living culture extending throughout the company, its suppliers and distributors.

6

INNOVATION

> C learly, the way to keep improving is to innovate.
> *—George C. Dorman, vice president, human*
> *resources, Westinghouse Electric Corp.*[1]
>
> I nnovation at 3M is strongly woven into our culture. However, we have learned that innovation aligned with total quality creates a winning combination leveraged toward competitive success.
> *—R. H. Kubinski, manager, corporate quality*
> *services, 3M*[2]

Ron Kubinski's words echo a common sentiment within 3M. A. F. Jacobson, previous CEO and chairman of 3M (and now chairman of The Conference Board's board), put it this way, "Quality and innovation. These are the tools for staying ahead in our increasingly competitive society."[3] Innovation has always been a key value at 3M, and therefore it was only natural

[1]Conference Board Report No. 909, p. 32.
[2]Personal communication with the author, January 14, 1992.
[3]From a 3M presentation, "The Quest for Excellence," provided courtesy of 3M Corporate Quality Services.

that innovation should provide a context and focus for the company's quality initiative. But the link between quality and innovation is not unique to 3M. In fact, it is a vital link for any quality practitioner, and companies without an innovation-oriented culture find it necessary to create one as they develop their quality programs.

The innovation-quality link is so important because quality improvement *is* innovation. Innovation is defined in the dictionary quite simply as, "the introduction of something new." Improvement means just that—the introduction of something new. It involves thinking up clever new ways to do things, and figuring out how to screen, nurture, develop, and implement these new ideas. Bottlenecks at any stage of the idea development process—and most companies have bottlenecks at *every* stage—will limit the company's ability to learn and change.

In a sense, quality is a broader vision of innovation. Innovation in the traditional management approach is often equated with technical research and development, and thus limited to the engineering and design departments. Innovation in the United States is traditionally technical in nature and focused on products. The quality culture focuses on improving *processes*—not only the processes of product development and production, but all the processes that make up the business. And so innovation must go on in every process, whether it be high-tech or low-tech, and whether it be concerned with products or with any of the various internal and external service activities that often make up the bulk of the work in any company.

Innovation and quality are in a sense two sides of the same coin. At 3M, Jacobson argues, "Quality belongs at the center of our drive for innovation—as a resource for innovation."[4] Companies without 3M's traditional emphasis on innovation might put this the other way around, making innovation

---

[4]Ibid.

a central resource for quality improvement, but in either case the link is a critical one. It does not much matter which side of the coin faces upward.

It takes innovation to generate the many new ideas needed for continuous improvement. Every improvement represents an insight into what is wrong with the old system, and a good idea concerning how to improve upon it. Further, *the rate of innovation* can be seen as a driver of the rate of improvement. We saw back in Chapter 1 that the faster-learning organization can outpace slower-learning competitors, as the Japanese auto companies did their U.S. competitors.

Managing the rate of learning is in a sense the same as managing the rate of innovation. Thinking and learning, questioning and imagining—these are the activities that generate new ideas and increase the rate of continuous improvement— and thus the activities that confer competitive advantage. 3M's vision of quality, formally defined as "continuous improvement in all business and support services at a rate of change that attains and sustains global leadership in their chosen markets," reflects the importance of the *rate* of learning and innovation.

Teams, discussed later in Chapter 11, are a useful tool both for generating and implementing ideas. They perform this role at Federal Express. As Fred Smith explains it, his company's Quality Action Teams have "enabled us to provide a structure that best utilizes the ideas of every employee, from courier to billing agent to vice president; from secretary to ops manager to senior vice president."[5] One way to up the rate of innovation is to use tools such as quality improvement teams that allow the company to harness the creative ideas and efforts of a larger percentage of employees. Once companies could afford to making thinking the work of specialists in the product development and planning departments. Now they

[5]Text of a December 5, 1990 speech, provided by the publicity office of Federal Express.

are compelled to put every employee's mind to work in order to achieve a competitive rate of improvement.

Intrapreneurship Programs for Harnessing Creativity

Intrapreneurship programs harness the ideas and energy of individual employees throughout an organization. They are based on the observation that entrepreneurs seem to be more creative, enthusiastic, and diligent innovators than their big-company peers. How can large organizations encourage their employees to innovate with the enthusiasm and success of entrepreneurs? There are many differences between a big company and an entrepreneurial one, and debate continues over the practicality of the concept. For example, many academics have attempted to show that entrepreneurs have a unique risk-taking personality their salaried peers lack. Hogwash. I've worked for both big companies and as an entrepreneur. The academic researchers are more likely measuring entrepreneurial *behavior* than personality, and behavior is in large part a factor of the environment. When big companies create the right kind of environment, one encouraging entrepreneurship and permitting entrepreneurs to receive rewards in proportion to their risks, their employees start behaving like entrepreneurs.

BELL ATLANTIC'S CHAMPIONSHIP CONCEPT

Bell Atlantic has had a company-wide quality program for several years now, and innovation is one of its cornerstones (in fact, even staff departments now develop their own innovative services and sell them both within and outside of the company). Especially striking is Bell Atlantic's formalization of the championship concept—their innovation program is designed to encourage and support individual champions of new ideas. Here is how Raymond Smith, Bell Atlantic's CEO, describes the program:

> We are committed to identifying corporate entrepreneurs, training them, and developing their ideas into new businesses. We do this primarily through our Champion program. The Champion program arose from one of our companies, Chesapeake & Potomac Telephone, and we spread it across the whole corporation in 1989. The program provides seed money, guidance, and training to potential entrepreneurs who propose new products and services. People at any level can make proposals. If projects are accepted, their proposers can run them. And they can invest a portion of their wages in the project, in exchange for the prospect of a piece of the action when their product has been marketed.[6]

The Champion projects follow a formal six-step process (presuming they make it over all development hurdles). This process sets the ground rules for entrepreneurship. One might say that rules are a violation of the essential freewheeling, independent spirit of entrepreneurship. But the program is designed to protect the entrepreneurial efforts of salaried employees (for example by insuring time and funding are available), and to maximize the success rate by adding the minimum in planning and review. Here is the process:

1. Proposals are submitted in writing for review by Champion staff in Bell Atlantic's Intrapreneurship Division.

2. Proposals are evaluated, partly through a self-evaluation by the champion submitting the proposal. If accepted, the champion is given special training in entrepreneurship and market analysis and given time and funds for development.

---

[6]Rosabeth Moss Kanter, "Championing Change: An Interview With Bell Atlantic's CEO Raymond Smith," *Harvard Business Review*, January–February, 1991, p. 127.

3. After three months, formal written assessments of progress are submitted to a committee of senior managers for review. (Good reports earn their authors cash awards.)

4. If ideas pass the screening, the champions are sent to work with the Business Development Group for six months for further development work and training. At the end of this period, the ideas are test marketed.

5. If test results are positive, they are brought to market by a product team. The champion often becomes the project manager and may work with this team for up to three years (in place of his or her previous job).[7]

This program is like a suggestion system gone wild, with the person making the suggestion given the opportunity and resources needed to carry the idea all the way to market. How well does the system work? It is proving a significant source of new products for Bell Atlantic. According to Raymond Smith, "In the first year, 36 Champions were accepted into the program. In 1989, 39 were added. By late 1990, there were about 33 products and services in the pipeline, several of them near the commercialization stage. Projects include Creative Connections, a line of designer phone jacks, Emerg-Alert, prerecorded emergency messages targeted to latchkey children and the elderly; CommGuard, a package of backup phone service in case of a system breakdown; local usage information services for all lines in a Centrex system, and a do-not-disturb service."[8] These are creative product and service ideas, and, most impressive, they are the brainchildren of Bell Atlantic's employees. Each was thought up and championed by an individual who, in the normal corporate culture, would have had no opportunity to put his or her good ideas to work for the

---

[7] Ibid.
[8] Ibid.

company. The greatest benefit of a program like this is not the added revenues such products may bring but the development of an entrepreneurial spirit in the company's corporate culture. The experience of championing an idea, or even watching a peer do so, is likely to make employees more assertive and enthusiastic when it comes to contributing new ideas of all sorts, not just new product or service ideas.

USING TACIT KNOWLEDGE
MORE EFFECTIVELY

One reason intrapreneurship programs hold so much potential for companies is that, as the philosopher Michael Polanyi once put it, "We can know more than we can tell." Much of what an individual knows is not articulated in a systematic, explicit manner. How, for example, do you hit a backhand in tennis? How do you recognize your child from a distance in a crowd? How do you make scrambled eggs that have just the consistency you like? These are examples of tacit knowledge— tacit as in the dictionary definition, "expressed or carried on without words or speech." A recipe for scrambled eggs is explicit knowledge. Without the tacit knowledge that comes from experience and feel, an inexperienced cook may make runny or tough scrambled eggs from that explicit recipe. And tacit knowledge, since it is not expressed in words or speech, is not easily communicated from the individual to the institution. Intrapreneurship programs, and quality programs in general, can be seen as a vehicle for turning valuable tacit knowledge into explicit knowledge. They harness the power of the individual's ideas by tapping into this reserve of tacit knowledge and applying it creatively to the generation of innovations and process improvements.

Professor Ikujiro Nonaka of the Institute for Business Research at Japan's Hitotsubashi University believes that Japanese companies are rapid learners because they use tacit knowledge more effectively than their U.S. counterparts. According to Nonaka, "To Western managers, the Japanese approach often seems odd or even incomprehensible." For example, he asks "Why is a beer can a useful analogy for a personal copier?" And he points out that this analogy resulted in a key breakthrough in the design of Canon's radical new minicopier.[9] The creation and use of tacit knowledge is a powerful tool for creativity and innovation. While the approach may be incomprehensible to many Western managers, I believe it makes perfect sense to managers of quality programs. The whole thrust of a quality culture is empowering the individual employees to innovate and improve the processes and products on which they work. The concept of tacit knowledge fits neatly into this underlying value of quality improvement.

Professor Nonaka tells a story that illustrates the value of tacit knowledge, and also shows how one Japanese company gives employees the kind of freedom and support needed to develop and apply tacit knowledge on the job:

> In 1985, product developers at the Osaka-based Matsushita Electric Company were hard at work on a new home bread-making machine. But they were having trouble getting the machine to knead dough correctly. Despite their efforts, the crust of the bread was overcooked while the inside was hardly done at all. Employees exhaustively analyzed the problem. They even compared X-rays of dough kneaded by the machine and dough kneaded by professional bakers. But they were unable to obtain any meaningful data.
>
> Finally, software developer Ikuko Tanaka proposed a creative solution. The Osaka International Hotel had a reputation for making the best bread in Osaka. Why not use it as a model? Tanaka trained with the hotel's head baker to study his kneading technique. She observed that the baker had a distinctive way of stretching the dough. After a year of trail and error, working closely with the project's engineers, Tanaka came up with product specifications—including the addition of special ribs inside

[9]Ikujiro Nonaka, "The Knowledge-Creating Company," *Harvard Business Review*, November–December 1991, p. 98.

the machine—that successfully reproduced the baker's stretching technique and the quality of the bread she had learned to make at the hotel. The result: Matsushita's unique "twist dough" method and a product that in its first year set a record for sales of a new kitchen appliance.[10]

Nonaka argues that knowledge is created in one of four ways: By transferring one person's tacit knowledge to another, as when Tanaka apprenticed with the hotel baker; by converting explicit to explicit, as when an analyst crunches numbers to produce a report; from tacit to explicit, as when Tanaka turned her new kneading expertise into a design specification; and from explicit to tacit. Presumably Tanaka and her colleagues gained tacit knowledge from their experience that they can apply in future product-development efforts.

U.S. companies traditionally manage the explicit-to-explicit style of knowledge creation fairly well. But they are not as good when it comes to generating tacit knowledge, converting it to explicit knowledge, and then applying the lessons learned to enrich the tacit knowledge of other employees. Nonaka argues that managers need to manage all four types of knowledge creation. In fact, he describes knowledge creation as a cycle that includes all four forms at different times. Here, in his words, is how the cycle, or 'spiral of knowledge', works, as illustrated by Tanaka's experience with the bread-baking appliance:

1. First, she learns the tacit secrets of the Osaka International Hotel baker (socialization).

2. Next, she translates these secrets into explicit knowledge that she can communicate to her team members and others at Matsushita (articulation).

3. The team then standardizes this knowledge, putting it

[10]Ibid.

together into a manual or workbook or embodying it in a product (combination).

4. Finally, through the experience of creating a new product, Tanaka and her team members enrich their own tacit knowledge base (internalization). In particular, they come to understand in an extremely intuitive way that products like the home bread-making machine can provide genuine quality. That is, the machine must bake bread that is as good as that of a professional baker. This starts the spiral of knowledge all over again, but this time at a higher level. The new tacit insight about genuine quality developed in designing the home bread-making machine is informally conveyed to other Matsushita employees. They use it to formulate equivalent quality standards for other new Matsushita products.[11]

This theoretical model provides a helpful context from which to view the various and diverse innovation and suggestion programs of Conference Board companies. Of course they can always be judged by their results—do they, like Bell Atlantic's Champions program, actually produce usable innovations? But they can also be tested by asking whether they generate new knowledge for the firm, and especially, whether they help translate tacit knowledge to explicit knowledge, and explicit to tacit knowledge. These two activities, articulation and internalization, are "the critical steps" in the spiral of knowledge according to Konaka. "The reason," he explains, "is that both require the active involvement of the self—that is, personal commitment. Ikuko Tanaka's decision to apprentice herself to a master baker is one example of this commitment."[12]

---

[11] Ibid., p. 99.
[12] Ibid.

Stop Thinking and Get Back to Work

The *individual* is the source of all ideas by which companies profit. While teams may provide the vehicle for accessing the ideas of individuals, we must not lose sight of the fact that the ideas have to spring from someone's mind in the first place. The normative forces at work in the traditional U.S. corporate culture discourage individuals from "sticking their necks out" and "taking personal risks." They discourage the vocalization of wild ideas or offbeat suggestions. And not only does the traditional corporate culture discourage individuals from sharing any ideas they may have, it discourages them from thinking—which is the action that produces ideas—in the first place.

Back in 1983, around the time Xerox was launching its first major company-wide quality program, professor Elliot Carlisle of the University of Massachusetts at Amherst wrote a story in which a manager finds a mentor in the person of an older, more experienced manager sitting next to him on an airplane. This mentor addressed the topic of thinking at work:

> You know," he mused, "when you get right down to it, it's almost impossible to get any real thinking done at work. Not just because of interruptions, but almost more importantly, the whole psychological and physical environment in which managers work tends to discourage contemplation and encourage activity . . . How many bosses would give a word of encouragement to a subordinate if they were to come upon him sitting at his desk, chair tipped back, foot resting on an open drawer, and staring into space with an abstract expression on his face? They'd be far more likely to ask him what the hell he is doing, and if the unfortunate replied, "Thinking," he'd probably be advised to stop thinking and get back to work.[13]

[13]Elliot Carlisle, *Mac: Managers Talk About Managing People*, Penguin Books, 1982, p. 12.

And if merely sitting and thinking for a moment could cause trouble, what employee in such a culture could possibly imagine an apprenticeship to learn how to bake bread?

The traditional corporate culture in most U.S. companies says "stop thinking and get back to work" in many ways. A favorite uncle of mine used to joke that his boss at the bank where he worked would say to him, "Every time you think, you weaken the organization." This was in fact one of my first and most lasting impressions of the corporate culture of big companies! I remember, as a child, being unable to see what humor in this remark would make all the adults laugh so hard every time they heard it. Wasn't thinking the *job* of employees? If they didn't think, what else could they be doing? But now, after working in companies where this kind of culture prevailed, I too can laugh at the remark. The challenge of quality programs is to create a corporate culture in which it is recognized that, every time employees think, they *strengthen* the organization.

OVERCOMING RESISTANCE TO NEW IDEAS

Ron Zarowitz, A Chrysler employee, had an idea that promised to strengthen his organization, and it took two years to get anyone even to listen to it. Here is how *Fortune* reporter Stephanie Losee tells the story:

> Ron Zarowitz had an idea. Struggling to hook up a car seat for his 2-year-old daughter one day in the early Eighties, he realized that a fold-down version of such a seat could be built right into the car and offered as an option. When he became a manager at Chrysler in 1985, he was well situated to push the idea—and did he ever push it. "I brought the idea up over and over again, and every time they said, 'Why would we want to do this?' " he recalls. Scores of memos followed, and top management at last agreed to discuss the idea in 1987. "It was in the discussion phase for two years," says Zarowitz. The first built-in child seats appeared this fall [1991], six years after Zarowitz

proposed them, as a $200 option in 1992 Chrysler minivans. The company says it's selling them as fast as it can make them—after missing the opportunity for years.[14]

To overcome this kind of resistance to new ideas, companies need both to make innovation a central value, and to establish specific programs designed to make it much, much easier for the individual to champion his or her own idea. Milliken is one company that has done a lot of work in the latter area.

Milliken, like 3M, has a history of technical innovation that has helped it expand the concept of individual innovation to all aspects of quality improvement. Here is a summary of the various programs Milliken uses to stimulate innovation by its employees (who are called Associates):

> Innovation is important at all levels of the organization, and Associates are encouraged to participate in programs which stimulate innovative actions. Programs such as "Evergreen" allow Associates to submit innovative actions which will reduce costs and improve profits. Our "Opportunity for Improvement" program allows Associates to communicate innovative approaches to improve the quality of product and service. And finally our "Corrective Action Team" system allows associates to work with peers, superiors, and subordinates in solving problems through a team approach. Innovation is recognized in many ways, but the ultimate recognition is provided through our Innovators Hall of Fame. Started in 1984, it has recognized associates from all levels within the organization.[15]

These programs, like those described earlier from Bell Atlantic, are good steps toward a corporate culture in which innovation and individual idea-generation are at the top of the list of priorities for everyone. But there are many other practices that can help, and it is interesting to see the diversity of

---

[14]"Closing the Innovation Gap," *Fortune*, December 2, 1991, p. 56.

[15]Background information provided by Terry May, director of public affairs, Milliken & Company, February 25, 1992.

approaches developed at various companies. In fact, the creativity with which companies have developed new ideas for stimulating the development of new ideas is itself a very encouraging sign!

Here for example is a very simple technique from Fuji Xerox for making individual thinking and ideas a valued part of the corporate culture. Hideki Kaihatsu, director of international relations for Fuji Xerox, says, "At Fuji Xerox, everybody has a small plaque on their desk with his or her initials on it asking "Why?"[16] Should a boss catch one of Fuji Xerox's employees sitting with "chair tipped back, foot resting on an open drawer, and staring into space" in the words of professor Carlisle's apocryphal mentor, he or she would know exactly what to do—simply point to the plaque, and go on thinking.

The link between innovation and quality improvement is neatly symbolized in these plaques. To achieve superior quality, companies must harness the innovative energies of their employees—all their employees. In a sense, both innovation and quality improvement boil down to the same simple act: Thinking. And the tendency for quality programs to stimulate thought and reward innovation may explain their success. This is certainly how James Fici, manager, quality planning, for Westinghouse's Baldrige-winning Commercial Nuclear Fuel Division, sees it. He says, "Total quality has helped us reinforce our overall position as world leaders in the marketplace. But, more important, it has given our people a new perspective. Our employees constantly come up with new ideas to improve things."[17]

[16]Conference Board Report No. 937, p. 9.
[17]Conference Board Report No. 937, p. 88.

Chapter 7

PARTICIPATION

A chieving greater employee involvement relates to the very fundamentals of how we manage. To foster more employee involvement and participation . . . is a major cultural change.
—Walt Burdick, senior vice president,
personnel, IBM[1]

P eople need to be recognized for quality improvements, whether
by a simple thank you or a cash bonus. Reward and recognition
are critical: If a work force doesn't share in the profits of their
improvements, they won't believe in the company's quality efforts.
—John Wilesmith, director, quality,
Rank Xerox Ltd.[2]

E very day I came to work and saw people so bored by their jobs
that they made thoughtless, dumb mistakes.
—Ralph Stayer, CEO, Johnsonville Foods, Inc.[3]

[1]As quoted in How Sharp is your Focus on Quality?, IBM Corp. 1991, p. 4.
[2]John Wilesmith, "Integrating Quality into Service Management," speech at The
Conference Board's Third Annual Quality Conference, April 2–3, 1990, New York.
[3]Ralph Stayer, "How I learned to Let My Workers Lead," *Harvard Business
Review*, November–December 1990, p. 66.

As the opening quotes suggest, employee participation has been essential to the success of quality programs at Conference Board companies. However, rather than plunge into details of the participation programs of IBM, Xerox and other large companies, I first want to relate the experiences of Ralph Stayer and the family business of which he is CEO, Johnsonville Foods, Inc.—a sausage manufacturer in Sheboygan, Wisconsin that employs approximately 400 people. The transformation his company made, from the traditional top-down command style of management to one that is now based entirely on employee participation, epitomizes the cultural transformation required by any organization that wishes to move to participatory management—and the cultural transformation that a move toward participatory management brings about. The lessons are especially relevant to those companies that are undertaking cultural change in order to advance their quality efforts.

Employee participation at Johnsonville Foods is more extensive than at most other companies, since this has been the primary focus of cultural change for more than a decade now. The company's quality efforts were a result of its efforts in the area of employee participation, while at most companies it works the other way around. Thus participation is the cornerstone of the quality program at Johnsonville Foods, just as training is at Corning or process is at Florida Power & Light. Johnsonville Foods proves that participation can actually be used to catalyze cultural change and bring about a quality culture.

Of Strategy and Sausages

Change began when Stayer realized that he was head of a business "that was in great shape and required radical change." It was in great shape in the sense that it was growing rapidly and making a profit. But Stayer was worried about his market position; he remembers that "we were a small, regional producer with national competitors who could outpromote, outadvertise, and underprice us any time they chose." He was also worried about the "host of local and regional producers small enough to provide superior service to customers who were virtually their neighbors." His strategic assessment told him that Johnsonville Foods was "too big to have the small-town advantage and too small to have advantages of national scale."[4]

THE GAP BETWEEN POTENTIAL AND PERFORMANCE

When Stayer looked for ways to offset this weak strategic position, he realized there was a significant "gap between potential and performance." The problem, in his words, was that, "Our people didn't seem to care. Every day I came to work and saw people so bored by their jobs that they made thoughtless, dumb mistakes. They showed up in the morning, did halfheartedly what they were told to do, and then went home." He conducted a survey of his workforce to explore this performance gap. Here is how he describes the results: "The survey told me that people saw nothing for themselves at Johnsonville. It was a job, a means to some end that lay outside the company. I wanted them to commit themselves to a company goal, but they saw little to commit to."[5]

Was Johnsonville Foods a worse place to work than most? No. Stayer's is an apt description of the workforce at many companies, and what distinguished Johnsonville Foods was the willingness of management to face this reality. In fact, employees are if anything more halfhearted and less committed than ever. A 1991 *Business Week* cover story reviewed the rising layoffs and high turnover in U.S. companies, found the

---

[4]Ibid., p. 66.
[5]Ibid., p. 67.

trend effecting white-collar as well as blue-collar workers, and declared that, "The once-solid foundation for millions of middle-class families—the corporate career—is in shambles. The Organization Man of the 1950s and 1960s is being replaced by the migrant manager and free-lance professional of the 1990s."[6] The lack of job security combines with the disenfranchisement of the traditional command-and-control organization structure to make most people's jobs seem undependable and meaningless. This is the somber backdrop against which commitment and participation must be fashioned in order for quality programs to take hold and grow.

The first step, at least for Stayer of Johnsonville Foods, was to recognize what the problem was—or *who* it was, to be more precise. Stayer concluded that, "The very things that had brought me success—my centralized control, my aggressive behavior, my authoritarian business practices—were creating the environment that made me so unhappy." This insight could just as well be applied to U.S. industry as a whole. The traditional management model helped U.S. industry grow and prosper for decades, but now stands in the way of further progress. All U.S. managers need to realize that the traditional management structure gives employees very little reason for commitment. Stayer's realization of this insight led him to conclude that, "I had been Johnsonville Sausage, assisted by some hired hands who, to my annoyance, lacked commitment. But why should they make a commitment to Johnsonville? They had no stake in the company and no power to make decisions or control their own work. If I wanted to improve results, I had to increase their involvement in the business."

A RECIPE FOR DISASTER

But as Stayer soon learned, participation means more than just turning the reins over to employees. "From now on," Stayer announced to his management team, "you're all responsible

---

[6]"I'm Worried About My Career," *Business Week*, October 7, 1991, p. 94.

for making your own decisions."[7] The result was disaster. They were unable to make the switch from followers to leaders. Two years later, all these managers had been replaced. And it was not only the managers who failed, it was also their CEO, Stayer. As he realized later, he did not really give up control by ordering employees to make their own decisions. Stayer analyzes his first try at participatory management as follows: "Deep down, I was still in love with my own control; I was just making people guess what I wanted instead of telling them."[8]

His story is a long one—it took him 10 years to perfect participatory management, and he still characterizes the change as ongoing. Along the way, he turned control of product quality over to the line employees. Where all sausages used to be tasted daily by management, now they are tasted by the employees who actually make them—a powerful symbol of the shift in responsibility. Teams formed on the shop floors to diagnose quality problems and fix them. Groups of employees tackled machine down-time, cutting it from 30 percent to 10 percent and freeing themselves of weekend overtime as a result. The line employees took on responsibility for individuals who did not perform well, firing some of them, and developed their own employee selection, hiring, and training systems. Now even major strategic decisions for the firm are made by employee teams in a group process. In short, the employee participation movement at Johnsonville Foods led the company into an entirely new way of managing, one that involved and pleased its employees and produced higher-quality product at lower cost.

How, finally, did Stayer do it? He didn't. He learned to stop directing employees and to start coaching them instead—and let the *employees* change the company. He realized, in his words, "that I didn't directly control the performance of the people at Johnsonville, that as a manager I didn't really manage people. They managed themselves. But I did manage the

[7]Stayer, ibid., p. 68.
[8]Ibid.

context." With this insight, his emphasis shifted toward designing and implementing systems that would encourage and support employee participation.

Quality control is one of those systems, and the move from inspection to built-in quality that underlies the U.S. quality revolution can be seen as a shift in the context of employee's work. At Johnsonville Foods, it took the simple form of giving employees responsibility for product tasting. With this context change, employees soon began to identify and tackle quality problems. They held morning meetings to taste products, and at these meetings began to discuss how to improve quality. They formed teams to work on problems. They began to take an active interest in related issues, such as costs and customer perceptions, and their requests for information in these areas led to the redesign of the company's information systems: More context changes that put cost, sales and marketing information in the hands of the line employees for the first time. Now, for example, complaints from customers are directed to the line employees who made the products, and they communicate directly with the customers to resolve problems (for example, by replacing products). And, most important, they apply what they learn from customer responses immediately in their work, to avoid the problems next time.

One of the innovations Johnsonville Foods developed was the 'coordinator' role. Instead of supervisors and middle managers, the company now uses coordinators, employees who lead teams and facilitate the management-level analysis and decision-making of the line employees. Senior management now focuses on training, coordination and support, rather than on making decisions itself. These changes help create the context needed for employee ownership of problems and decisions.

Now Stayer reports that "Everyone at Johnsonville discovered they could do considerably more than they had imagined. Since they had little trouble meeting the accelerated production goals that they themselves had set, members raised the minimum acceptable performance criteria and began routinely to expect more of themselves and others."[9] The more responsibility employees took for their own work, the better they performed, and the more rewarding their work was to them as well as to the company. As employees performed better, so did the *company*, rewarding the employees with higher earnings and greater job security. Now, according to Stayer, employees' "general level of commitment is as high or higher than my own."[10]

Participation and Quality

Conference Board Quality Council members and Baldrige Award winners all emphasize participation (although, oddly, employee involvement accounts for only 4 percent of 1992 Baldrige Award point values). While few have gone as far as Johnsonville Foods, all have taken participation far beyond the prescriptions of the traditional management paradigm. Employee participation is a strong and constant theme at successful quality practitioners, and many seem to be headed down the same trail Johnsonville Foods has already broken.

This emphasis on participation makes sense, because ultimately it falls to the individual employees to implement any quality program—the managers cannot do it alone. The linkage between personal participation in quality improvements and the company's overall quality effort is made clear in Kodak's use of 'personal quality-improvement projects.' Ralph Rosati, former director, corporate quality, for Eastman Kodak Company, explains how this mechanism works:

> It's human nature to make more progress on a problem if it's "legitimized" by being made a project. A project can more effectively compete for attention, personnel, facilities, and ser-

[9]Stayer, ibid., p. 83.
[10]Ibid., p. 83.

vices. Everyone in management at Kodak, including our Office of the Chief Executive, is working on specific, clearly defined personal quality-improvement projects.

For example, Rosati, explains,

Bill Prezzano is Group Vice President and General Manager of our Photographic Products Division. The major elements of his personal quality project are to cut the traditional product realization cycle time in half within two years and to foster a process for technology planning that is consistent with corporate business strategies.[11]

The ownership of quality improvement that comes with a personal quality-improvement plan is an important step toward full employee participation. While Rosati did not elaborate on how the personal plans are prepared, a fully participatory approach would require each individual to write his or her *own* plan. And, of course, the idea would have to be extended from management to all employees.

James Houghton, CEO of Corning Inc., equates participation with teams, seeing teamwork as the best way to create employee participation in the quality process. According to Houghton, "For us, participation means active membership on a quality team . . . The secret is simply to encourage participation. The best encouragement is to tell the employees that what they think and do has value to Corning; that we will listen to and develop a better way of doing things." This means the teams need to participate in meaningful change at Corning, and that management must be willing to implement the teams' ideas.

TAKING EMPLOYEES' SUGGESTIONS SERIOUSLY

Originally, participation at Corning meant putting a suggestion in a box. Suggestion boxes are the traditional vehicle for employee participation in management decisions in most

[11]Conference Board Report No. 909, p. 16

companies. And they never worked well. According to Houghton, "We had an employee-participation system in which employees put their suggestions into a box on the wall. This system, for us, proved ineffective." A suggestion box on the wall obviously falls far short of full employee participation in management decision-making, and it is easy to see how employees might not take suggestion boxes seriously. In fact, suggestion boxes have come to be seen, with considerable cynicism, as a symbol of unresponsive, dictatorial management. But there is nothing inherently wrong with the suggestion box as a communications medium. After all, letters are put in mail boxes, and they generally reach their destination and generate a timely response. The problem with suggestion boxes turns out to be the behavior of the *recipients*, not the medium itself. And this issue, while it may seem trivial at first, captures the essence of the broader problem of employee participation neatly within it.

The easiest way to see that something intriguing lies behind the failure of suggestion boxes is to look at some comparative statistics. Professors Dean Schroeder of Valaparaiso University and Alan Robinson of the University of Massachusetts, Amherst, who have studied Japanese continuous improvement programs, report a startling observation:

> Japanese companies received almost 48 million improvement proposals from their employees in 1986, while their counterparts in the United States received about one million. Toyota alone received 2.65 million suggestions from its employees that year.[12]

This is not the kind of statistic that is reported on an annual basis, so we must do our best to imagine what current statistics might look like. I suspect that the gap is not as great, but still

---

[12]Dean M. Schroeder and Alan G. Robinson, "America's Most Successful Export to Japan: Continuous Improvement Programs," *Sloan Management Review*, Spring 1991, p. 74.

exists. At least at Corning, management discovered one of the secrets to making those suggestion boxes work: Responding. If a friend never answers your letters, you will eventually stop writing. Same with suggestions; and at most companies, employees gave up and stopped writing years ago. But when management responds, participation rises dramatically. Houghton describes this phenomenon at Corning as follows:

> Last year we tried a new system. Our 25,000 employees gave us 16,000 improvement suggestions (ten times more than previous years)—an average of one improvement suggestion per minute, day and night, for the year. Last year we used over 8,000 suggestions (more than 50 times the number of suggestions used in previous years). Our only rule for this new method is that a manager must respond to the employee's suggestion within one or two weeks.[13]

The response rule forces managers to read and consider each suggestion, thus upping the rate of adoption. And it forces a rapid response to the suggestion, thus giving the employee meaningful, timely feedback. Perhaps this feedback works because it is an explicit recognition of the employee's contribution. Recognition turns out to be vital to participation.

Recognition of Employee Participation

At Corning, as at other companies with quality-improvement programs, recognition of employee participation is considered key. Houghton explains Corning's approach; "The new system also includes different forms of recognition. We use, among other things, celebrations and parties as forms of recognition."[14] Federal Express also emphasizes recognition, but favors awards over other forms. At Fed Ex, employees or teams

---

[13]Conference Board Report No. 937, p. 23.
[14]Ibid.

may receive letters of appreciation or cash awards through six separate award systems. There are Bravo Zulu awards, Golden Falcon awards, Circle of Excellence awards, Hall of Fame awards, Five Star awards, and Star/Superstar awards. Each award program has formal rules, nomination processes, and so forth, and every winner receives extensive recognition within the company.[15] In a recent Conference Board survey of large U.S. companies with quality programs, 85 percent of the 158 respondents make a practice of giving awards to individuals and teams. Seventy-five percent offer unit or plant-wide awards. Noncash awards prevail, but slightly more than 30 percent offer both cash and noncash awards to individuals and teams and 15 percent make both available to units or plants.[16]

Thus we can safely say that the award-and-celebration approach to recognition is common at many companies with successful quality programs. A great many award dinners, team recognition days, and so forth are held at these companies. But recognition needs to go beyond these periodic public events, in two directions. First, recognition needs to become part of the daily work environment. Managers need to acknowledge the contributions of their employees, and, perhaps even more important, the *efforts* of their employees to contribute. Whenever anyone tries to use a new quality tool or technique, whenever anyone makes an effort to participate in quality improvement, this effort needs to be reinforced immediately through acknowledgement and praise. This is informal recognition, and it is no doubt vital, yet undeniably hard to manage.

Second, recognition needs to touch the employee on his or her bottom line. Johnsonville Foods now uses a compensation system that allows employees to participate in the company's *profits*, as well as the decisions that produce those profits. Profit-sharing is perhaps the greatest step any company can

[15]Information supplied by public relations office, Federal Express, January 1992.

[16]Conference Board Report No. 974, p. 7.

take toward full recognition of employee's contributions. Ironically, profit-sharing plans are falling out of favor now—many companies experimented with them in the last two decades, and saw little impact on employee behavior or performance. This was no doubt because the programs were implemented independently, without the supporting context of a quality initiative and a cultural shift to participatory management. In the context of quality programs, profit-sharing makes good sense. As Arthur B. Nichols, consultant and former director, quality management, for Hoechst Celanese Corporation, puts it, "If we expect everyone to make a 'commitment to continual improvement,' then everyone should have the opportunity to share in the fruits of the improvement they help to bring about."[17]

Profit-sharing links participation to the employee's compensation, making it an effective motivational tool. A similar degree of impact can be achieved by linking participation to performance appraisal and promotion. In fact, the three strategies are often seen together. No employee can miss the message when participation in quality-improvement efforts is tied to compensation, performance appraisal, and promotion! In the Conference Board survey cited above, less than half of the respondents report that they tie promotion to participation. Of these, about 60 percent tie participation in quality efforts to employee's compensation. And 75 percent tie quality participation to performance appraisal. It is interesting to note, however, that these practices are more prevalent among companies with older quality programs. Apparently companies move toward participation-based compensation as they gain experience in the implementation of total quality.

So far we have focused strictly on a narrow meaning of participation—the involvement of a firm's employees in decision making and change at the company. But participation can mean a great deal more than employee involvement. In quality

---

[17]Conference Board Report No. 909, p. 11.

programs, other groups are often asked to participate as well. For example, suppliers may play a central role in the improvement process. The task of gaining their active participation is in many ways parallel to the task of stimulating employee involvement, and can be equally difficult. Even customers may have to become involved, to participate in the quality improvement process. And when participation of customers and suppliers is considered, it becomes necessary to find a new, unifying vision that allows management to work on participation issues in their many, diverse forms.

Participation as Partnership

When you look at participation as a partnership, it is a lot easier to make sense out of the need to stimulate participation in diverse groups. This is how David Luther, senior vice president and corporate director, quality, describes Corning's strategy to build participation, both by Corning's workforce and its suppliers. The partnership concept helps Corning's management take a consistent approach to participation issues with all these groups. Here I have collected several statements made by Luther in order to present a fuller picture of what partnering means and how it is pursued at Corning:[18]

> Quality forms the basis for a network of partnerships. And companies need partnerships to move forward with quality.
> In our continuous quality journey, we have come to four conclusions:
>
> 1. Total quality consists of growth stages.
>
> 2. Partners are needed to move through these stages.
>
> 3. To make partnerships work, a company must develop mechanisms that address attitude, environment and the process of total quality.

[18]David B. Luther, "Continuous Quality Improvement: The Ever-Widening Network," speech at The Conference Board's Third Annual Quality Conference, April 2–3, 1990, New York.

4. Managing partnerships requires trust, effective communication and the ability to lead for the long-term.

[Corning identifies three phases of quality: Start-up, Breakout and World Class Quality]

Corning would not have progressed beyond the start-up stage if it hadn't formed partnerships with customers, co-workers, and suppliers.

This talk of partnering sounds good, but is it just talk? If so, there will be no true participation, because participation needs a certain degree of equality and mutual respect to occur. Participation is a form of sharing. To partner effectively with employees, suppliers, customers and others, Corning must share with them: Share the change process, share authority, share ideas and resources. This is a radically different way of defining the company's relationships, and at Corning it is more than just talk. To see what I mean, listen to what some of Corning's suppliers, customers and employees have to say about their partnership with Corning.

Robert Pombrio is vice president, manufacturing, at Pfizer Minerals, a Corning supplier. He describes his company's relationship with Corning as unique. He says, "Perhaps our relationship with Corning is excellent because we are very similar companies, but in different businesses . . . We forged the partnership for three reasons: Corning is a large customer; Corning people did their homework, presenting us with cogent proposals; and Corning's commitment to total quality was enthusiastic and contagious . . . From the beginning, we interwove the two companies as tightly as possible. Pfizer people began attending Corning's Quality Institute, and there was active interaction between the two managements. Our shared philosophy of continuous improvement has paid off and proves that partnerships work."[19] This description of a "shared philosophy" between two lightly interwoven companies is

---

[19]Remarks from a panel discussion at The Conference Board's Third Annual Quality Conference, April 2–3, 1990, New York.

dramatically different from the traditional supplier-customer relationship. Corning and Pfizer are true partners, sharing their expertise and vision as they both work to improve quality.

A similar form of partnering links Corning to some of its customers. According to customer Kenneth Arnold, president-North America, Catalytic Systems Division, Johnson Matthey Inc., "The partnership between Corning and Johnson Matthey emerged because managements saw that the opportunity for cooperation would provide benefits for all. Our plants are now linked by a computer system so we can share information on production schedules, inventories and planning. Interestingly, the difficult times have strengthened our alliance. We have developed trust." Corning and its customer participate together in the customer's production process, and in its quality improvement efforts as well. Arnold explains that, "As a result of our partnership, Johnson Matthey has made significant improvements in its plant efficiency, in its quality and in its ability to serve the customer." And these are striking statements. By partnering with its customer, Corning has added great value in these areas, which are far broader and more important than any value it can add simply by supplying component parts. By sharing its quality improvements, Corning allows its customers to participate in a process that benefits them as well as Corning, and thus builds a deeper, longer-lasting relationship with the customers than any traditional supplier-customer relationship.[20]

What about employee participation? Can it be seen in the same context as supplier and customer partnerships? Yes, according to Lawrence Bankowski, national president, American Flint Glass Workers Union, AFL-CIO. He explains that, "Our union represents most of the hourly employees at Corning." These employees have an unusual partnership with management, one that was created for and by the quality process. According to Bankowski, "In 1983, Corning began its

[20]Ibid.

total quality system and the intention was to train every employee. Since then, our union and Corning's leadership have become committed to total quality. David Luther and I regularly conduct quality reviews at plants nationwide. We interview workers at all levels about what is right or wrong with the process. And a pattern has emerged in the responses. The American worker wants to produce quality and to work in a partnership with management. But this worker must have a supporting environment to do this. Corning has created this environment and we applaud its ongoing support." Part of the participatory environment for Corning employees is a system that gives employees direct access to goal-setting at the company. In this partnership, management and employees share responsibility for corporate strategy. Bankowski says, "In 1989, we negotiated a system of goal-sharing in which management and the union will draw up company goals together. We know this process works and we are committed to it." This is an example of the sharing of power and authority that participatory management requires.[21]

Employee participation is for real when employees are partners with management (and the company's owners) in the quality improvement process. Partnership is a powerful concept because it implies ownership. As Ralph Stayer of Johnsonville Foods learned, delegating responsibility will not produce employee participation. As he puts it, "The goal was not so much a state of shared responsibility as an environment where people insist on being responsible."[22] Partners insist on being responsible, because they have as much to gain or lose as any other party to the partnership. Award programs and delegated decisions will not create this level of participation alone. They must be part of a broader, more sweeping cultural change that results in the replacement of traditional hierarchical relationships with partnerships, both within the firm and in the supplier and distribution channels beyond it.

[21] Ibid.
[22] Stayer, Ibid., p. 69.

CHAPTER

8

COMPETITION

he importance of the Baldrige Award is not getting it but the process of competing for it.
—*Royce Benjamin, senior quality associate, Ford Motor Company[1]*

What role should competition play in the creation of a quality culture? Leading quality practitioners send mixed signals on this question. On the one hand, most practitioners eschew competition in favor of greater cooperation, arguing that the best way to get employees to work better is to get them to work *together* better. On the other hand, the most prominent symbol of America's quality revolution is a competitive award, the Malcolm Baldrige National Quality Award; and a new generation of derivative awards, such as New York State's Excelsior Award and a variety of industry awards and company-sponsored supplier awards, are now coming on line.

The mixed feelings toward competition are encapsulated in a comment from Royce Benjamin, of Ford's corporate quali-

---

[1]Conversation with the author, January 29, 1992.

189

ty office, who says that, "We don't believe in awards. We agree with Deming's philosophy that competition and individual recognition don't belong in a quality program. But our purchasing department has found that the Q1 Award is a good way to energize our suppliers."[2]

The truth is that American companies *are* competing vigorously for quality awards, and if competition is a problem, then the country's quality efforts must have a *big* problem. However, as we will see, a certain amount of competition seems to be healthy, and can serve as a motivator to cooperation and the adoption of continuous improvement processes.

THE BALDRIGE AWARD AND THE QUEST FOR QUALITY

When IBM Rochester won the Malcolm Baldrige National Quality Award, Steve Schwartz was asked to give a report to the management committee [see Exhibit 8-3 for information on the Baldrige award]. As senior vice president of Market-Driven Quality, Schwartz had plenty to say on the topic—and more than a little justification for boasting. However, the message he brought was not so much congratulatory as cautionary. Here is how he put it: "We have two feet firmly planted on the yellow brick road. That is the really good news. The sobering news is: The Emerald City is nowhere in sight. We have a very good beginning, but we have a long way to go."[3]

It is difficult to see the Baldrige Award as just a beginning, especially if you have just lived through the grueling process of competing for it. But while it is a good catalyst for change, it provides no stopping point for contestants, even the winning ones. By now it must be obvious that quality itself is a process—a never-ending process in all likelihood. So just what does a Baldrige mean? What can be accomplished in the real

[2]Ibid.
[3]IBM publication: *Think* No. 6, 1990, p. 22.

world of business-to-business competition, beyond the media's spotlight, by applying for the Baldrige Award? And what can we learn from others who have applied and from the application process itself? These are important issues for any company to consider as it pursues total quality. For one thing, quality awards are proliferating—there are now many state awards, industry awards, and even single-company vendor awards for which a company can compete—and this means managers must decide what role, if any, competition for awards should play in their quality process.

But there is one other point that emerges, or ought to emerge, from the Baldrige experience. And when Steve Schwartz described winning as a way to plant your feet firmly on the yellow brick road, he foreshadowed this final and critical point. Because the Emerald City at the end of this road, as anyone who has seen The Wizard of Oz will recall, is a hoax. There is no all-powerful wizard, only a small-town con man in disguise, and the unhappy pilgrims on that road eventually discover they must rely on themselves to solve their problems, not the wizard. That's the *really* bad news, and a similar disillusionment awaits any company that pursues a Baldrige, Deming or any other quality award in the hope that this external certification will bring some good magic to their business and industry. As Royce Benjamin at Ford puts it, "The award tends to look like a finish line; people are tempted to stop improving once they reach the award level. But of course there is no finish line."[4]

The problem with competitive awards is that there is no finish line. The award ceremony cannot confer everlasting competitiveness. However in business, if not in movies, a problem always represents an opportunity. And this problem provides a wonderful opportunity to discover hidden resources within oneself and one's company.

You may recall that the Wizard did help out, in his own

[4]Conversation with the author, January 29, 1992.

way; the pilgrims discovered their own solutions *through the quests he sent them on.* And that may be the most important thing about a trip down the yellow brick road. It often takes an Emerald City on the horizon, and an externally-inspired journey, for a company to discover the many wonderful resources within its own walls. Thus the final and most important point about the Baldrige (and awards in general) is that it provides a suitable goal for a quest. It is the Holy Grail, Golden Fleece, or Emerald City around which a quest can be organized and made compelling. The reward itself is secondary to the quest. It doesn't really matter whether there is a Holy Grail, or a Wizard of Oz—what matters is that you go on a journey in search of one. Which means that, while it is tempting to critique details of the application and examination process (as many are now doing), it is really much more important to focus on the company's journey than this object of its quest. The award is not a destination at all, but simply symbolizes the ultimate destination, which is a truly customer-focused, flexible, innovative, learning organization that is able to renew itself through an ever-accelerating rate of continuous improvement. Is such a thing possible? We don't really know, and nor should we care, as long as the journey continues to provide benefit to the company.

This point seems to be echoed in the thoughts of one of the Baldrige judges, W. Kent Sterett, executive vice president of Southern Pacific Transportation Company. He argues that "The Baldrige Award was established to generate knowledge, not to emphasize the act of winning. Winners are not limited to recipients of the National Quality Award. A winner is any company that applies the tools and techniques of the quality process to improve its competitive position."[5]

But skeptics might point out that for every winner there is a loser. Competitive awards by their nature brand most entrants as losers. Is this a constructive approach? If everyone is

[5]Conference Board Report No. 979, p. 43.

supposed to be a winner, then awards should be given to every company that achieves a certain level of performance or that meets certain criteria for quality process and culture. A national quality award need not be competitive—it could be modeled on a certification-type exam instead. We just happen to have adopted a competitive model at the national level, and this model is now spreading throughout states, trade associations, and individual companies, making a competitive approach the national standard. Not everyone thinks this is a good idea.

In fact, the Baldrige Award has served as a focus for the argument against a competitive approach to quality improvement. The majority of winners have been large companies, like Xerox, Cadillac, Motorola, and Federal Express, who have leveraged the award through extensive publicity and advertising. It is clear that winners try to make the most of the award— and why not, when they invest so much in the application process? It is estimated, for example, that Xerox's winning application required the full-time efforts of 20 people with a budget of $800,000 to complete. With this level of effort, it is easy to see how the award might be viewed as an end in itself.

To Compete or Not to Compete?

The power of a goal for the company's quest is important, but need it be a *competitive* goal? Certainly the ultimate aim is to be more competitive in world markets, but is this best achieved by pursuing competition for awards? Many managers argue that the heightened intra-industry and intra company competition fostered by awards is unhealthy and competes with other quality objectives, especially cooperation and teamwork.

Cooperation is a pervasive, if subtle, theme in every quality program. Previously-competitive individuals and departments come together to break down bottlenecks in the business process and to cooperate in teams. Suppliers and buyers develop long-term, cooperative relationships and walk the quality and innovation paths together. Unions and managements agree to cooperate in job redesign, training, and quality circles. And participative decision making forces cooperation and sharing of authority from the corner office to the factory floor. In many cases, the new cooperative spirit even crosses company borders—witness the cooperation required for company-to-company benchmarking and the unprecedented sharing of shop talk in the Conference Board's Quality Councils, for two examples of intercompany cooperation.

A variety of academic studies support the notion that cooperation in the workforce is more productive than competition. One study of 4,000 people by psychologist Janet Spence (of the University of Texas at Austin) concluded that competitiveness often interferes with achievement. Another study, this one comparing cooperative educational methods with competitive ones, found that the cooperative approach usually produced higher student achievement. And a classic experiment by Peter Blau (of the University of North Carolina and Chapel Hill) pitted two groups of interviewers at an employment agency against each other. In one group, interviewers were instructed to share all information with each other. In the other group, interviewers were instructed to compete rather than cooperate. No information was shared. This group was less successful than the cooperating group; it failed to fill as many jobs as did the cooperators. In general, experimental evidence favors the belief that greater cooperation leads to better performance.[6]

With an emphasis on cooperation and teamwork in quality programs, and with the academic evidence stacked against competition, it is hard to understand why competition for awards should be permitted. Might not this competition interfere with the cooperation needed for effective quality im-

---

[6]Robert McGarvey, "The Competitive Edge," *USAir* Magazine, February 1992, pp. 30–36.

provement? To explore this issue, we will visit a company that bases its quality improvement program on a highly competitive inter-divisional quality award—making it perhaps the most competitive of all U.S. quality practitioners. The company is Bausch & Lomb, an upstate-New York neighbor of Corning and Xerox, whose quality programs we have already encountered. B&L's commitment to quality is more recent, and perhaps not as visible as its neighbors'—for example, its 1990 annual report to shareholders includes only a brief mention of quality. But the impact, while subtle, is strongly visible in the company's focus on product quality and customer satisfaction. What the annual report *does* show is customers: Dozens of them are illustrated and profiled in full-page inserts, reflecting a fundamental shift at B&L toward a customer-driven definition of performance.

THE BAUSCH & LOMB QUALITY AWARD

B&L has been working on total quality programs in its various divisions for four or five years now, and one of the most important results is that every division now does extensive customer research, and is evaluated in part according to how its customers rate it. The company first encountered total quality programs when some of its divisions worked with 3M, back in 1987, to adopt their methodology. Since then, each division (including the eyewear, international, and thin films divisions) has pursued its own independent quality improvement efforts. Ritchie Thomson, director, quality assurance, for B&L's International Division, explains that "Every division used different consultants; overall, B&L has probably tried every quality program available."[7]

This is typical of the company—its divisions operate relatively autonomously and its managers typically describe it as

---

[7]Conversation with the author, February 5, 1992.

"highly divisionalized." (I once attended a meeting at which the quality directors from two B&L divisions were present, and was greatly surprised to find myself introducing them!) And to go along with the company's decentralized approach, it is highly competitive as well. Every year, for example, a Chairman's Award is given out to the division that performs best against its financial objectives. With this corporate culture as a starting point, it is perhaps not surprising that Thomas McDermott, president and COO, chose to promote quality by introducing a new annual award based on the Baldrige criteria.

The award is administered by the one-person corporate quality office (it's small size is another indicator of B&L's decentralized approach). According to the competition's organizer, Richard Brandt, director, corporate quality, "The culture of this organization is basically competitive. By making these awards competitive, we mobilize the entire organization." He, like other managers at B&L, agrees that the intra-company competition is unusual, explaining that "Most people we meet say this is not a very smart thing to do because it creates so much tension and pressure." But Brandt feels that it is appropriate for his company. He argues that "It's a powerful motivator in this organizational culture."[8] Ritchie Thomson of the International Division, whose British origins perhaps give him more objectivity about the United States than indigenous managers, argues that the underlying culture in this *country* is highly competitive. He thinks the Baldrige Award works on the national level for the same reason the Quality Award works with the B&L, "The Baldrige Award fits the U.S. culture. It's very competitive. The guys at the top of U.S. companies *want* to win. The award is very motivating."[9] I believe this makes B&L's experience a useful case study for the rest of the country.

[8]Conversation with the author, February 5, 1992.
[9]Ibid.

HOW B&L RUNS ITS QUALITY AWARD

B&L's quality award is open to three categories of business units: Large business units (like international or eyewear), small business units (one subsidiary from each international region can compete), and staff units. While participation is voluntary, McDermott's emphasis on participation is sufficient to insure that all the major divisions and staff units generally participate each year. In the 1991 competition, approximately 20 applications were received by Brandt.

The preparation of these applications is a big deal—a really big deal. In fact, the competitive atmosphere seems to generate as much *intra*-divisional cooperation and teamwork as it does inter-divisional competition—which incidentally may account for the success B&L has had with this program. I spoke with the quality directors of several divisions in early February, a few days before the awards were due, and the applications were their major concern at that time. In fact, the preparation of quality award applications takes as much staff time and management involvement as might any annual plan, and the application is, in effect, an opportunity for quality planning and self-assessment at each division. Rich Schick, vice president, quality, for the eyewear division, explains that each division writes a quality plan annually, in June, and that the award preparations provide an opportunity to review progress against this plan halfway through the year. According to Schick, "What this process does is call into question anything we said in our quality plan six months before."[10]

Another benefit of the application process, according to Gordon Donahue, director, corporate quality, for the Thin Films Technology Division, is that it "forces use of external, quantitative measures of performance."[11] Each division must has proven a powerful lever, pushing the divisions to develop their own approaches to customer satisfaction measures and

[10]Ibid.
[11]Ibid.

other measures of quality progress. International, for instance, now uses an annual customer survey that comes as close as possible to providing a consistent measure across twenty countries and in almost as many different languages (the trick, according to Thomson, is to execute locally, and "although the mechanism differs from country to country, that's OK as long as it is consistent from year to year."[12]). The international survey, like those of other divisions, is standardized to provide useful trend analysis from year to year.

Applications are not to exceed 15 pages in length, although supporting documents can be referenced. This means the applications are less than half the weight of a typical Baldrige application, but much less background information is needed so the meat of the application is only a little lighter. Applications are judged (and thus written) according to the Baldrige Award criteria and weightings, which, incidentally, are a moving target. A number of changes in category weightings were made in 1991. Exhibit 8-1 gives the Baldrige categories and weightings for both 1990 and 1991.

B&L uses its own managers and corporate officers to evaluate applications. According to company documents, "Each submission will be scored by a panel of trained examiners from participating non-competing units . . . The examiners will forward the top three submissions in each category on to a panel of officers from participating units for final judging."[13] Dick Brandt of B&L believes the use of managers as judges is one of the strengths of the program. For one thing, "There is a tremendous involvement of our senior managers."[14] This sends a message throughout the company, of course, and also helps senior management learn more about the company's quality efforts. The use of middle managers for selection of

[12]Conversation with the author, December 20, 1991.
[13]From material used to train 1991 Quality Award judges, courtesy of B&L's Corporate Quality office.
[14]Conversation with the author, December 30, 1991.

Exhibit 8-1

Category	1990	1991
Leadership	100	100
Information & Analysis	60	70
Strategic Quality Planning	90	150
HR Utilization	150	150
QA of Products & Services	150	140
Quality Results	150	180
Customer Satisfaction	300	300
Total	1000	1000

Source: National Institute of Standards and Technology, United States Department of Commerce.

finalists gives the corporate quality office an opportunity to provide several days of training to these managers. According to Brandt, this is unusually effective training; "Training the evaluators is a benefit—they get to *apply* their knowledge, which is the best way to learn."[15]

There are any number of practical details that must be resolved to execute a Baldrige-style award process; more than are appropriate to go into in this forum. But one issue that is of exceptional interest is whether to use on-site inspection, as is done for the Baldrige Award. At B&L, the judges do not go on-site, but instead score entirely based on the written submissions. Does this practice compromise the objectivity of the award? It is a critical question, because an award like this will not motivate if it is seen as unjust or biased. Brandt argues that the use of senior managers as judges "eliminates the need for site visits because the penalty for being found untrue is so high at this level that we don't have to worry about it."[16]

---

[15]Conversation with the author, February 5, 1992.
[16]Ibid.

THE IMPORTANCE OF CUSTOMERS
AND QUALITY

While direct falsification seems pretty unlikely, there is still the possibility that a better-written presentation might win out over a weaker one on the strength of communication skills, especially if the competitors are not far apart on the seven Baldrige criteria. Ritchie Thomson argues that the skill with which the application is prepared is part of the game. His International Division won the Quality Award in 1990, and according to Thomson, "We elevated the standards by submitting a beautifully-designed brochure rather than the standard loose-leaf binder." In fact, the application *is* very well designed. Its gold, blue and white cover, for example, repeats a key sentence from the company's value statement, "The importance of customers and quality," in dozens of languages. The effect is striking:

L'IMPORTANCE DES CLIENTS ET DE LA QUALITE

DIE BEDEUTUNG VON "KUNDEN UND QUALITAT"

L'IMPORTANZA DELLA CLIENTELA E DELLA QUALITA

HET BELANG VAN KLANTEN EN KWALITEIT

VIKTEN AV KUNDER OCH KVALITET

. . . and so forth. But Ritchie is quick to add that the glitz had another motive—this brochure was in fact distributed around the world to let B&L's international staff and distributors know about the company's progress on various quality measures. And he believes that his division won the award because of the progress it made in its Total Customer Responsiveness (TCR) quality program during the year, not just because the information was well packaged.

Rich Schick of the eyewear division says that, "If there is any problem, it's that the process doesn't encourage us to talk about what we are doing wrong." (This is certainly an issue

EXHIBIT 8-2 1991 BAUSCH & LOMB QUALITY AWARD

Criteria	50% Performance	Additions	Deductions
Quality Assurance of Products & Services			
• Effectiveness of systems for assuring quality in all operations • Effectiveness of approach to continuous quality improvement	Effective approach to assure quality of goods and services based on process design and control including purchased parts and services	• Evidence that unit has improved the effectiveness of its design process and shortened its design-to-introduction cycle • Certification of key processes/vendors (internal/external) • Quality assessment of its systems, processes, practices, products and services	• Reliance on inspection, not quality at source • Limited evidence to support application of QA techniques to staff/service functions
Quality Results			
• Measurement of product and service through eyes of customer, compared to levels in competing firms	Thorough and objective measurement; Competitive product quality; Improvement goals in key quality indicators achieved	• Demonstration of improvement in supplier quality levels • Sustained improvement in business processes, support services, and product quality	• Anecdotal information • No trends • Key quality indicators do not include competitive levels or targets

201

Eхнвгт 8-2 (*continued*)

Criteria	50% Performance	Additions	Deductions
Customer Satisfaction			
• Knowledge of customer requirements and demonstrated success in meeting them • Measurement of unit's customer satisfaction and indicators of adverse customer response	Knows who customers are and has effective methods to monitor satisfaction. Commitment to customers to promote trust and confidence in its products and services. Tracks adverse indicators (complaints, returns, repairs, warranty costs, etc.)	• Favorable trends compared to industry or benchmark norms • Positive trends in gaining customers and customer and account retention and market share • Effective process for determining product and service features and the relative importance of these features to end users • Effective mechanism for deploying individual and team goals to improve processes which determine customer satisfaction/adverse indicators	• Customer satisfaction inferred, not measured • Limited deployment of customer satisfaction goals

Criteria	50% Performance	Additions	Deductions
Leadership			
• Visible support of quality and involvement in improvement	Management team provides effective leadership which is visible throughout organization, and to customers and suppliers	• Regular communication of quality progress • Evaluation of the extent to which quality values have been adopted	• Limited evidence to support priority of quality • Lack of approach to promote cooperation across levels and different functions
Information & Analysis			
• Data bases and analysis to support quality planning • Methods adequate to support a responsive, *prevention-based approach* to quality improvement	Evidence of effective development and management of data to support the quality system	• Proactive approach to measure quality in all functions • Use of competitive comparison and benchmarks to support quality planning, evaluation and improvement	• Quality measures not from point-of-view of ultimate customer • Employees do not have access to relevant quality data

Exhibit 8-2 (*continued*)

Criteria	50% Performance	Additions	Deductions
Strategic Quality Planning			
• Integration of customer requirements/ operational/strategic planning • Prioritizing of issues/ concerns into long-term goals and short-term objectives	Development of consistent, realistic customer-oriented goals and objectives	• Acceptance of goals which will raise quality of standards beyond competition in key operations of the unit • Projection/target levels for key quality indicators	• Linkage of quality and business goals unclear • No evidence of integration
Human Resource Utilization			
• Means for all employees to contribute to quality improvement	Effective mechanisms for promoting full participation and an environment conducive to quality leadership and personal growth	• Positive trends in involvement in teams, suggestions, and training • Goals and actions to increase employee authority to act (empowerment)	• Portions of employee base not involved • Lack of feedback to and recognition of employees

with the Baldrige Award as well.) Because the goal is to win, the emphasis is on presenting the division's quality program in the best possible light. This may lead to avoidance of problem areas. However, in general he feels that, "This process is extremely healthy. The effect of the competition internally is good, in that there's a natural tendency to think *you're* the best. When somebody else wins, at first you think the judging was unfair, but then you look at what you are doing wrong." He sees the award process as a stimulus for "constructive self-criticism."[17]

Baldrige judges use a complex scoring system in which points are built up as the applicant is evaluated on hundreds of specific criteria. But Baldrige judges receive extensive training, and applicants pick up the tab for lengthy on-site visits. If it is to be applied within a single company, this process needs to be simplified. B&L has designed a scoring system that is pleasingly simple (Exhibit 8–2 on pgs. 201–204.). The judges first evaluate an applicant against "50 percent performance" criteria on each of the seven categories. If they meet these simple criteria, they receive half the total points possible for the category. Next the judges make additions or subtractions to the 50 percent score based on additional criteria. For example, an application receives 50 percent of total leadership points if management "provides effective leadership which is visible throughout the organization, and to customers and suppliers," according to documents used in the training of B&L's judges. Additional leadership points can be awarded if there is "regular communication of quality progress," and if there is "evaluation of the extent to which quality values have been adopted." Deductions may be made if there is "limited evidence to support priority of quality" or for "lack of approach to promote cooperation across levels and different functions." That's it. Clearly a simpler approach, and while it would not do for a national quality award, it is certainly useful for a company award.

[17]Ibid.

HOW TO SCORE YOUR OWN COMPANY'S QUALITY PROGRAM

Readers whose companies have quality programs will find it fairly simple to score their own companies using this simplified method; the full judges' instructions appear in Exhibit 8-2. This self-assessment is a useful exercise, and a number of companies have instituted formal self-assessment processes. American Express's corporate quality staff will help divisions

EXHIBIT 8-3 BALDRIGE AWARD FACT SHEET

According to the United States Department of Commerce, The Malcolm Baldrige National Quality Award "was established by Congress in 1987 to promote quality awareness, to recognize quality achievements of U.S. companies, and to publicize successful quality strategies. Two awards may be given annually in each of three categories: manufacturing, service, and small business. In conjunction with the private sector, the National Institute of Standards and Technology developed and manages the award program."[22]

U.S. Commerce Secretary Robert A. Mosbacher explains that, "The award is not given for specific products or services. However, as part of the award process, an applicant must describe its company's methods for assuring the quality of goods and service. In addition, applicants provide details on achievements and improvements in six other areas: leadership, information and analysis, strategic quality planning, human resource utilization, quality results, and customer satisfaction."[23]

Winners of the award are:

1988   Motorola Inc., Commercial Nuclear Fuel Division of Westinghouse Electric Corp., Globe Metalurgical Inc.
1989   Milliken & Company and Xerox Corp. Business Products and Systems
1990   Cadillac Motor Car Division, IBM Rochester, Federal Express Corp., and Wallace Co., Inc.
1991   Solectron Corp., Zytec Corp., and Marlow Industries

[22]*United States Department of Commerce News,* October 9, 1991.
[23]Ibid.

Exhibit 8–3 (*continued*)

Applications and information can be obtained from:

Malcolm Baldrige National Quality Award Office
A537 Administration Building
NIST
Gaithersburg, MD 20899
(301) 975-2036

Funding for the administration of the award is raised from the private sector by The Foundation for the Malcolm Baldrige National Quality Award.

To compete for the award, a company or business unit must meet the following deadlines (based on 1991 procedures—contact the administrators for updates or changes):

March 15	Submit "Eligibility Determination Form" with a $50 fee.
April 3	Submit Application Report with the review fee—$3,000 for manufacturing or service companies and $1,000 for small businesses. Companies reporting on more than one separate business unit need to submit Supplemental Sections and pay an additional fee of $1,500 for each.

The *review process* generally proceeds as follows:

April-June	First-Stage Review. At least four members of the Board of Examiners will decide whether to refer the application on for consensus review.
June-August	Consensus Review. A second examination determines which applications will receive site visits.
September	Site Visit Review. At least five members of the Board of Examiners provide on-site verification of the Application Report and make their own report to the Panel of Judges.
October	Final review of all evaluation reports by the Panel of Judges leads to selection of winners, which is presented to the Secretary of Commerce in the form of recommendations.
November	The Secretary of Commerce accepts the judges' recommendations and the awards are presented by the President of the United States.
December	Feedback reports are distributed to all applicants.

perform a detailed quality self-assessment upon request, and Johnson & Johnson has instituted a self-assessment program that "helps operating units strengthen their competitive advantage by measuring their total quality performance against the recognized world-class criteria of the Malcolm Baldrige Quality Award," according to company literature on the program. Specifically,

> In a one-day workshop, operating unit managing directors, presidents, management boards and other senior managers learn about the Baldrige Award criteria; conduct a self-assessment of the organization regarding one or more of the criteria; and develop an action plan for the appropriate next steps.[18]

While self-assessment does not necessarily require a competitive award system such as B&L's, self-assessment certainly is one of the beneficial side-effects of B&L's program. Every competing unit must assess itself as it prepares the evidence concerning its performance on each of the Baldrige criteria. And of course this self-assessment is put into perspective by the assessment of the judges—who in a way perform another kind of self-assessment, since they work for the same firm as the judged.

Self-assessment, and assessment in general, is certainly one of the benefits of competitive quality awards. A competition forces a certain objectivity on the self-assessment process. Whether it is at the company or business unit level, self-delusion will not hold up long in the face of competition. This is one of the advantages of the B&L-type company award, and of course of national awards such as the Baldrige as well. Better to risk disappointment in a contest like this than in the marketplace, where results really matter.

The competitiveness of the markets is in many ways the best argument in favor of competitive awards. Managers pursue total quality programs precisely because they wish to make

[18]"The Johnson & Johnson Total Quality Self-Assessment Program," provided by Sue Jacobs, Johnson & Johnson Quality Institute, January 8, 1992.

their companies more competitive in the marketplace. They hope, like Xerox, to regain lost market share, and they hope, like Motorola, to capture share in difficult markets like Japan as a direct result of the quality process. In this fundamental respect, every quality process is highly competitive. Further, the tendency of quality processes to look outward for superior models against which to benchmark can be seen as fundamentally competitive. Gordon Donahue, B&L's vice president, quality, in the Thin Films Technology Division, makes this argument in defense of his company's competitive awards. He says, "I don't think competition is bad at all. One of the things you do in quality is benchmark against the world's best; now isn't that competition?"[19]

In reality, competition is embraced to some extent by most companies with quality programs—not just competition in the marketplace, but also competition within the firm as a way to motivate employees and business units. In a recent Conference Board survey of 158 U.S. manufacturing and service firms with TQM in place, "Respondents report extensive use of quality award programs," this according to the report on this survey by Conference Board researcher Kathryn Troy. She reports that, of large companies with quality programs, "Eighty-five percent give awards to individuals and teams, and 75 percent offer unit or plant-wide awards. Noncash awards prevail, but slightly more than 30 percent offer both cash and noncash to individuals and teams and 15 percent make both available to units or plants."[20]

RESOLVING THE COMPETITION/ COOPERATION DILEMMA

We saw in the beginning of this chapter that B&L's competitive approach was criticized by managers from other companies. Yet, as the survey results prove, there is a competitive ele-

[19]Conversation with the author, February 5, 1992.
[20]Conference Board Report No. 974, p. 7.

to most quality programs. The difference in many cases is that B&L puts competition front and center, using the award as its primary tool for motivating the autonomous division managers to implement their own quality processes (and obtaining significant commitment to quality as a result). At other companies, the quality effort is more likely to be driven by a corporate plan and vision, and to follow an agreed-upon process and approach. Nonetheless competition still plays a role—probably a bigger role than most managers would acknowledge.

The reason that managers are hesitant to acknowledge the importance of competition is that competition appears to stand in the way of cooperation, and cooperation is undeniably one of the most striking aspects of a successful quality program. Yet contenders for the Baldrige, like B&L's competing divisions, are proving that the competitive quest can lead to greater cooperation and teamwork. The only way to win a quality award is to pursue the goal together, as a group— individual achievement is not even one of the Baldrige criteria. And, just as heightened teamwork and cooperation is required to win a quality award, so is it required to achieve competitiveness in the firm's marketplace. Competition may be an unpleasant reality, but it is a reality nonetheless, and quality programs can benefit by acknowledging this truth.

However, competition must be managed. The *level* of competition must be managed. If left to their own devices, individual business units, teams or managers often develop competitive rivalries that reduce the effectiveness and efficiency of their company's business processes. Like harried commuters who struggle to be first through an intersection, they may lose site of the ultimate objective and create a kind of organizational gridlock that keeps everyone from getting home in time for dinner. In the company, as on the road, short-sighted rivalries and personal competitiveness certainly lead to reduced cooperation and a misdirection of effort. These traits are bad for the company—at least when expressed inappropriately. In the opening of this chapter, Royce Benjamin of Ford said that his company subscribed to Deming's philosophy toward competition—meaning Ford is opposed to competition. It is helpful to see what Deming says on the topic. He uses a list of fourteen key points to describe the transformation of management methods that must accompany the new quality paradigm, and of these, several speak to the issue of competition:

- Drive out fear, so that everyone may work effectively for the company.

- Break down barriers between departments.

- Eliminate slogans, exhortations, and targets for the work force . . . Such exhortations only create adversarial relationships, since the bulk of the causes of low quality and low productivity belong to the system and thus lie beyond the power of the work force.

- Eliminate management by objectives. Substitute leadership.[21]

Competition can create fear, build barriers, create frustration and disenfranchisement, and provide an unhealthy and ineffective substitute for real leadership. If management declares a contest in which two factories compete to see which can achieve a higher numerical rating on some measure of productivity or profitability, the resulting competition will *not* produce continuous quality improvement. The fact remains that the end result of any quality program has to be enhanced competitiveness in the marketplace. And this goal is best served by enlisting the entire workforce in the effort to be more competitive. Thus, at a relatively centralized company, company-wide cooperation must be directed at company com-

---

[21]As quoted in Rafael Aguayo, *Dr. Deming: The American Who Taught the Japanese About Quality,* Simon & Schuster, 1991, pp. 124–5.

petitiveness in the marketplace. In other words, management must keep competition at the company level. In a decentralized company such as Bausch & Lomb, where each business unit competes in its own market, cooperation needs to result in greater competitiveness at the business unit level. Thus management may wish to permit competition at the business unit level, or even to encourage this level of competitiveness, as B&L does through its quality awards. But to manage the level of competition requires not only the pursuit of company awards, like the Baldrige, or the creation of business unit awards such as B&L's—it also, and perhaps more importantly, requires that management eliminate competition wherever it is inappropriate. It may be that the pursuit of a quality award, at a level that mirrors the real competition in the company's marketplace, provides a good opportunity to eliminate other levels of competition and replace them with cooperation.

The process of applying for the Malcolm Baldrige National Quality Award tends to encourage cooperation within the company or division applying for it. It is often seen as an external yardstick against which to measure the progress of a quality program, and as such tends to replace competitive yardsticks from within the organization. In this sense the Baldrige functions much as benchmarking does to broaden the context against which the organization judges itself. This use of the Baldrige is illustrated in the comments of managers from two winners. C. E. Vogel, Manager, Total Quality, Westinghouse Commercial Nuclear Fuel Division, explains that, "We heard about the Baldrige Award and decided that the criteria would be a good way to make an assessment of how well we were doing. The professional, objective people coming in would be able to tell us whether we were doing well or not. Even though our goal was to find out where we were, we wound up winning."[22] William T. Lesner, staff assistant to manufacturing engineer, Cadillac Motor Car Division of GM,

---

[22]Conference Board Report No. 990, p. 33.

reports, "The Baldrige Award proves to us that we're on the right track and motivates us to work even harder to attain our mission, which is to once again make Cadillac engineer, produce and market the world's finest automobiles."[23]

It is hard to criticize competition that leads to these kinds of results. At both companies, the process of competing for a quality award focused attention on an objective external yardstick, allowing the organization as a whole to judge its progress and requiring it to work together as a team. This competition helped the organizations become more competitive in their markets, but it certainly did not lead to greater competitiveness among the individuals within the organization. Competitiveness in the general sense, meaning a tendency to compete rather than to cooperate, does not have any role in total quality management. But competition, when used to foster greater cooperation within the organization and to make the organization more competitive in its markets, can be an effective tool in the pursuit of quality.

[23]Conference Board Report No. 990, p. 15.

9

LEADERSHIP

L eadership from the top is absolutely essential.
   —*Paul Allair, chairman and CEO, Xerox[1]*

I n any organization, leadership is key to the quality process.
   —*Douglas Anderson, director, corporate*
   quality service, 3M[2]

A ccording to a survey by the Forum Corp., a consulting firm, 82 percent of FORTUNE 500 executives believe their corporate strategy is understood by "everyone who needs to know." Alas, Louis Harris research finds, less than a third of employees say management provides clear goals and direction. When the Hay Group asked what kind of information workers wanted more of from top management, the troops checked "reliable information on where the company is headed" and "how my job fits into the total."
   —**Fortune** *magazine[3]*

[1]From an October 1, 1991 speech by Paul Allaire, transcript provided courtesy of Xerox Corp.
[2]Conference Board Report No. 979, p. 33.
[3]Alan Farnham, "The Trust Gap," *Fortune,* December 4, 1989, p. 57.

A quick visit to the business section of any bookstore reveals that leadership is a hot topic. Approaches range from pop psychology to inspirational exhortations from gurus and 'proven' leaders—including Attilla the Hun! On the academic side, the number of research reports on leadership climbs every year. Managers wishing to become charismatic leaders have available a great many self-help guides that, in a modern echo of the Dale Carnegie tradition, promise to make them stronger, better, more powerful people. But that is not the issue. Leadership, at least as it is practiced in successful quality programs, is more about doing one's job differently than becoming a different person.

As the opening quote from *Fortune* suggests, the largest performance gaps in leadership are in the fundamentals. Most employees do not even know which way their leaders are going, so it will not do much good to work on the person-alities of the leaders. Charisma and forcefulness are secondary to communication, at least when communication is not hap-pening as it should. The *Fortune* review cited above goes on to show that the communication problem is extensive, and is not getting any better either: "When Opinion Research Corp. of Chicago surveyed 100,000 middle managers, supervisors, pro-fessionals, salespeople, and technical, clerical, and hourly workers of FORTUNE 500 companies . . . it found the lines of communications fraying. With the exception of the sales group, employees believed top management now was less willing to listen to their problems than five years earlier. The groups felt top management accorded them less respect."[4] The various surveys suggest that better leadership may boil down to something as basic as better communication between the leaders and the followers.

---

[4]Ibid., p. 57.

Sending Strong, Consistent Messages

In IBM's quality program, communication is considered an important leadership tool, and the priority is on sending a strong, consistent message to all employees. According to Schwartz of IBM, "For communications to be effective, it is essential to have a steady, consistent drumbeat on Market-Driven Quality throughout the corporation. Every publication, every speech, each video or internal television program is an opportunity to reinforce the message. We have a logo for Market-Driven Quality which shows up in publications, correspondence, on awards and in meetings. The effect is cumulative, and powerful."[5]

In addition to the strong link between leadership and communication, there are also fundamental linkages between leadership and participation. Employee participation can and must increase dramatically before a quality culture can be achieved. And participation means both responsibility and *authority* to act on that responsibility. Because employee participation spreads authority downward in the organization, it seems at first glance to work counter to leadership. This is because, in our traditional management paradigm, we equate leadership with power. The more power, both personal and organizational, the more effective the leader. A strong leader is often called a "powerful leader." Yet how can a leader increase his or her power, while at the same time giving away power to underlings to increase participation? The two goals conflict; except at companies with successful quality programs, where both increased participation and stronger leadership are observed simultaneously.

---

[5]Speech by S. B. Schwartz, Goal/QPC Conference, Boston, November 12, 1991. Transcript provided courtesy of IBM.

Participative Leadership

One way to resolve this apparent conflict is to look at what academic studies of leadership reveal. A new school of thought, termed situational leadership theory, holds, according to professor Jane Goodson of Auburn University at Montgomery and her colleagues, that "the critical situational factor that . . . determines preferred leadership style is the task-related readiness of followers," and that "readiness is defined as the extent to which a follower has the ability and willingness to accomplish a specific task."[6] In other words, the state of the followers is critical to the effectiveness of the leader. This makes intuitive sense. There have to be followers for there to be leaders, just as their have to be leaders for there to be followers. And if, by shifting authority away from the leader, participation increases the readiness of the followers to follow, then leadership is served as well. Contrary to conventional thinking, participation and leadership can be made to pull in the same direction. They do not have to conflict. As Steven Schwartz, senior vice president, Market-Driven Quality at IBM, puts it, "Empowerment doesn't reduce the role of the leader. Delegation doesn't mean abdication."[7]

Not only will increased participation help make leadership more effective, but effective leadership will made participation more effective. In fact, leadership is critical to achieving the high-participation organizations that are required for continuous improvement. This finding comes from another aca-

---

[6]Jane R. Goodson, Gail W. McGee, and James F. Cashman, "Situational Leadership Theory: A Test of Prescriptions," *Group & Organization Studies,* Vol. 14, No. 4, December 1989, p. 447. Be forewarned, however, that in the world of academics points such as these are the subject of lively, even acrimonious, debate. In this case, the authors do their level best to disprove the theory as previously presented by Hersey and Blanchard *(Management of Organizational Behavior,* Prentice Hall, 1988), and show that some of the previously-accepted prescriptions for leadership style do not hold up in their study. Never mind. The key point, that the situation is important as well as the leadership style, is not refuted.

[7]Speech by S. B. Schwartz, Goal/QPC Conference, Boston, November 12, 1991. Transcript provided courtesy of IBM.

demic study, a survey of hundreds of senior managers at large industrial companies by Denis Collins of the University of Pittsburgh and two collaborators. They found that, "although other reasons are often cited, the primary missing ingredient in the forecasted managerial evolution toward participative systems is a lack of transformational leadership. Until this is developed, installation and success of such systems will remain limited."[8] They also found that, at most companies, leadership style is "paternalistic" in their terminology, but that most of the managers believe they *ought* to be using a "participative" style instead. Exhibit 9-1 on page 220 defines these terms and two other generic leadership styles, *authoritative* and *consultative*.

Exhibit 9-1 represents a spectrum, ranging from the most authoritative and top-down style of leadership, on the left, to the least, on the right. At present, according to the survey, most managers *implement* the paternalistic style of leadership, yet most believe that the participative style of leadership is what their organizations *need*. This opinion is borne out by the experiences of successful quality practitioners, who are moving, on all of the factors listed in the exhibit, from the traditional paternalistic model to a more participative model.

THE SEARCH FOR ALTERNATIVE MANAGEMENT STYLES

Interestingly, there is also increasing recognition of the fact that women naturally tend toward a participative style of management, compared with men's traditional style of leadership—thus making the gender reference in the term 'paternalistic' an apt one. For example, Professor Judy Rosener of the University of California, Irvine, reports that in a study of successful female managers, "women leaders made frequent reference to their efforts to encourage participation and share

[8]Denis Collins, Ruth Ann Ross, and Timothy L. Ross, "Who Wants Participative Management? The Managerial Perspective," *Group & Organization Studies,* Vol. 14, No. 4, December 1989, p. 422.

Exhibit 9-1[9]

Leadership styles:

Factors	Authoritative	Paternalistic	Consultative	Participative
Where responsibility for achieving co.'s goals is located.	Mostly at top	Top and middle	Fairly general	At all levels
What the usual direction of information flow is.	Downward	Mostly down	Down & up	Down, up & sideways
How accurate the upward communication is.	Usually inaccurate	Often inaccurate	Often accurate	Almost always accurate
The extent of trust and confidence in subordinates.	Virtually none	Some	Substantial	A great deal
How free employees are to talk to their supervisors about their jobs.	Not very	Somewhat	Quite	Very
How involved subordinates are in decisions related to their work.	Never	Occasionally	Generally	Fully

[9]After Collins et al., Table 2, p 431–2.

power and information—two things that are often associated with participative management." Rosener's study showed, in her words, that "Women managers . . . have proven that effective leaders don't come from one mold. They have demonstrated that using the command-and-control style of managing others, a style generally associated with men in large, traditional organizations, is not the only way to succeed." I recommend her article, the study of female leadership styles, and indeed the promotion of women into leadership roles, to managers looking for alternatives to the traditional, paternalistic approach to leadership that predominates in American companies.[10] The search for alternatives, and for managers who can implement them, can be difficult. David Luther, senior vice president and corporate director, quality for Corning, complains of the difficulty of this search when he says, "We seek leaders and coaches, not bosses and managers; this is a particularly tough search."[11] The search may become easier as more women are considered for leadership roles in U.S. businesses.

TRANSFORMATIONAL LEADERSHIP

Returning to the study by Collins from which Exhibit 9-1 is drawn, I am struck by the fact that the surveyed managers recognize the need for a new leadership style, a more participative style of leadership. Yet they still use a style of leadership that is very far from this goal. As the authors of the study conclude, there is a clear need for "transformational leadership," leadership that transforms the way the company operates by changing all the factors measured in the study: Responsibility, information flows, trust, and self-control over job design. These are fundamental determinants of corporate cul-

---

[10]Judy Rosener, "Ways Women Lead," *Harvard Business Review,* November-December 1990, quotes from pp. 119, 120.

[11]David B. Luther, "Continuous Quality Improvement: The Ever-Widening Network," speech at The Conference Board's Third Annual Quality Conference, April 2–3, 1990, New York.

ture, and to change that culture, to make it more competitive and participatory, leaders must systematically set about the task of transformation. Transformational leadership is a powerful notion—powerful because of the insight it offers us, not the personal power it gives leaders. It has little to do with traditional notions of leadership and personal power. Most of those inspirational books on leadership are therefore not of much use. Nor, for that matter, can the academics tell us how to implement transformational leadership—formal documentation in the research literature generally lags behind actual practice. To understand what this new transformational leadership entails, we have to return to our model companies, the quality practitioners of The Conference Board's Quality Councils and similar companies where leadership has already been used to transform organizations. At these companies, leaders are learning to use participation and leadership hand-in-hand to nurture cultural change.

Leadership by Championship: From the Top Down

If you want your leadership to transform your organization, the most direct way to accomplish your goal is to become the main catalyst and champion for this transformation. That is what a number of senior executives have done, and, when done well, it seems to be the most successful model. It requires the senior manager, usually, the CEO, to become the company's leading quality crusader.

Ronald Schmidt is chairman, president and CEO of Zytec, a leading maker of power supplies for computers and one of the 1991 Baldrige Award winners. Since Zytec began its quality journey in 1984, Schmidt has been an active and visible champion. By focusing his own energy on the quality program, and by working closely with employees on it, he has effectively focused the entire organization on quality-directed organizational change. These excerpts from Zytec's 1991 Baldrige application reveal some of the leadership strategies Schmidt and his top managers used:[12]

- Meetings were held with every Zytec employee to increase knowledge of Deming's points [upon which Zytec bases its program], and many employees have attended half-day, two-day, and four-day Deming seminars. As a result, Deming's 14 Points for Management guide Zytec's actions, from long range strategic planning to employee empowerment to leadership.

- In 1988, Zytec's CEO and the vice president of marketing and sales visited Japan on a TQC study mission. As a result of this trip, Zytec initiated a process called Management By Planning (MBP). The process involves employees in establishing long range plans and short-term objectives . . . Zytec's senior executives set corporate objectives to guide the process, then lead the six cross-functional teams that review and develop individual plans, by key functional areas, for presentation to employees . . . Nearly every employee is on a MBP team working on at least one objective.

- The CEO plays "catch ball" with each department to coordinate establishing their objectives, monthly goals, and action plans. During monthly operations review meetings, senior management reviews progress on the MBP corporate objectives . . . If a department needs help, a senior executive is assigned responsibility for providing whatever is needed to improve the process.

- Senior management is actively involved in quality training.

---

[12]Provided by Karen Scheldroup, Baldrige Office, Zytec, January 13, 1992.

- Senior executives meet often with customers and suppliers and participate in benchmarking competitors and world-class companies.

The hand of management is strong in this company, as evidenced by the prominent role senior management plays in setting corporate objectives, for example. And, by championing the quality program himself, teaching quality courses, travelling to Japan to study quality methods, acting as ball-catcher for each of the company's 33 departments, and participating directly in benchmarking efforts, Schmidt places himself at the center of the change process. However, he does this in a nontraditional manner—this is not the conventional paternalistic leadership style described above, but something closer to the Deming ideal upon which Zytec based its quality program.

The company has adopted Deming's 14 points, or, as Deming terms them, "methods for management of productivity and quality." Point 7 is, "Institute leadership." Deming elaborates; "The aim of leadership should be to help people and machines and gadgets to do a better job." This, according to the Deming philosophy, requires that management "put everybody in the company to work to accomplish the transformation. The transformation is everybody's job." It is a peculiarly participative vision of leadership, with leadership by top-down objectives replaced by worker-defined objectives for example, and numerical production goals and merit ratings replaced by pride of workmanship.

Despite (or perhaps because of) Schmidt's heavy involvement in the quality effort, individuals and individual divisions are actively involved in setting their own goals and managing their own work. A number of Zytec's departments have no managers—they are managed instead by teams of production workers. Zytec uses education as a way to strengthen participation and empower employees. Its Multi-Functional Employee program rewards employees for the number of skills they acquire.[13] Zytec seems to emphasize both top-down leadership and bottom-up management at the same time.

Another 1991 Baldrige Award winner, a manufacturer of heat exchangers, Marlow Industries describes its approach to quality as a "top-to-bottom" approach. As at Zytec, Marlow's quality program is championed by the company's CEO and president, Raymond Marlow. He chairs the company's TQM council and "maintains daily responsibility for quality-related matters."[14] Marlow has only 160 employees, and Zytec about 800. Perhaps their small size explains the effectiveness of the leader-as-quality-champion strategy at these companies. Does it work at larger companies?

Apparently it does. David Kearns of Xerox acted as champion of the quality initiative from its beginnings, back in 1979, until his departure in 1991. Paul Allaire, Xerox's current chairman and CEO, emphasizes the importance of senior management's championship of quality. For example, he states that,

> Leadership from the top is absolutely essential. First, senior management must own the quality strategy. Leadership can't be delegated. Nor can it be relegated to a staff function. In fact, our top 25 executives played a hands-on role in designing our strategy back in 1983. I believe that a common denomination among those companies who have successfully implemented TQM is a leadership that has a deep understanding and commitment to quality. Second, senior management must lead by example. Commitment must take the form of action as well as rhetoric. Managers must walk like they talk. This is tough for most of us who are used to being "above the fray."[15]

While it is a difficult transition, it is apparently a necessary one. It is necessary in part because the new approaches to leadership and participation change the way companies are

[13]Information supplied by Karen Scheldroup, Zytec.
[14]Company literature.
[15]From an October 1, 1991 speech by Paul Allaire, transcript provided courtesy of Xerox Corp.

organized. Where the paternalistic model uses a vertical organization with many layers of management, the participative model uses a more horizontal organization. As George Fisher, chairman and CEO of Motorola, puts it, "we need to work more participatively within the organization and more cooperatively across organizations and functions. A vertical organizational chart misses the external world. It takes a horizontal organization to serve the customer."[16] And a horizontal organization requires every manager, especially those on top, to shift their style from paternalistic to participative. It necessitates an entirely different kind of relationship with subordinates and peers. If senior management does not make this change in its role, it will, unwittingly, stand in the way of the changes other managers and employees must make to accommodate the new, horizontal structure and the new information flows that accompany it.

TRAINING MANAGERS TO LEAD

One way to make sure senior managers, and all managers, champion quality is to train them in the skills of transformational management. This is what IBM does. Steven Schwartz, senior vice-president—Market-Driven Quality at IBM, explains how education was used to kick-start his company's new quality program: "At the outset, we asked every employee and manager to attend two days of Market-Driven Quality awareness education—plus two days of transformational leadership training for the management team." This is the most direct approach: If you need transformational leadership, train managers in transformational leadership. Something this important is better not left to chance. Yet in most companies, training is used for lower-level employees, not senior managers.

---

[16]George M. C. Fisher, "Measuring the Unmeasurable," *World: The Magazine for Decision Makers* (published by KPMG Peat Marwick), No. 2, 1990, p. 5.

IBM also found that leadership training should not be limited to senior managers. After all, participative leadership is a two-way street, requiring participation and openness of both the leader and the follower. And, in principle, managers should be learning from employees even as employees learn from managers; the two groups have an interest in transforming each other, since they must walk down the quality path together. Schwartz reports that training employees in leadership, along with their managers, is effective. He says, "We found that having employees attend those leadership classes with their managers is very effective. Last year, worldwide, about 60 percent of our employees also went to transformational leadership training with their management team."[17]

At Florida Power & Light, there are three three-day courses in leadership: Leadership for Managers, I, II and III. They train managers both in the basic tools of quality, and in the details of the leaders' role—for example, FPL trains managers how to lead quality improvement teams.[18]

Johnson & Johnson also uses training to teach managers how to lead the quality process. The training is part of the company's Total Quality Self-Assessment Program, which "helps operating units strengthen their competitive advantage by measuring their total quality performance against the recognized world class criteria of the Malcolm Baldrige National Quality Award," according to a company publication. The training includes a management orientation that "highlights the critical role leadership plays in total quality implementation."[19] And this message is also emphasized by Johnson & Johnson's senior managers. Chairman and CEO Ralph Larsen explains that "Our belief in the Quality Implementation Process is evidenced by the resources allocated to its implementa-

---

[17]Speech by S. B. Schwartz, Goal/QPC Conference, Boston, November 12, 1991. Transcript provided courtesy of IBM.
[18]Conference Board Report No. 959, p. 22.
[19]"The Johnson & Johnson Self-Assessment Program." Source: Sue Jacobs, Johnson & Johnson Quality Institute, January 8, 1992.

tion. Jeff Nugent has been appointed Vice President of Worldwide Quality Improvement, and I, personally, chair the Quality Improvement Steering Committee that will provide overall corporate direction and emphasis. The other committee members . . . represent the Executive Committee, as well as senior executives from each of the sectors and key corporate functions."[20] In other words, all the company's senior managers are also leaders of the quality initiative.

IF MANAGERS WON'T, WHO WILL?

A contrary, but telling, point in favor of top-level leadership of the quality function is that there does not seem to be any good alternative. If senior management does not champion quality, who will? Quality has been the province of quality-control engineers for decades, and they were unable to transform their companies, despite the fact that in many cases they knew perfectly well that catching bad quality—what they did—was inferior to building quality in. The QC inspectors and engineers do not have sufficient clout to transform their organizations. Nor, most likely, do corporate quality offices.

In a growing number of cases, senior managers have created corporate quality offices as the first step of a quality program. (A 1990 survey of 52 large companies by recruiters Battalia & Associates found that almost half had established executive-level quality offices in the last two years.[21]) The quality staff are given a pat on the back and told to implement total quality throughout the organization. But, without a corresponding turnaround in the way senior management leads, their efforts constantly clash with the existing culture. This ought to be apparent, but, as an *Industry Week* review of the topics concludes, "a disquieting number of U. S. executives apparently are still barely aware of [quality's] techniques and

[20]Source: Sue Jacobs, Ibid.

[21]Gilbert Fuchsberg, "Gurus of Quality Are Gaining Clout," *The Wall Street Journal,* November 27, 1990, p. B1.

impact."[22] These managers may not grasp the difficulty of the challenge, and may not realize that they are sending mixed messages on quality.

The experience of Darla Mendales, vice president of corporate quality management at Fidelity Investments, is illustrative. When she took office in 1989, senior executives first suggested she promote quality by distributing buttons and mugs. Mendales explains that, "They wanted to turn it into a marketing campaign." More than that, management continued to emphasize objectives that conflicted with quality goals. For example, in 1990 the performance of Fidelity representatives was still measured according to their productivity, and they complained that the new quality objectives from Mendales' office were inconsistent with their performance measurement system. This problem is representative of many that a new quality program encounters, and the ability of any corporate quality staff to deal with such problems depends in large measure on the support for quality at the top.

The fact that Mendales continues to make progress can be attributed as much to growing top-level support as to her tenacity. No corporate staff has the power to transform a company by itself—its role must be to support the transformational activities of management, rather than to carry the baton of change single-handed. This is no doubt why Ralph J. Rosati argued in his role as director, corporate quality, at Eastman Kodak Company, that "if there is a single essential element, I believe it is getting and keeping top management involved."[23] The sentiment is echoed by Richard Dulude, Group President, Corning Glass Works, who states that, "Quality starts at the top. Quality demands an ongoing commitment from top management. It can't be just a put-on attitude, a slogan."[24] Or a mug or button, as Fidelity's managers learned.

[22]Thomas M. Rohan, "Sermons Fall on Deaf Ears," *Industry Week,* November 20, 1989, p. 35.
[23]Conference Board Research Report No. 909, p. 17.
[24]Conference Board Research Report No. 909, p. 25.

THE LEADER AS HELPER:
ROLE MODELING

One of the statements from Zytec's Baldrige application described the manager's job as providing help. That is a participative view of leadership, not an authoritative one. The manager is a resource for the employee, ready to step in for problem-solving or to contribute ideas and resources. This kind of leadership works very well in the larger company too. Xerox includes two leadership tools in its quality toolbox whose purpose is to help managers play this leadership role: inspection and role modeling. Inspection is . . . well, perhaps it is best to see these tools in action rather than to simply talk about them. Here is a fictional quality tour given a Xerox manager in a management parable Xerox uses for training. This manager is visiting John Jones to learn how his department uses quality tools, including inspection and role modeling, and the two have just returned to Jones' office after visiting other parts of the department. The visitor, you, have been listening to Jones as he has a long phone conversation with his manager. Jones has just hung up the phone, and you are now discussing the conversation.[25]

"Sounds interesting," I said.

"It was. Two more quality tools in action."

What I had overheard didn't sound to me like Quality tools. I said cautiously, "Which two?"

"Two related ones, both concerned with communication: inspection and role modeling."

"You were being inspected just then?"

He smiled. "Sounds so military, doesn't it? But, of course, it's not. My manager was using the Quality tool of inspec-

[25]From *Quality Tools: The Present Builds Our Future,* USMG Quality Office, Copyright 1988, Xerox Corporation. Reproduced by permission of the company.

tion to do what it's designed for: to get a clear picture of what is happening in an employee's area and to assist when necessary. As it happens, as a result of his questions he saw an opportunity we hadn't even realized was there, and he passed on some information my team can really use. That might not have happened if he hadn't been using inspection."

"Pretty informal inspection," I said. I had pictured inspection as more defined, even rigid. Checklists. Written reports.

"That was informal, yes," Jones said. "Certainly there's a place for more formal inspection as well. But I think frequent, oral check-ins about Quality give managers a more accurate picture of how Quality is working in their area."

"I agree," I said. "Although now that I think of it, there are some people I haven't spoken to in a while . . . there might be some help or encouragement I could offer them."

"Or they could offer you," Jones said. "Inspection means communication up and down the reporting ladder."

I said, "You mentioned two Quality tools involved in that phone call. What was the other one? No, wait, let me guess—it was role modeling."

"Right. Role modeling is still the best way to convey to people what is really important in a work environment, as opposed to what managers say is important. My manager's questions to me, as well as his own use of quality tools, signal strongly, 'This is the way we work around here.' "

These two tools, inspection and role-modeling, are designed to create the two-way communication needed for participative management, and to teach quality management by example. Role modeling is a powerful form of leadership. It is what the leaders of companies like Zytec, Marlow, 3M and Xerox are doing when they become the champions of quality within their own companies. Although the companies may be too big for them to work directly with every employee, their use of these two tools helps create the same kind of leadership throughout the organization. Every interaction with managers below them reinforces quality management and trains managers in transformational leadership. And these managers spread the vision to quality champions beneath *them*.

Furthermore, it is not a one-way flow. Even as quality techniques and information are passed down through role-modeling and inspection, other information is passed upward, and a new, more open approach to information is taught throughout the company. Effective quality leadership stimulates connection-making, the sharing of information over boundaries such as department walls and levels of management, and one of the jobs of the transformational leader is to role-model this new approach to information-sharing.

Inspection does have a military sound to it, as the fictional Mr. Jones points out, but that is deceptive. It is designed and intended as a helpful tool, not a threatening one—and must be used to help, not threaten. The same can be said of role modeling. The key to the success of these leadership tools, and to the use of managers as quality champions, lies in the fact that the leader uses tools such as these to *help* employees, not to boss them around.

The Need for Continuous Improvement

Leadership of the quality process is best provided by the senior managers of a company, as we have seen. And leadership, in the context of a quality program, must be used to transform the company's style from the traditional paternalistic to the new participative leadership model. What is needed is transformational leadership. These are easy points to make in writing, but no doubt hard to live by. The changes described in this chapter cannot happen at once, throughout the company, and even if they did, there would no doubt be a new vision of leadership requiring additional changes. That is what continuous improvement is all about. Therefore it makes sense to track management progress in the area of leadership, to quantify the extent to which leadership is helpful and participative, and to hold managers responsible for improvement in their leadership performance.

LEADERSHIP EVALUATION

Accountability for leadership performance? It sounds like sacrilege. The fact of the matter is that, while the performance of line and service employees is routinely measured, and their compensation often tied to those measures, management has generally avoided such close and scientific scrutiny. (As a result, most people, including many managers, are not sure exactly what managers *do*.) Perhaps this lack of accountability is one of the reasons why most academics who study organizational change find managers the most resistant to change. However this lack of accountability is coming to an end if Federal Express is any indication. At FedEx, every managers' leadership is now evaluated *by their employees* through an annual survey (employee surveys are combined to permit anonymity). Not only that, but the managers are required to develop a plan of action that addresses any weaknesses revealed by the survey, and to start implementing it within six weeks. Managers are held strictly accountable, by their employees, for the leadership they provide those employees.

Exhibit 9-2 gives a list of questions used in Federal Express's leadership survey. This may be a useful benchmark for other companies wishing to institute a leadership evaluation system. And readers may also find it interesting to use the instrument to evaluate the leadership provided in their company, both by their boss and by senior management in general.

EXHIBIT 9-2 SURVEY QUESTIONS USED TO MEASURE LEADERSHIP AT FEDERAL EXPRESS

(Managers are scored by employees on the following scale: Strongly agree, agree, sometimes agree/disagree, strongly disagree, and undecided/don't know.)

1. I feel free to tell my manager what I think.
2. My manager lets me know what's expected of me.
3. Favoritism is not a problem in my work group.
4. My manager helps us find ways to do our jobs better.
5. My manager is willing to listen to my concerns.
6. My manager asks for my ideas about things affecting our work.
7. My manager lets me know when I've done a good job.
8. My manager treats me with respect and dignity.
9. My manager keeps me informed about things I need to know.
10. My manager lets me do my job without interfering.
11. My manager's boss gives us the support we need.
12. Upper management (directors and above) lets us know what the company is trying to accomplish.
13. Upper management pays attention to ideas and suggestions from people at my level.
14. I have confidence in the fairness of management.
15. I can be sure of a job as long as I do good work.
16. I am proud to work for Federal Express.
17. Working for Federal Express will probably lead to the kind of future I want.
18. I think Federal Express does a good job for our customers.
19. All things considered, working for Federal Express is a good deal for me.
20. I am paid fairly for the kind of work I do.
21. Our benefit programs seem to meet most of my needs.
22. Most people in my workgroup cooperate with each other to get the job done.
23. There is cooperation between my workgroup and other groups in Federal Express.
24. In my work environment we generally use safe work practices.
25. Rules and procedures do not interfere with how well I am able to do my job.
26. I am able to get the supplies or resources I need to do my job.
27. I have enough freedom to do my job well.

Exhibit 9-2 (*continued*)

28. My workgroup is involved in activities to improve service to our group's customers.
29. The concerns identified by my workgroup during last year's SFA feedback session have been satisfactorily addressed.

Source: Federal Express

I also highly recommend using it for *self-evaluation* by, first, asking any employees reporting to you to fill out a questionnaire based on the exhibit and give you a statistical summary of their results (to protect their individual identities). Then, before you look at these results, use the instrument to evaluate yourself (giving the scores you think employees would give you), and compare the two results. Do you see your leadership as your employees do? In most cases, managers and supervisors will discover a significant perception gap! The gap reflects the survey findings, quoted in the opening of this chapter, that most managers actually use a paternalistic leadership style, yet recognize the need for a participative style. If the statements in the FedEx survey describe your management style accurately, then you have made the transition to a participative style of management. If not, the statements that do not fit you can provide the basis for your own improvement plan.

Management Leadership: The Most Critical Area

Most of the Quality Council companies, and certainly most of the Baldrige winners, agree that strong, transformational leadership must be provided from the very top of the organization in order to create the far-reaching cultural and organizational changes required for total quality. And a number of these companies go one step farther, arguing that management leadership is the *single most important element*. I am not sure if this theory is universally true, but it deserves attention nonetheless. For many companies, at least, transformational leadership is the most important driver of organizational change. Here, by way of conclusion, is how Jack Fooks, (former) vice president, corporate quality and productivity, describes leadership at Westinghouse Electric Corp. In his view, a company's leader needs to champion change (he describes Westinghouse's chairman during the development of its quality program, John Marous, as "our fanatic"), and also needs to lead by example. Marous subjected himself to testing and developed his own quality improvement plan, much as the managers at Federal Express do, in behavior that makes powerful use of the two tools Xerox teaches its managers, inspection and role modeling. And Fooks argues that the best way to overcome communications problems and spread the quality vision throughout the company is for leadership to behave in a way that is consistent with the vision. Here is how Fooks describes leadership at Westinghouse.[26]

> The most critical element in building a total quality culture is *management leadership*. People look to managers to set agendas. The first requisite for culture building is a *fanatic* to drive the process. John Marous, Westinghouse's chairman, is our fanatic. He embodies the process in everything he says and does; Morris sets examples across the corporation. Inside the company, he drove us with the George Westinghouse Total Quality Awards. And Marous insisted that he be tested in a Total Quality Fitness Review, after which he initiated an improvement plan for himself as chairman. This was all quantified in an effort to set standards for the chairman. These actions send powerful signals to the troops.
>
> During the quality improvement process, the first step for management leadership is to establish the vision, and, then, to commit the organization to the vision—from the top down. Do janitorial services understand the vision as well as the chairman? Most important, it is essential to remain consistent to the vision, both in word and action.

[26]Jack H. Fooks, "Culture Change and the Quality Organization," speech given at The Conference Board's Third Annual Quality Conference, April 2–3, 1990, Grand Hyatt, New York.

Chapter 10

TRAINING

T raining . . . was not something we could deliver like milk and expect people to consume spontaneously. It was not simply a matter of instructing or giving people a chance to instruct themselves. We had to motivate people to want to learn, and that meant overcoming complacency.

—William Wiggenhorn, corporate vice president for training and education, Motorola[1]

I f you went to work for some of our high-performance factories, you'd find your pay level depends on what skill level you reach. We're paying for what you *know*, not what you do.

—David Luther, senior vice president and corporate director, quality, Corning Inc.[2]

Q uality University is a philosophy [as well as a training center]. It's a total approach to customer satisfaction that begins with dedication to the growth and development of American Express employees—and results in commitment to meeting the expectations of American Express customers.

—From a brochure for American Express's employee training program

[1]William Wiggenhorn, "Motorola U: When Training Becomes an Education," *Harvard Business Review*, July-August 1990, pp. 71–83.
[2]Personnel communication with the author, January 1992.

As quality programs bring greater employee participation and responsibility, they make greater demands on employee skills. More and better skills are required, both in the specifics of quality methodologies and in more general areas like math and communications. Quality demands a great deal of the workforce, and companies are finding that extensive training is required to bring their workforces up to the required level. William Wiggenhorn of Motorola explains that, "Ten years ago, we hired people to perform set tasks and didn't ask them to do a lot of thinking. If a machine went down, workers raised their hands, and a trouble-shooter came to fix it . . . Today, we expect them to begin any trouble-shooting themselves."[3] When a quality program asks people to start doing "a lot of thinking," training becomes one of the most important components of the quality strategy. Thinking is in large part a learned behavior.

Corning predicates its entire quality effort on training, as we saw when we reviewed the importance of vision in Chapter 2. While other companies may have different visions of quality, *all* quality programs demand a significant training commitment. Training helps focus the company on customers. Training is one of the best ways to fill up individuals' toolboxes with the many techniques and methods of process improvement. Employees need to be trained. Management needs to be trained—often before any other steps can be taken toward total quality. Suppliers need to be trained, and so, sometimes, do customers. In fact, most of the companies mentioned so far in this book have special training programs for suppliers and key customers. Corning runs a one-day Visitor Quality Orientation on the third Tuesday of every month. IBM has a similar monthly program for suppliers at its Market-Driven Quality Institute. Ford's supplier training program has spun off into an independent nonprofit called The American Supplier Institute. And every company has at least one major training center for

[3]Ibid., p. 71.

employees—from Motorola U. to Xerox's training facility in Leesburg, Virginia, millions of employees have already received in-depth training on how to design and use quality improvement processes. In fact, there has never been as large a mobilization of corporate resources in the field of management training.

THE PROBLEMS WITH QUALITY TRAINING

The unprecedented investment in quality training reflects two problems, one of them more avoidable than the other. First, one cannot get around the fact that quality programs require a paradigm shift. The pursuit of quality requires a great deal more than the adoption of a handful of new techniques. All employees have to be brought up to speed in the new paradigm. This is a challenging goal; it takes a lot more than a half-day seminar to change the way people think about their work. And the longer they have been working under the old management ways, the harder it is to change the way they think. One quality manager I interviewed for this book said that senior managers were the hardest to train for the simple reason that the total quality paradigm conflicts with twenty or thirty years of past experience and learning. Even when an experienced manager ascribes to the quality principles, it can be difficult for him or her to break old habits of thought and action. According to my anonymous informant, "It won't be until a whole generation of managers have worked for 20 years on process improvement that you will see full adoption of total quality." It is remarkably hard to change one's *modus operandi*, and new ways of learning and managing are adopted gradually and with difficulty, even when a company and its managers make change a top priority.

The second problem is that U. S. schools have not trained new entrants to the job force in the skills and concepts needed to participate in quality improvement processes. As Motorola's chairman, Robert Galvin, recently put it, "Quality principles and practices represents a branch of knowledge that is missing from almost all of our new hires."[4] In fact, the nation's business schools may even be providing *negative* training by emphasizing notions from the old management paradigm that conflict with the principles of total quality management. (As we have seen repeatedly, the old wisdom is often in opposition to the new.) The failure of business schools to teach quality is really a factor of time—too few programs have been in place for too little time for academia to have studied the practices and incorporated them into teaching. The business school curriculum normally changes only in response to the development of a field of scholarly research and the maturation of a new generation of researchers and teachers interested in the new field. However, this traditional change process may be dysfunctional, and from business' (the customers) perspective a reduction in the cycle time for development of new academic fields is in order.

The Total Quality Forum, a group made up of both academic and business leaders, represents many of the foremost American practitioners of quality. At a recent meeting sponsored by American Express, IBM, Procter & Gamble, Ford, Motorola, and Xerox, the forum concluded that "many academic institutions have been slow to incorporate TQM into their core curriculum and their own administrative practices." The group is actively encouraging schools to incorporate TQM into the training they provide future managers, on the theory that,

> This situation is bad for us all. Business bears the burden of educating and, in some cases, re-educating new hires. This not only represents an additional cost but also perpetuates a competitive disadvantage. And academic institutions that are slow to embrace TQM, at best, miss the opportunity to lead change and, at worst, run the risk of becoming less relevant to the business world.[5]

[4]As quoted in Fortune, January 13, 1992, p. 14.
[5]"An Open Letter: TQM on the Campus," *Harvard Business Review*, November-December 1991, p. 94.

This quote is from an open letter signed by the CEOs of the six sponsoring organizations,[6] which is a pretty good indicator that business sees the issue as a major problem. On the other hand, every problem represents an opportunity, and companies have been making the most of the opportunity to retrain employees and managers in the principles and practice of quality improvement. And although each company's program has unique elements, there is remarkable unanimity on the fundamentals of how to undertake this task. A Conference Board survey of training practices at Quality Council member companies, performed (and initially reported) by Kathryn Troy, a senior research associate in The Conference Board's Quality and Productivity Program, identified many of these common elements in quality training. The best way to describe quality training is therefore to look closely at the results of this study.[7]

HOW QUALITY COUNCIL COMPANIES TRAIN

The research program was initiated by members of the U. S. Quality Council, and enabled them to compare and contrast their own training programs to those of firms with quality processes at a similar stage of advancement—incidentally making this an interesting example of the benchmarking philosophy in practice. The survey's most obvious finding is that training has become a vital element in efforts to raise employee awareness, to equip them with problem-solving and statistical skills, and to prepare managers and supervisors to build work teams and facilitate group dynamics. The specific training needs flow from a company's strategy and plans—often

---

[6]James Robinson of American Express, John Akers of IBM, Edwin Artzt of P&G, Harold Poling of Ford, Robert Galvin of Motorola, and Paul Allaire of Xerox.
[7]The following description draws heavily on Conference Board Report No. 959 by Kathryn Troy.

through a formal assessment of existing capabilities versus those required to implement the quality plans—and they must also reflect corporate strategy.

Employee needs are factored into the training equation through a variety of methods, but the annual performance review process is probably the most important. However, the trend may be away from supervisor-prepared reviews and toward self-evaluation. At American Express Travel Related Services, managers are responsible for preparing a training plan for each employee reporting to them, *based on a discussion with the employee.* Individual-by-individual assessment of training needs is becoming standard in companies with mature quality programs—both Corning and IBM now prepare training plans for each individual, and at Corning managers are expected to prepare their *own* training plans.[8] The idea is that each employee needs to take responsibility for their own training, and this starts with what the academics call meta-knowledge, or an awareness of both what you do and do *not* know. Research shows that managers generally underestimate their uncertainty by a large margin—they are overconfident in their own knowledge. But in cases where better meta-knowledge is a priority, individuals are able to improve their understanding of what they do not know.[9] Hopefully the adoption of self-assessment and self-planned training will have a positive impact on employees' meta-knowledge as well as their knowledge.

The effectiveness of training is, as we have already argued, based both on how well it meets individual training needs and how well it aligns with corporate strategy. There are both individual and company-wide knowledge gaps that need to be closed. The question of aligning training with corporate strategy was considered important by council members, and

---

[8]Based on January, 1992 conversations with David Luther of Corning and Frank Keegan, Senior Quality Advisor, IBM.

[9]J. Edward Russo and Paul J. H. Shoemaker, "Managing Overconfidence," *Sloan Management Review*, Winter 1992, pp. 7–17.

they gathered several examples that might be considered positive role models against which to benchmark.

Ford's overall quality training strategy focuses on three key corporate priorities:

- Implement management and operating practices consistent with the company's vision. (At Ford this means the formal statement of mission, values and guiding principles, and especially the notion that continuous improvement is everyone's job, as articulated, for example, in Ford's Policy Letter #1, which is distributed to every employee.[10])

- Meet customer needs and expectations.

- Achieve continuous quality improvement.

Training policy is monitored continuously by senior executives from each business unit, such as the Quality Strategy Committee, which represents the 30 top executives from all functional disciplines within the company's North American Automotive Operations. Thus for Ford there is a strong top-down component to training which helps keep it focused on corporate goals and needs.

First Chicago's quality training focuses on the company's "commitment statements," which define the basic focus and emphasis of quality improvement efforts and the training that supports these efforts. Here are the commitment statements used at First Chicago:

- Our commitment to the customer is our highest priority. (Customer focus training is an important area of the curriculum, and includes courses titled Leading Customer Focus and Creating Customer Focus.)

---

[10]Based on a conversation with Royce Benjamin, Senior Quality Associate, Ford Motor Company, January 29, 1992.

- "Our commitment to our people is the key to our success." (Training emphasizes development and job skills, including courses titled Process Improvement and Tools and Techniques.)

- "Our commitment to teamwork means working together within and between businesses." (Courses in facilitation and teambuilding, and the practice of taking courses *with* one's team, are designed to focus on building teamwork.)

- "Our commitment to integrity, excellence and professionalism in all we do." (To support this company commitment, training is offered in courses such as Training in Quality Awareness, Managing for Excellence and Leadership Strategies.)

At Xerox, the annual quality strategy assessments are used to evaluate quality training within each operating unit, giving management an opportunity to realign training with corporate strategy. Assessment activities of special relevance to training are as follows:

- Benchmark data on training are compiled from Fuji Xerox and leading U. S. and overseas companies and feedback is provided to senior staff at operating units, including quality officers, quality training managers and the corporate quality office. (This means senior management can compare Xerox's quality training to that of other companies.)

- Prior to implementation, training strategy is validated via personal interviews with Xerox line management. (This is an example of internal customer research, using a qualitative research technique that, like the transaction studies discussed in Chapter 4, is likely to reveal any problems from the customer's perspective.)

The importance of alignment between training and management strategy cannot be overstated. But I will try. Council members emphasize the importance of setting training strategy by gathering data on needs through a top-down/bottom-up process. This means, for example, that performance reviews are an opportune vehicle for the bottom-up assessment of employee training needs, and also that employee surveys and exit interviews can provide good bottom-up input. However, it is vitally important that corporate mission, goals and strategies should be factored into the process of developing training strategy, preferably with the involvement of top management or a senior-level training task force. Top management needs to be involved in the initiation of a quality training program, and council members also stress that top management must *stay* involved. Continued management involvement elevates the status of the training process (and, admittedly, training is traditionally a low-status backwater at many U. S. companies). In Corning, members of top management are the first class in each new training course; in a number of other firms, a top executive kicks off every quality training course.

CURRICULUM DECISIONS: WHAT TO OFFER

One of the fundamental issues in any training effort is what courses to offer. We have just reviewed some of the practices whereby content input is obtained both from the top and the bottom of the company. It is also helpful to look at the range of courses offered in Quality Council companies today. One of the first conclusions a survey of course content reveals is that it is not always possible or even desirable to separate quality training from other company training courses. As Newt Hardie, Milliken's vice president, quality, explains, "All training is quality training, but in the traditional view some courses are more directly associated with quality."

The notion that all training is quality training is a striking one, and deserves exploration before we go into the specifics of the courses that are more directly associated with quality. While surprising at first glance, the notion is a natural extension of the principle that continuous improvement requires more rapid learning at both the individual and company levels. And faster learning can be driven in part through training, and of course must be supported by training. As a simple illustration of this point, David Luther of Corning gives this example of how his company might implement its commitment that every employee spend 5% of their time on training. He says, "For example, a forklift driver in Germany may need to know more about maintenance. It's their job to go out and get the training."[11] Training on forklift maintenance has nothing to do with total quality, but the idea that the driver of a forklift ought to know how his machine works flows from the quality paradigm. That driver "owns" the process of moving stuff around with the forklift, and he or she can make this process run more smoothly by making sure the forklift does not break down. Also, *the driver is responsible for his or her own learning process*—that's why Luther says it's the driver's job to go and get that training. Which makes it training's job to support the driver's learning process by supplying training on forklift maintenance. The lesson is that the quality paradigm changes the way everyone *thinks about* training, which effects both quality-related courses and all other courses.

Nonetheless, Quality Council members have had to add a considerable number of specialized quality courses to their training curricula. Typical quality courses, according to council members, include:

Quality Awareness. Targeted at helping employees understand the basics, these courses define total quality and its relationship to the corporate culture. Employees are introduced to the quality improvement process, the costs of quality, problem solving, teamwork, an emphasis on customer satisfaction, and so on.

[11] Interview with author, January 7, 1992.

Team Building. Courses stress a cooperative approach to goal setting, identifying and solving problems, project implementation and evaluation, and related topics. Managers learn group dynamics skills and are trained in group leadership.

Process Management Training. These courses help employees and managers learn the tools and techniques needed to define, document and continuously improve processes while moving toward a goal of zero defects.

Customer Awareness Training. Courses are designed to help employees and managers become attuned to the demands and expectations of markets and product or service users. (The lessons learned can be applied to every employee's immediate customers, the consumers of that employee's work, whether they be internal or external customers.)

Quality Measurement. These courses equip employees and managers with the tools to gauge the impact of poor quality on basic processes and functions, to establish controls, develop and apply cost systems, and to test activities and processes against internal standards.

Statistics Training. These courses are designed to refine the ability of employees and managers to engage in continuous improvement of processes, to design experiments, and to reach decisions based on collection and analysis of data.

VOLUNTARY OR MANDATORY?

Knowledge in each of these areas equips trainees with both the conceptual tools—the inspiration—and the hands-on tools needed to act on that inspiration. And since this knowledge is necessary for the practice of quality improvement, one might expect companies to make training on each topic mandatory for all employees. However, training has historically been voluntary at most U. S. companies, and in fact the training department traditionally had to market courses internally in an effort to entice employees to sign up. Further, the popularity of courses often determined whether they were repeated, so in effect the curriculum was determined by a bottom-up popularity contest. This does not seem appropriate when a company is trying to manage a paradigm shift—some forced training at least will be necessary. But Council members do not always agree concerning the extent to which training ought to be mandatory rather than elective. In fact, a wide range of options were observed in the Conference Board survey.

At Corning, quality training is a condition of employment. Corning probably goes farther than any other company toward making training mandatory, although, as we saw above, it also gives individuals considerable input by encouraging them to perform their own needs assessments. Corning defines a set of required courses for every employee—the requirements vary by job level. First Chicago makes several basic courses mandatory. These include Management Practices, which is mandatory for all managers, and Customer Focus training, required of all customer contact personnel. The goal at First Chicago is a minimum of 40 hours of quality and job skills training for all employees, and this goal will soon be raised to 80 hours. IBM also makes basic training in quality mandatory for all employees. Everyone goes through the company's Market-Driven Quality curriculum. Milliken makes several courses mandatory for different groups. Managers and some administrators must take Human Relations and Public Speaking courses. Non-managers and manufacturing managers must take Basic Statistical Process Control. And senior and middle management are required to take Benchmarking. 3M uses a trickle-down approach; all supervisors and managers are trained in total quality management concepts, and they in turn are expected to train their employees.

ALLOCATING TRAINING HOURS

One of the most basic issues, at least once the curriculum is defined, is how to allocate training time. There is not enough time to train everyone thoroughly in every topic of possible relevance to a quality effort, even if, as at Corning, a full 5% of employees' time is devoted to training. Thus allocation decisions are critical, and must reflect training priorities for the firm and the individual. In the introductory stages of the total quality process, firms place a priority on courses which help employees understand and accept new practices. Training is allocated so as to support the effort to forge a new mindset in employees. "Training is the beginning of the learning journey in total quality. We link training to the concept that quality is a basic business strategy," is how Dr. Paul Batalden, vice president for medical care at Hospital Corporation of America, puts it.[12] As the process takes hold, there may be a shift in emphasis, with training focused on skill-development and enhancement. In fact, the choice between these two general areas—skill training and attitude change—is the most basic and important of allocation decisions. When and how each should be pursued is an interesting question.

JOB SKILLS AND KNOWLEDGE—
THE TOP TRAINING CATEGORY

Overall, Council-member firms currently place the greatest emphasis on training employees in job skills and knowledge— this category represents at least half of the training time reported for most firms in the Conference Board survey, and 85 to 90 percent of the training hours at Corning, IBM, and 3M. At Xerox, all employees attended a four hour course in quality orientation during 1984 to coincide with the launch of the firm's strategy. As each Xerox unit started its own program in the 1984-1988 period, employees participated in 48 hours of training which included 4 hours devoted to introductory quality, 8 hours to mission and team building, and 16 hours focused on problem solving. Additional Xerox training time is allocated to a range of topics, including interactive skills, process

---

[12]Conference Board Report No. 959, p. 10.

improvement, measuring quality, benchmarking, and facilitation of team processes.

Allocation of training time is part of the larger issue of how to allocate all employee time, and in general more time is allocated to training as quality programs mature. At Johnson and Johnson, for example, job skills and knowledge have always accounted for about 65 percent of training activities, but employees now receive more training in this area because the *total* time allocated to training has doubled in the last few years.

ATTITUDE TRAINING

Training time allocated to attitudinal change at Council firms is, on average, less than a quarter of the total. Service organizations such as HCA, First Chicago and American Express stress customer knowledge, sensitivity and awareness in their training—which definitely requires an attitude change given the low standard of customer service in our culture. Ford focuses its attitude training on building employee participation and involvement.

The IBM philosophy is that education can play a role in attitudinal change, but that the role of managers at the executive, functional, and department levels is equally important. Managers are encouraged to initiate attitude change, and to use education to support their efforts rather than as a substitute for them. Corning and Westinghouse placed greater emphasis on attitudinal change during the start-up of their quality efforts than they do currently. "Training was introduced as the change agent to make quality happen," explains David Luther of Corning, and as a result, behavioral and attitude training accounted for three-fourths of all training at first. However, according to Luther, "Today the ratio is reversed and close to 90 percent of training time is spent on job skills and knowledge."

PERSONAL BEHAVIOR CHANGE

Training in personal behavior change is offered primarily to managers and supervisors. The leadership aspect is stressed: "Applying total quality strategy requires a change in behavior from a managing to a leading role," says Aleta Holub, vice president and manager, quality assurance, for First National Bank of Chicago. Attitude training is essential as managers attempt to make the transition to leaders. (We saw in the previous chapter that Ford provides special training sessions just to teach managers how to lead a process improvement effort.)

The degree of centralization possible in the training function seems to be determined by how diverse and decentralized the company is in its general organization. At Ford, for example, factors such as product diversity and worldwide geographic dispersion dictate a decentralized approach to quality training. The responsibility for selection and delivery of training lies with line management in the individual Ford units, and central control is only indirect; line managers receive guidance and support from the corporate quality and employee relations functions.

INNOVATIVE WAYS OF DELIVERING TRAINING

Corporate training traditionally consists of a lecturer, an overhead projector, and rows of desks or tables. Although this may not be the best way to engage the trainees, the classroom model is still the most common vehicle for training in most companies. IBM, Xerox, Milliken, HCA, and American Express report that between 60 and 80 percent of their quality training is classroom based. 3M's emphasis is a little different—it uses workshops that emphasize participation and make greater use of hands-on activities as well as multimedia presentations.

When a company has a central training institute or center (as do Xerox, Ford, Corning, IBM and Westinghouse), this center generally takes responsibility for designing quality courses. At worst, this centralization may mean a more consistent and professional approach to the traditional classroom training model, and at best, it may lead to innovations in training delivery such as 3M's use of participative workshops.

EFFICIENT . . . BUT NOT EFFECTIVE

The idea of innovation in training may seem farfetched at first, but the fact is that traditional approaches to training are not especially effective (although they may be efficient). After all, the classroom-based training provided throughout the U. S. public school system has proven to be efficient but remarkably *in*effective, and there is no good reason to assume that traditional teaching methods should work any better in a company than they do in the public schools. In fact, I believe that innovation in training is likely to be one of the next important drivers of the quality improvement process. For one thing, more effective training methods may well be necessary in order to increase the rate of organizational learning significantly beyond the levels already attained by quality practitioners.

Corning, already a leader in quality training, is making a commitment to innovate in the area of training effectiveness—in part because it is hard to see how it can continue to increase the time employees spend in training much beyond the 5 percent level it has recently attained. David Luther of Corning, who has already been quoted more briefly on the topic of training (in Chapter 3), describes his company's plans as follows:

> We established our first five-year goal in '86—that every employee spend 5 percent of their time on training. And we're here, we reached it this year. Now our new five year goal is to double the measured effectiveness of training. This is an ambi-

tious goal. It's going to take some innovation. We don't know how to do that yet.[13]

While the answers are not yet clear, it is likely that increased effectiveness will come from further modifications of the traditional classroom model of training. (New approaches to training using self-paced, interactive computer modules, participative group learning, and so forth have yet to be incorporated into many corporate training programs.) For this reason, and because of the critical role training innovations will play in the future of quality improvement programs, it is particularly helpful to look at some of the specific methods companies are now employing to deliver their quality training. Creativity and innovation are already in evidence in the training methods of many companies. And the Quality Council survey provides useful material on this subject. Here are details from several companies as reported by their training staff in the survey.

Corning
Training is delivered in four ways:

- Classroom training provided by the company. These are proprietary courses that are considered "core" and very important, including Corning's Quality Institute and other training that the company is satisfied it does well.

- Classroom training delivered by local colleges. Under contract with Corning, a local college center in the headquarters area develops and delivers many training courses. David Luther says that "This unique and innovative approach so far has worked very well."

- Classroom training given by employee instructors at unit sites. About 400 employees have been taught to teach.

[13]Interview with author, January 7, 1992.

According to Luther, "They have become the secret weapon of quality . . . the morale boost is world class, for them and their students."

- Outside delivery vehicles. This includes an on-line, fee-based service which responds to employees' subject matter requests with an informed guide to the best courses, whether in-house or offered by outside organizations. Luther sees a further emphasis on outside vendors; the goal is "To off-load all training that can be better done by others."

First National Bank of Chicago

- Classroom training is provided primarily by corporate training with the remainder delivered by a "train the trainer" approach. The company hopes to continue to move further toward training delivery by line management.

- On-the-job training is supplemented through follow-up by trainers who coach employees and insure that both employee and manager are best applying the employee's newly-learned skills.

- Quality seminars and conferences are used to provide outside "third party endorsements" of the quality process. A key goal is to promote employee buy-in, but the experience also facilitates idea gathering and benchmarking.

Florida Power & Light

- Classroom training is the primary vehicle, but a variety of innovative methods are used to make it more effective, including use of line personnel as well as instructors, an FPL-produced video, group exercises, study groups, lectures, case studies, and special projects.

- On-the-job training is accomplished through quality improvement team meetings and unit/department meetings. Other approaches have included Japanese Union of Scientists and Engineers (J.U.S.E.) counselor clinics, and internal television.

- Other resources include the corporate library collection of literature and video materials for self-study. Computer-based training is under consideration.

IBM

- Classroom training represents the bulk of all quality education. Whenever feasible, classroom training is offered at the employee's location.

- Live interactive television broadcasts from central studios to selected sites are the second most common means of delivering education.

- On-the-job training typically occurs in conjunction with formal training mechanisms, and in the context of existing business and performance requirements.

- Self-study methods include programmed learning, audio and video cassettes, computer-based training, and interactive video-disc.

- Participation in symposia, forums, professional society meetings, graduate work study, and professional development is supported. Generally, such participation is voluntary, but IBM does appoint selected professionals to be the corporate representative in specific cases.

Westinghouse

- The Productivity and Quality Center provides classroom training which represents about 30 percent of total quality training. No outside resources are used.

- Classroom training is also provided at the local level to fit needs and practices of individual company units.

- The corporate training department provides courses at off-site locations with both in-house and outside support.

- Special total quality conferences are sponsored by internal corporate councils.

- External seminars and courses are supported as the need is perceived by local management.

These descriptions of training methods point to innovations in a variety of areas. The use of line managers and specially-trained employees to perform training; the selective use of independent seminars and conferences; development of interactive television training; use of computer-based, video-disc-based, and library-based self-training; the use of group-based cases and projects to increase participation in the classroom: These are all examples of innovations in training. It is with new ideas and techniques such as these that Corning will be able to double the effectiveness of training in the next five years.

EVALUATING THE EFFECTIVENESS OF TRAINING

How to measure the effectiveness of training is a difficult issue, and clearly one that needs to be resolved before significant innovation can take place. Just as a quality improvement needs to be tracked in customer perception via benchmark surveys, formal evaluation of training is required to find out what, if any, effect it has had. The conventional approach to evaluating training is the "smile test," as Luther puts it—trainees are asked to fill out an evaluation form at the end of the training. And if the training is given high ratings, it is deemed effective. But the real goal of training is to improve job performance, rather than to win popularity contests, so there is considerable room for improvement in evaluation methodology. At Corning, and in fact at many other companies as well, there is a movement toward more substantive measurement techniques, and according to Luther the movement follows these steps:

1. Smile test,

2. Six month retention,

3. Skill improvement,

4. Job performance improvement.

Corning now uses measures in all four categories. The fourth level, direct measurement of job performance improvements resulting from the training, is the trickiest by far. It is generally difficult to isolate the training from other variables that affect job performance. As a result, there is considerable room for innovation in this area of measurement.

When companies go to the extra trouble required to actually evaluate job performance following training, they are in a position to quantify the return on training investment for the first time. Does training workers in quality improvement methods actually improve their work? Is it a good investment? In principle, yes, but in practice, training does not always have a positive return. Motorola performed a detailed study to learn how and why performance reflects training, and the results suggest that the broader context is as important as what goes on in the classroom. Here is how William Wiggenhorn, corporate vice president for training and education and president of Motorola University, describes it:[14]

> We asked two universities to evaluate our return on investment. They identified three groups [of trainees]:
>
> • In those few plants where the work force absorbed the whole curriculum of quality tools and process skills and

[14]William Wiggenhorn, "Motorola U: When Training Becomes an Education," *Harvard Business Review*, July-August 1990, p. 75.

where senior managers reinforced the training by means of new questions appropriate to the new methods, we were getting a $33 return for every dollar spent, including the cost of wages paid while people sat in class.

- Plants that made use of either the quality tools or the process skills but not both, and then reinforced what they taught, broke even.

- Finally, plants that taught all or part of the curriculum but failed to reinforce with follow-up meetings and a new, genuine emphasis on quality had a negative return on investment.

This is an interesting experiment, and in all likelihood the results can be extended to other companies. Effectiveness was influenced largely by two factors at Motorola: How thoroughly the subject of quality was taught, and how well quality training was reinforced by management when the trainees went back to work. This is an important lesson for all companies; quality training is only as good as quality management— it must be reinforced and integrated into daily work through an effective quality process.

A second and quite different finding from Motorola is also likely to be of relevance to any company undertaking a quality improvement process. William Wiggenhorn tells the story of Motorola's decision, in 1985, to open a new cellular manufacturing plant in the U. S. rather than to take it offshore. The company felt that, with effective quality management and training, the higher-cost U. S. workforce could be sufficiently productive to cancel out any advantage that a lower-cost Asian workforce might have. This was to be an important test of the ability of quality training to make U. S. labor competitive. Wiggenhorn explains that, "Our workforce in Arlington Heights, outside Chicago, knew new radio technology, and given the similarities, we believed these workers could make the bridge to cellular. In addition, they had improved quality tenfold in the first five years of training and were well on their way to doing it again." However, before committing to the new cellular facility, Motorola decided to do a quick assessment of this workforce's capabilities and training needs. As Wiggenhorn describes it, "We did a quick math assessment to see exactly where we stood with regard to further training. The scores were a shock. Only 40 percent passed a test containing some questions as simple as "Ten is what percent of 100?" Wiggenhorn goes on to discuss the implications:

> The Arlington Heights work force was going to lead the company into global competition in a new technology and 60% seemed to have trouble with simple arithmetic. We needed a work force capable of operating and maintaining sophisticated new equipment and facilities to a zero-defect standard, and most of them could not calculate decimals, fractions, or percents.[15]

But then, with further analysis, Motorola discovered the real reason behind the poor math scores. According to Wiggenhorn, "The real cause of much of this poor math performance was an inability to read or, in the case of many immigrants, to comprehend English as a second language."[16] This was good news in the sense that maybe math skills were not quite as bad as the first test suggested, but awful news in the sense that language skills were requisite for operating the new equipment, much of which required interacting, in English, with on-site computers. Digging even deeper, Motorola discovered that the work force had relied heavily on middle-managers and supervisors for help with language and math problems, and that the prior quality improvements had been made in spite of considerable math and language barriers. In fact, a company-wide evaluation revealed that half of Motorola's 25,000 U. S. manufacturing and support people did not have math and language skills at or above a seventh grade level. What had started as sophisticated quality training now

[15] Ibid., p. 77.
[16] Ibid.

became a matter of basic skills training, and Motorola has moved into extensive basic-skills training for its workforce, including a heavy involvement in collaborative programs with schools and colleges. The lesson is that quality training cannot be viewed apart from the broader training efforts of a company, and in fact many companies will find that basic skills training is necessary in order to make the quality training fully effective.

This lesson holds true for management as well. The practice of quality improvement demands a higher level of skill from everyone in the company—generic skills as well as quality skills. For example, Kaspar Cassani, an executive vice president with IBM, observes that "strategic knowledge within the company cannot be isolated in one person or staff: Executives must develop cross-functional expertise to understand how a decision by one department affects others."[17] Quality improvement demands both that employees and their managers learn new tools, and also that they use *old* tools far better than many of them are accustomed to. Which means that training is inevitably a major component of any quality effort. As John Hudiburg, chairman emeritus of Florida Power & Light, puts it, "A company must be prepared to spend a great effort and enormous resources over a long period of time to educate all employees."[18]

One final word of warning is in order before we leave the topic of training. Precisely because training is such a large-scale project, touching everyone in the organization and, when done right, requiring a tremendous investment of time, energy and capital, it can on occasion displace other activities that are also vital to a total quality effort. This warning is sounded by Dr. Donald M. Berwick, a Baldrige Award judge and currently president of the Institute for HealthCare Improvement:

---

[17]Conference Board Report No. 909, p. 40.
[18]From a presentation at the Conference Board's Third Annual Quality Conference, April 2–3, 1990, New York.

Be aware of consultants who push training as *the* element of TQM. Training packages are relatively easy to develop and very profitable to sell, and some consultants create the illusion that if the work force is properly trained, all else will follow. This is not the case. Training is an essential piece of quality management, but there are other pieces. Consultants who say training will solve your problems don't understand your problems.[19]

The same might be said of any of the other elements of a total quality program that we discuss in this book, although apparently it is a more common problem in the area of training. At the risk of angering the consultants who specialize in only one of these key elements, it must be stated that none is sufficient on its own to bring about a total quality culture or to initiate a high rate of continuous improvement. As important as is training, it must be accompanied by a great many other initiatives to have a significant and lasting impact on corporate culture.

[19]Conference Board Report No. 979, p. 46.

HANDS-ON QUALITY IMPLEMENTATION

In a sense, every one of the factors associated with successful quality programs is a tool. But as we have seen, some, like visualizing and planning quality, are most closely associated with direct management intervention. Others, like participation, competition, or training, are indirect in their action. They bring about change largely through their impact on the corporate culture and the individual employees that make up, and are shaped by, that culture. In this section of the book, we will address four success factors that are direct, hands-on quality tools.

Teams, benchmarking, measurement, and process management are the day-to-day activities that individual employees pursue in the effort to implement a company's quality vision. Each encompasses a variety of techniques and methods that, with the proper management focus and quality culture, are capable of rendering change by increasing quality and lowering cost. These then are the areas in which the high-minded vision of senior management is finally translated into specific actions that affect the value added for customers and other constituents. When a quality initiative is translated to direct action by a broad base of employees in these four areas, business practices begin to change at a rapid rate, and the journey from inspiration to practice can finally be considered complete. For now. Of course, it is necessary to repeat this journey endlessly in order to achieve continuous improvement, but first things first!

11

TEAMS

We have over 2,200 different quality teams with names such as: "Quality Improvement" teams, "Quality Circles," and "Corrective Action" teams. Some teams work in perpetuity. Others are ad hoc teams that solve a particular problem and then move on. These teams are restricted only by the employee's imagination.
—James Houghton, CEO, Corning Inc.[1]

Some of the stories companies tell about their teams make for wonderful reading. They are so excited by the results, they cannot stop talking about their teams. Here are representative stories from Cadillac and Johnson & Johnson:

> Over 60 percent of our employees serve on teams—a 600 percent increase since 1985. We have nearly 600 work teams in our plants involving 5,000 people. One example of a plant team is our "Grow the Business" teams. These teams are comprised of skilled and unskilled hourly people as well as salaried workers, primarily engineers, whom we've empowered to look at ways to grow the business through continuous improvement

[1]Conference Board Report No. 937, p. 23.

and end sources. One of these teams worked with our SE [simultaneous engineering] teams to improve the design of the product and process. The design they worked on was the 1990 rear compartment pan. The total annual savings of their design was $52 million.[2]

A product development team of two dozen people at Johnson & Johnson's Ethicon, Inc. subsidiary in Somerville, New Jersey developed a new ophthalmic needle for use in eye surgery. Comparable product introductions had taken two years or more, but this team brought its product, CS Ultima, to market in only nine months. According to the company, "The improvement in CS Ultima in ease of penetration, a key performance attribute for the surgeon, was measured at more than 50 percent. Also, in pursuing continuous improvement, a multiplant team examined the total process and was able to improve the initial process yield three-fold in one year."[3]

The results speak for themselves: The Cadillac team cut expenses by $52 million a year. The Johnson & Johnson team cut the product development cycle by two thirds. They achieved a 50 percent improvement in customer-defined performance and a productivity increase of 300 percent.

THE STATE OF THE TEAM

Teams are increasingly widespread in business, and are used for a diversity of purposes. As the story above suggests, teams are capable of achieving remarkable quality improvements. However, teams are not automatically included in companies' quality programs—they are difficult to establish and manage, and many companies with early-stage quality initiatives have not fully adopted the team approach. Further, the type and duration of teams, the ways in which they are managed and rewarded, and other details differ widely from company to

---

[2]Rosetta M. Riley, Director of Customer Satisfaction, Cadillac Motor Car Division. Conference Board Report No. 990, p. 38.

[3]Company literature supplied by Sue Jacobs of the Johnson & Johnson Quality Institute, January 8, 1992.

company. Because of the diversity of approaches, it is interesting to step back a little from our narrow sample of Quality Council companies and look at what a broader sample of U.S. companies are doing with quality-improvement teams.

A recent Conference Board survey sent to the nation's largest 1000 firms gives us just such a view: A picture of how teams are used among the 158 responding firms. This survey is referenced periodically throughout the book, and it bears noting that its 16 percent response rate is considered normal for a mail survey. However, respondents include most of the firms from the sample that had significant quality programs, rather than a random representation of the sample. (After all, what company without a quality program would bother to fill in a questionnaire about quality programs?)

I am going to let Kathryn Troy of The Conference Board summarize the survey's findings on the question of how and to what extent, teams are used in the quality programs of this sample of the largest 1000 U.S. companies.[*] You may notice that she includes unattributed quotes throughout her remarks. These are the comments of respondents, usually the managers of quality programs, and it is customary to keep their and their firm's identities anonymous in surveys of this kind. (See Exhibit 11-1 for a graphical summary of survey results.)

How U.S. Companies Use Teams: The Conference Board Survey

Teams often release the creative energies of those closest to the work processes in a way that can help prevent or solve quality problems, cut across departmental and functional barriers, surface new ideas, and ultimately produce better products and services. Together with training, our survey participants identify teams as heading the list of valuable involvement

---

[*]Based on Conference Board Report No. 974.

Exhibit 11–1 Summary of Survey Results

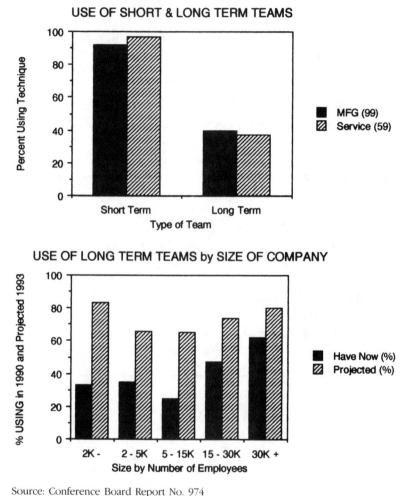

USE OF SHORT & LONG TERM TEAMS

MFG (99)
Service (59)

USE OF LONG TERM TEAMS by SIZE OF COMPANY

Have Now (%)
Projected (%)

Source: Conference Board Report No. 974

techniques. "Training is essential for culture change, teams for implementation," reports a diversified manufacturer.

Teams vary in purpose and duration. Short-term teams, such as a task force, may meet over a brief time span to investigate issues, solve specific problems or make recommendations on a discrete set of activities. Quality circles are groups which promote employee involvement and problem-solving relevant to immediate work-related needs. They are impermanent and may be disbanded or reconstituted as needs change. Virtually all manufacturing and 90 percent of service respondents have short-term teams. Typically, teams involve 50 percent of the firm's senior managers, 40 percent of middle managers and first-line supervisors, and 30 percent of non-managers.

SHORT-TERM RESULTS

Respondents laud short-term teams because they "involve people at all levels and give tangible results quickly." They are focused, task-oriented, meet regularly, are reinforcing and improve morale. Says one participant; "Task teams make bottom-line improvements which stimulate line management commitment."

Roughly 40 percent of respondents have long-term teams. This proportion rises to 60 percent among those firms rating themselves near the top in Baldrige award-readiness, and plunges to 20 percent among participants who say they are less than halfway there. In general, the longer the TQM process has been in place, the greater the likelihood that such groups will exist.

LONG-TERM WORK GROUPS

"Short-term teams were useful in the beginning to learn to solve easier problems, then we expanded into self-managed work groups for long-term benefits," says a manufacturer. Again, the firms with the oldest processes seem somewhat less likely to use long-term teams than those in the next age group. In the oldest group, 4 of the 11 respondents who do not have long-term teams plan to start them within two years. Two firms are "very satisfied" with their progress toward involving employees, and the remainder are only "moderately" satisfied or dissatisfied with their progress.

The largest firms—those with more than 15,000 employees—are also more likely to have long-term teams than are smaller firms, but half of the smaller group plan to implement such teams within three years. Typically, half of top management, about a quarter of middle managers and first-line supervisors, and a fifth of nonmanagers are involved in long-term teams. (These figures are medians). Greater involvement at upper-management levels may be tied to the fact that long-term teams are started at the top of the organization and need time to work their way through management layers to workers. Since such teams tend to be the mark of a mature TQM process, there has not yet been sufficient time to complete the cascading process.

POWER OF LONG-TERM TEAMS

Members of long-term teams not only recommend action, but have the power to implement solutions. In some cases, team members are workers in the same department who meet periodically (e.g., weekly) to monitor quality, set schedules and control costs. Some teams are vertically structured, with representatives from many different levels of the company who focus on changes in a particular product line or issue (such as new technology) over time. In a more evolved team model, workers may be cross-trained and enabled to take on a variety of responsibilities as needs shift. In addition to monitoring quality, scheduling and cost-control, team members take on some managerial tasks. They plan, hire and interact with customers and vendors. The managerial/supervisory role is transformed into that of leader. Team leaders become coaches, counselors—the pointmen for the group.

Respondents note that autonomous long-term teams show management's confidence in employees. "When you indicate confidence, employees take ownership and feel responsible." Moreover, teams focused on improvement commit their members to a joint effort rather than to a "program." In sum: "Teams (both autonomous and supervisory/participant) are very effective when supported with a consistent problem-solving methodology. They get people to concentrate on root causes in a continuous-improvement thought process," says a computer company executive.

INTERPRETING THE RESULTS

Troy's finding that most companies start with short-term, task-oriented teams is interesting. These teams generally have problem-solving autonomy, but *not* management authority. They recommend solutions or improvements, and management makes the final decision. They are therefore a partial move toward the truly autonomous work-group teams that tend to manage their own functions in more mature quality programs. As such, they might be criticized as representing a half-hearted adoption of participatory management. Until work groups are given authority to manage their own functions over the long term, and until their managers switch from supervising individuals to coaching a team, participation is not 100 percent.

However, the short-term teams seem a very desirable intermediary step, creating a forum for applied learning and giving employees on-the-job experience in the use of quality improvement tools and in collective decision making. They should not be dismissed out of hand. Further, they are obviously much easier to implement than long-term self-managing teams—the main reason they are more prevalent. And short-term teams will always have a role in companies, even ones that have moved to fully participatory management. Many projects are simply short-term in nature, and only require temporary attention. In addition, some projects do not need management authority in the first place. Some teams are convened simply to provide a communication vehicle among different functions or groups, bridging the gaps that can slow the business process or product development process as it moves from one functional area to the other. Such teams have no need of authority—giving them authority would only make them compete with the authority of the functional groups they bridge.

Teams Break Down Barriers to Customers

In Chapter 4, we discussed the power of the internal customer concept. Every process has an output, and every output is consumed by someone. That consumer is the process's customer. Many departments within a large company produce outputs consumed only by other departments within the company. These internal consumers are their customers—and if they can treat them like real customers, the overall business process will benefit, along with the external customers that it serves. But this is easier said than done. Internal barriers and rivalries can be as resistant to change as was the Berlin Wall. Teams, according to Douglas Anderson, director, corporate quality at 3M, can bring these walls down:

> In the past, the sales force sometimes protected customers from other people at 3M. Similarly, plant managers protected the plant from customers, the sales force or other employees. These barriers have fallen. Now people interact openly with suppliers and customers.

The barriers that keep employees from contact with customers are also a concern at Union Pacific Railroad Co., where teams are used specifically to address this problem. Kent Sterett, former assistant vice president—quality, explained how their customer team program works: "Union Pacific organized around a concept that we benchmarked from Xerox: The central focus of the operation is the customer. Team UP represents all the people, organizations and locations that serve an individual customer. Team members are identified by name, rank and location; and the customer knows who each person is." In addition, Sterett explains that "We involve our employees, customers and suppliers in our teams. . . . We cannot decide what our customers want; they must be involved."[5]

The management hierarchy is another source of barriers in the traditional top-down organization. Most of the communication is confined to hierarchical layers. Line employees talk, and complain, to each other. Supervisors talk with other supervisors. Middle management sticks together, and top managers can't seem to get anyone to listen to them—not even other senior managers! Much is made of the top-down and bottom-up flows of commands and information, but this communication is relatively light compared to the sharing that occurs routinely and informally *within* each layer. Teams, it turns out, can also be effective in breaking down the class and caste walls that reduce vertical information flow in the traditional hierarchical structure. Again according to Douglas Anderson of 3M,

> Our hourly people participate on teams with supervisors, middle management and executives, including meeting with customers. 3M's senior management travels with our sales force, making customer calls as colleagues, not as executive vice presidents. In short, we have developed strong inside and outside customer relationships.[6]

Product development is another area where the traditional barriers need to be eliminated, and where teams can help make the change. The traditional development process has been likened to a bucket brigade, as the product concept is

---

[5]From remarks by W. Kent Sterett at The Conference Board's Third annual Quality Conference, April 2–3, 1990, New York.
[6]Conference Board Report No. 979, pp. 33–34.

passed first from one functional area of the company to another. It *is* like a bucket brigade, except it is even less efficient, because in product development the buckets were often spilled and sent back down the line for refilling before making it to the fire. For example, if designers' specifications did not suit the manufacturing department, the design would be handed back for another round of revisions. Errors and costs accumulate rapidly on a bucket brigade such as this, and, perhaps even more troubling, opportunities for insight via cross-functional collaboration are not realized.

The multifunctional product development team does away with these barriers. Thomas Patrick, marketing and product planning director for GM's Baldrige-winning Cadillac division, refers to the old bucket-brigade style of product development as *over-the-wall engineering*, in reference to the practice whereby each department threw its design over the wall to the next department. And he calls Cadillac's new approach, which uses multi-functional teams to eliminate those walls, *simultaneous engineering*. Here is how he describes the change at Cadillac:

> Our cultural change began in 1985, when we introduced a new philosophy at Cadillac, and throughout General Motors . . . One that dealt with how vehicles should be designed, engineered, and manufactured. We call it simultaneous engineering. In the past, we all used a very methodical, sequential process to develop our products. You might call it "over-the-wall" engineering.
>
> For example, a stylist would dream up a car—a car that was innovative, unique and distinctive. But once completed, the design would be "thrown over the wall" to product engineers . . . who, in some cases, might not be able to fit the available major components within the parameters, and to do so the design would have to be compromised.
>
> Product engineering would then throw the design over the wall to manufacturing . . . who would now have to figure a way to produce what product engineers had designed. This way of doing business eventually became out of alignment, because

each time we threw that project over the wall, we lost something . . . in time, cost, and most importantly in customer satisfaction.

Today, our teams have representatives from every function— engineering, manufacturing, human resources, financial, materials management and so on. Some include hourly, as well as salaried members and 75 percent of our teams include suppliers.[7]

BUSINESS TEAMS AND BARRIERS

The theme of breaking down barriers is picked up by Jeffrey Siebenaller, director of quality management, Chemical Group, Hoechst Celanese Corp., when he discusses the role of teams at his company. He reports that, "High Performance Teams are an important way to reach our goal of eliminating barriers, bringing down the walls, and creating effective cross-functional teams." He goes on to describe some of the benefits the teams have provided, and to discuss his company's commitment to management by teams.

Resulting benefits certainly occur in the form of improved resource utilization, reduced administrative waste, a high degree of market focus and, most importantly, unprecedented responsiveness to the needs of customers. Hoechst Celanese across most of our business areas has moved extensively away from the typical functional organization to having business teams, with multiple function membership, controlling their own destiny, and, in so doing, having complete control and accountability on the business process.[8]

When teams start breaking down the walls between departments and functions, the horizontal structure of the business organization inevitably changes. And when long-term

---

[7]Quoted from remarks by Thomas Patrick at The Conference Board's 1991 Marketing Conference, October 29–30, 1991, New York.

[8]Quoted from remarks by Jeffrey S. Siebenaller at The Conference Board's 1991 Marketing Conference, October 29–30, 1991, New York.

teams begin managing themselves—as do the High Performance Teams at Hoechst Celanese with their "complete control and accountability"—the vertical reporting structure is effected as well. Organizational structure exists to define *how people work with each other*. That is its simple but essential purpose—an easy fact to overlook. When looked at this way it is obvious that teams, which are also all about how people work with each other, should have an impact on organizational structure. They do. Siebenaller of Hoechst Celanese goes on to explain that, with the formation of self-managing long-term teams in his company, "The traditional organization in many areas becomes obsolete as these high performance teams move away from singular, directive-based reporting relationships, to activities and decisions driven by consensus, collaboration, or consultative interface."

If teams are making the traditional organization obsolete at Hoechst Celanese, it is clear they have power to change corporate culture everywhere. As the Conference Board survey revealed, teams are considered key, along with training, to employee participation in the quality improvement process. And, even beyond that important role, teams also contribute by improving the decision making and innovation of employees. Properly supported, well-run teams simply do better work than individual employees. As Siebenaller puts it, "One outcome is particularly clear. Better decisions are made from teams than from one singular perspective."[9]

Facilitating Teams

Most managers who talk about their company's use of teams do not go into the specifics of how to manage an *individual* team. Teamwork is not natural to most employees or companies. The traditional meeting protocol can easily take over

[9] Ibid.

when a team is convened. After all, a team meeting looks a lot like a traditional staff meeting—and will be no more productive unless the behavior of the individuals is dramatically different. Mark McCormack of *What They Don't Teach You at Harvard Business School* fame once wrote "I would like to find the guy who first said, 'There is no such thing as a stupid question,' and force him to sit through the monthly meeting cycle of any major corporation."

Douglas Anderson, director, corporate quality services for 3M, says that "Teamwork is not a working method that comes naturally in our society. It must be learned. 3M, like most American companies, has systems in place to stress and reward individual efforts and achievement more than group accomplishment. Undertaking quality improvement projects on a team basis needed new insights into group behavior, from top management on down." To address this need, 3M "provided a multitude of courses and techniques on group processes, dynamics and motivation to increase understanding of group activity. We then tied group training and management techniques, such as performance management, to tangible programs that are quality related." Anderson reports that, "These strategies have accelerated the integration of teamwork within the company."[10]

How do you move from the traditional meeting format, in which the manager at the head of the table dominates the proceedings, to one in which every member of the team participates actively and creatively? Like 3M, many Conference Board companies have found it necessary to provide specific training courses in facilitation in order to help teams make this behavioral transition. Some go as far as hiring expert facilitators to come in and work with teams for their first few meetings. Techniques like brainstorming, the Gordon/Little method, and the Nominal Group Technique also help teams learn

---

[10]Company document by Douglas Anderson, "Quality, A Positive Business Strategy," provided courtesy of Corporate Quality Services, 3M, January 1992.

how to work collaboratively.[11] Attention to the group dynamics within the team will benefit team performance.

There is considerable variation in the performance of teams, and some teams fail to produce significant innovations despite hundreds of hours of work. What makes some teams more successful at product development and innovation than others? It is tempting to quote the opinions of seasoned managers in answer to this question, but a recent study by professor Hans Thamhain of Bentley College indicates that managers do not always know what makes teams work. Thamhain reports that, "of the fifty influence factors mentioned by managers as drivers or barriers toward innovative team performance . . . only fifteen of these were found to be statistically significant."[12] The others may be red herrings, proving that one's instinct is not always on target when it comes to managing high-performing teams.

Thamhain's study points to fifteen critical success factors, not all of which currently receive management attention in most firms. The most important were task-related factors, including plans, leadership, autonomy, experience, and visibility. Also important are people-related factors: work satisfaction, mutual trust, good communications, minimal conflict, and minimal personal risk. Organization-related factors of importance are stability of the team, resources available, high management involvement, stable goals and priorities, and ample rewards and recognition.

Attention to these success factors, and to the facilitation of individual teams, can make a significant performance difference—likely to be important in companies, such as those described here, that have hundreds or thousands of quality teams.

---

[11] These three techniques are described in Hiam, *The Vest-Pocket CEO: Decision-Making Tools for Executives,* Prentice Hall, 1990.

[12] Hans J. Thamhain, "Managing Technologically Innovative Team Efforts Toward New Product Success," Journal of Product Innovation Management, Vol. 7, March 1990, pp. 5–18.

Chapter 12

BENCHMARKING

We took competitive analysis one step further and came up with what we now call competitive benchmarking. It's an intense, in-depth study of what we think is our best competition. It's a continuing, never-ending process, and it's an integral part of our new and stronger emphasis on quality.

—David Kearns, ex-Chairman,
Xerox Corporation[1]

Leaders of companies that have moved rapidly and successfully have reached out and stolen shamelessly from the best. They see what others have done well and seize the ideas that fit their own organizations.

—W. Kent Sterett, executive vice president,
Southern Pacific Transportation Company,
and a Baldrige Award judge[2]

'Benchmark' is defined by the dictionary as "a mark on a permanent object indicating elevation and serving as a reference in topographical surveys." This meaning has nothing to do with benchmarking.

[1] As quoted in a company document, *Competitive Benchmarking: The Path to a Leadership Position*, Xerox Corporation, 1988.
[2] Conference Board Report No. 979, pp. 43–44.

But from the original meaning the word has come to be used more broadly, either to indicate "a point of reference from which measurements may be made," or to describe "something that serves as a standard by which others may be measured."[3] Both of these meanings capture the sense of benchmarking as it is practiced. Benchmarking refers to the use of a superior standard of practice against which to compare and improve one's own practices. Companies benchmark against other companies, and plants, departments and divisions of companies benchmark against other units of their own company. The search for superior models against which to benchmark can be limited to one's own company, to a single industry, to all companies within a region or nation, or to every available organization worldwide. Benchmarking can be a collaborative sharing of ideas and practices between two groups or companies. It can also be a one-sided affair, as when a company reverse-engineers one of its competitor's products to see what makes it tick.

If benchmarking has nothing to do with the original dictionary meaning of 'benchmark,' why does this chapter start with that definition? Because it is important to recognize, and reject, a hidden assumption the word carries with it. A benchmark is, traditionally, a firmly-fixed, dependable point of reference—a brass plate cemented into the crest of a hill, for example. Topographers can count on the constancy of such a benchmark for their map-making and exploration. The landscape is *not* fixed, of course: Continents drift, mountains uplift and erode, seas rise and fall, and glaciers cavort over continents—but on geographic time, not our time. Topographers can safely ignore the changes in the landscape when placing and using their benchmarks. Change is too slow to be of any practical concern.

Standards of business excellence used to be located on a

---

[3]*Webster's New Collegiate Dictionary*, G. & C. Merriam Company, 1977.

similar landscape. There was a proper way to run a modern production line, order-processing center, or customer service window, and there were people and companies who could claim long-lasting expertise in each of these areas. While practices no doubt evolved and improved, the changes were incremental and could be ignored for long periods of time. The landscape, and one's standards of excellence, could safely be assumed to be fixed from day to day and quarter to quarter. The standards in the textbooks were still valid ten years later when the students reached middle management ranks. The companies that were the best at something a decade ago were probably still the leaders a decade later. Benchmarks were fixed, well-known points, and maps based on them could be banked upon. This is no longer true.

We have touched on the subject of flexibility already, and have seen how the business environment presents increasing challenges to firms. Flexibility and learning are now required of organizations because the environment changes more rapidly. As a result of this more rapid rate of change, the benchmarks do not behave as if they are fixed any more. Take a standard for granted or rely on an accepted assumption, and it will come back to haunt you. It is as if the map-maker were to wake up one morning and find the continents drifting miles every day. Unless he can make maps much more quickly, they will not be of much use. The benchmark that used to identify the crest of a hill may now be in the bottom of a valley.

If this were to happen, topographers would have to spend more time putting new benchmarks in place. They would have to re-explore and re-map the terrain routinely. Those venerable brass plaques might be replaced by less permanent markers whose value would be judged by how recently they were placed, rather than how permanent they were. Topographers would have to behave like journalists, chasing the landscape around. And if this happened, the original meaning of 'benchmark' would be quite inappropriate to topographers. This is just what has happened to the business landscape and to the business managers who map and travel it, and this is why the permanence implied by the term is so inappropriate.

Now the game is to find the newly-emerging high points and be the first to place a benchmark on them. The *act* of benchmarking is important, rather than the benchmark itself. Benchmarking is an active endeavor, whereas the benchmark is, at least to topographers, an inactive, permanent thing: the two represent absolute opposites. This is apparent in how Xerox defines benchmarking: As "the continuous process of measuring our products, services, and practices against our toughest competitors or those companies renowned as industry leaders."[1] Benchmarking, at least in the modern business environment, is a *continuous process*, not a fixed point of reference. Another internal document interprets this definition for Xerox employees, saying that, "The point—always—is to *use* the information gained [through benchmarking]. Competitive benchmarking is not just additional paperwork. It is *action*."[5]

For this reason the best way to start our presentation of the topic of benchmarking is through some of the action stories of Xerox's benchmarking, examples of how teams have gone out exploring and come back with a new benchmark for their company to improve against.

COMPARING MANUFACTURING COSTS

This is where Xerox's benchmarking process began, back in 1979, and although the methodology is more sophisticated now, the early results were nonetheless of great value to the

---

[1] Quoted from a Xerox employee-education publication, *USMG Partnership: The Way We Work*, 1988, p. 35.

[5] *Competitive Benchmarking: A Practical Application*, Xerox USMG Quality Office, 1990, p. 3.

company. Here is how Robert C. Camp describes it (Camp is manager, business analysis, U.S. Marketing Group, Business Services, at Xerox and author of the book used internally at Xerox for benchmarking):[6]

> In 1979, Xerox initiated a process called competitive benchmarking. It was started by our manufacturing operations unit to examine and evaluate manufacturing costs. Selected product comparisons were made; mechanical components were taken apart and scrutinized . . . We formalized comprehensive benchmarking with the analysis of copiers produced by the Japanese Xerox affiliate, Fuji-Xerox, and later with other Japanese-manufactured machines. These investigations confirmed that U.S. manufacturing costs were substantially higher. When the manufacturing cost was completely analyzed it revealed that competitors were selling machines for what it cost Xerox to make them. Our U.S. manufacturing therefore quickly shifted to adopt these externally set benchmark targets to drive its business plans.

This dose of reality was critical to the subsequent turnaround at Xerox. Charles Osborn, who studied Xerox as a Harvard Business School Research Associate, explains that the benchmarking program "became a way of informing all Xerox employees of salient market information and using that knowledge to build targets for key improvements." In his opinion, the product cost analysis "focused Xerox's attention outward into the marketplace, enabling Xerox study teams to discover, for example, how Japanese competitors were using shorter development cycles to realize lower product costs."[7] In other words, the relationship between speed and cost of development made clear in Westinghouse's cost-time profile, discussed in Chapter 5, was first discovered at Xerox through this benchmarking effort.

---

[6]As quoted in Conference Board Report No. 937, pp. 35–36.
[7]Harvard Business School Case No. 9-189-134, p. 2.

THE L. L. BEAN STORY

Xerox visited clothing and outdoor equipment catalog-company L. L. Bean to learn how they handled order fulfillment, and learned a great deal that could be applied to a copier/parts warehouse as well as a clothing warehouse. Xerox also, quite accidentally, created what has become the prototypical benchmarking story. Every major business magazine has mentioned the Xerox-L. L. Bean story at least a dozen times in the last few years. But I will describe it briefly because it is rarely described accurately in the business press. In fact, to make sure it is given justice, I will let Camp describe it:

> When Xerox (a copier company) first informed our management that we were going to assess ourselves against L. L. Bean (an outdoor specialty company), there was disbelief. But we had much to learn from them. The L. L. Bean statistics that dealt with their warehouse order picking (the picking of the customer's order) showed that they were able to do it almost three times faster than Xerox. We wanted to know why. The answer was that they had a computerized order sorting process. This allowed L. L. Bean to accumulate the same item. Then, the picker would gather the total number of that item at once and then fill each order with the appropriate number requested. L. L. Bean made a conscious effort to sort the orders and minimize the picker's travel distance.[8]

This story illustrates a key point about benchmarking. Companies in very different businesses often perform similar processes, and can therefore share innovations. Another example Camp gives is the bar code, an innovation which manufacturers were slow to adopt: "The bar code was a proven practice in technology, developed in the grocery industry more than a decade ago. Here, anyone doing functional benchmarking could pick up a way to be more error-free and productive in data capture than with either key entry or manu-

---

[8]As quoted in Conference Board Report No. 937, p. 42.

al practices. Functional benchmarkers could have implemented this and gained superior performance of some type."[9] However, according to Camp, industrial firms were slow to see the relevance of the innovation even after hospitals adopted the bar code for patient record tracking and libraries for book tracking. The idea that grocery stores and libraries might have something to teach companies like Xerox and IBM probably seemed, at first glance, ridiculous. As in the L. L. Bean benchmarking effort, management might well feel "disbelief" at first, and this is no doubt why the innovation took so long to work its way into industry. At Xerox, people sometimes use the analogy of 'cutting windows' when describing benchmarking. It is a way to open up views onto firms, such as L. L. Bean or the grocery industry, and it is especially powerful when you cut windows where they are least expected.

The L. L. Bean story illustrates the dangers of the old 'benchmark' concept and the permanency it implies. This story has made its way, in simplified form, into the mythology of management, and as it is told over and over again, both listeners and tellers may come to see it as a reassuring example of permanence. The implication is that, once Xerox found and applied the L. L. Bean benchmark, the job was done and the story over. However, even as this story is retold, Xerox has moved on to newer benchmarks for its order fulfillment process. In reality, the benchmark has shifted, as it inevitably must in a changing environment where constant improvement is the price of admission and relative speed of improvement the key to success. Yes, Xerox learned how to deliver its products much faster by benchmarking against L. L. Bean. But then customer research revealed that customer satisfaction measures were still suboptimal—about 70 percent. Root cause analysis pointed to uncertainty of delivery time as the cause. Even though the products came faster, their arrival was not sufficiently *predictable* to satisfy today's customers. A new

---

[9]Ibid., pp. 40–41.

improvement cycle was begun, with a new team, new bench-marks, more modifications. Xerox added tracking of each individual product and part as it moved through the distribution process (an innovation that was first applied on a large scale by Federal Express). Now salespeople can tell customers exactly where their products are and when they will arrive, and the customer satisfaction measure is up from 70 to 90 percent.[10]

MEASURING CUSTOMER SATISFACTION

This is a recent example of competitive benchmarking at Xerox, and it illustrates the expansion of the quality effort from manufacturing to other functions, a trend that is driving change now at Xerox and most of the other companies discussed in this book as well. In the area of customer satisfaction, Xerox uses extensive surveys to see how it stands against all its competitors. These provide a period-to-period measure both of competitive standing and of progress versus prior results. Competitors that rank highest on specific customer satisfaction measures are targeted for benchmarking efforts, and often provide ideas for improving Xerox's practices as they relate to that measure. Customers often can provide the clues needed to improve Xerox's performance versus a superi-or competitor. This requires the kind of aggressive customer research we explored in Chapter 4. For example, Peter Waas-dorp, manager, customer satisfaction, for Xerox's U.S. Market-ing Group, explains that, "Even though a customer may indi-cate overall satisfaction with Xerox, if he or she has expressed dissatisfaction on any single item we will be in touch with that customer."

The integration of customer research and benchmarking

---

[10]Alexander Hiam and Charles D. Schewe, *The Portable MBA in Marketing,* Wiley, 1992, p. 45.

is an interesting and necessary development when benchmarking is applied to customer satisfaction, as Waasdorp's emphasis on survey research technique suggests. He goes on to explain that Xerox has "standardized questions in an effort to benchmark best practices globally." And, according to Waasdorp, "We maintain 15 months of customer satisfaction information that people have access to; this amounts to about 160,000 surveys. We are able to cut this information by product and by function, which enables us to work back to root causes of customer dissatisfaction issues."[11]

The benchmarking efforts in the area of customer service revealed a number of root causes affecting satisfaction, according to Waasdorp:

- Xerox focused largely on equipment and service—a hardware orientation.

- Xerox did not fully comprehend the customers' decision-making process.

- Xerox took a problem-oriented approach rather than simply asking customers if they were satisfied.

- Xerox was good at counting customer problems but not good at resolving them (the service recovery issue we first raised in Chapter 4).

- Many would-be internal Xerox users of the customer satisfaction information had difficulty gaining access to it.

The identification of root causes such as these through benchmarking provided direction to quality improvement efforts in the way Xerox interacted with its clients and in how it acquired and used information on customer satisfaction.

[11]From remarks appearing in full in Conference Board Report No. 979, p. 17–18.

A Formal Methodology:
The Xerox Model

Press information distributed by the administrators of the Baldrige Award states that, "In its quest to elevate products and services to world-class status, Xerox BP&S [Business Products & Services, a 1989 award winner] devised a benchmarking system that has, in itself, become a model." With this ringing endorsement, it seems appropriate to describe Xerox's methodology in detail. Here, evidently, is one of those best practices against which companies from all industries can benchmark.

Xerox recognizes four fundamental types of benchmarking, differentiated by where the benchmark is located. According to Robert Camp, "*Internal benchmarking* is a comparison of your internal operations to other internal operations. *Competitive benchmarking* is a competitor to competitor comparison. *Functional benchmarking* holds great potential for Xerox. In this instance, industry specifics are not important; instead we compare function against function across wide sections of different industry types. *Generic benchmarking* [a type of functional benchmarking] looks at business processes. There are a number of fundamental business processes in any major business such as taking an order, creating an invoice, servicing customers, satisfying customers. There is a limited set of generic business processes that should be benchmarked to find the best of the best industry practices."[12]

Although the Xerox benchmarking model has been held up as the global standard against which other companies ought to benchmark *their* benchmarking, it proves a moving target for the researcher. I have in front of me, as I write, transcripts of several talks by Xerox managers in which the process is described or diagramed; differently in each case. And a half-dozen training manuals and other company docu-

---

[12]Conference Board Report No. 937, p. 40.

ments also add to the confusion, as each seems to describe a process with more or less steps, bearing different names, and appearing in different order. Perhaps there is a lesson in this. No benchmark can be considered a constant, not even the benchmarking procedure itself! I will present below the most representative and detailed version from those at hand, with the warning that Xerox's practice in this area is no doubt both somewhat variable and subject to periodic improvements. This version requires ten steps:

1. *Identify what is to be benchmarked.* A team selects a product, a service, a process or a practice; even a level of customer satisfaction. The goal is to determine whether the area of interest is managed the best way possible.

2. *Identify comparative companies.* Benchmarking partners can be other operating units within Xerox, Xerox competitors, or noncompetitors who are judged the leaders in the area to be benchmarked.

3. *Determine data-collection method, and collect data.* In true "apples-to-apples" fashion, teams determine what measurements will be used in the benchmarking process. [These are termed 'metrics' at Xerox, and a listing of commonly-used metrics appears at the end of this chapter.] Then a trip is often made to the selected company, and face-to-face exchanges are conducted with principals in both firms. Often, a tour of the benchmarked area is included.

4. *Determine current performance levels.* Once the team has gathered the necessary data and compared them with current performance levels, the results are analyzed. Generally, they reveal a negative or positive performance gap (and the negative performance gaps are of course the most useful, as they indicate that the benchmark does indeed achieve superior performance).

5. *Project future performance levels.* The benchmarking team forecasts the expected improvement by the company under study, and sets the new Xerox goals based on this forecast of the benchmark. This step ensures that the Xerox goals will still equal or perhaps exceed the performance of the studied organization following the time it takes to implement the team's findings.

6. *Communicate benchmark findings and gain acceptance.* The team presents its methodology, findings, and proposed strategies to senior management. This information is also communicated to employees who will be asked to help implement the new strategies.

7. *Establish functional goals.* After concurrence, the team then presents final recommendations on ways in which the organization must change, based on benchmark findings, to reach the new goals.

8. *Develop action plans.* The team develops specific action plans for each objective, and develops strategies for obtaining full organizational support. (Obtaining buy-in from everyone affected is important.)

9. *Implement specific actions, and monitor progress.* The plans are put into place. Data on the new level of performance are collected. Adjustments to the process are made if the goals are not being met, and problem-solving teams may be formed to investigate.

10. *Recalibrate benchmarks.* Over time, the benchmarks are reevaluated and updated to ensure that they are based on the latest performance data from the benchmarked company.

As step three suggests, benchmarking is often done with the consent and collaboration of the benchmarked organization. Benchmarking is not supposed to involve spying, and

Xerox tells its employees to avoid misrepresenting themselves or trying to gain confidential information on competitors. Employees are instructed to identify themselves as Xerox employees and to check with Xerox legal staff before using any questionable information-gathering procedures.[13]

The initiation and/or coordination of benchmarking is one of the little-recognized but vitally important roles of the new corporate quality offices and their directors. Especially in functional benchmarking against noncompetitors, the corporate quality offices are able to negotiate reciprocal access to confidential information and details of operating procedure that are not generally discussed with outsiders. This practice is growing rapidly, and is one of the more surprising about-faces in management behavior spawned by the quality revolution. A decade ago, competitor intelligence was a hot new field, and companies were busy obtaining a small amount of competitor information at great expense and, often, through dubious and questionable methods. Now they are opening their doors to each other and permitting teams from other companies to gather a great deal of information at very little cost and through totally above-board methods (note however that Xerox provides employee training in how to handle benchmarking visits and what information *not* to discuss). However, the new openness does not completely replace practices (at least the legal practices) of competitor intelligence. They are also of value in benchmarking. For example, companies like Xerox are encouraging employees to engage in information-gathering about competitor practices when they talk with customers, salespeople or distributors, and these informal channels of information often turn up useful benchmarks.

---

[13]According to company document, *Competitive Benchmarking: A Practical Application,* USMG Quality Office, Xerox Corp., 1990, p. 19. Also see the detailed discussion by Robert Osterhoff, Manager, Customer Satisfaction and Quality Real Estate/General Service Division, Xerox, in Conference Board Report No. 990, pp. 22–25.

Informal Benchmarking

We have already seen the formal side of benchmarking at Xerox—the methodology that benchmarking teams use in their craft. But how does one integrate this methodology into the daily routine? The idea of extensive research projects, often involving far-away companies, can seem impractical to the average manager, who's average in-box is no doubt overflowing with memos, requests, problems and phone messages. A major benchmarking project is a serious interruption of this routine, and not something to be undertaken lightly—or frequently, for that matter. Or is it?

Like quality in general, benchmarking is both a formal set of procedures and a state of mind. And managers who embrace the benchmarking concept find they can implement it often in informal ways, as well as through the occasional major benchmarking project. The best way to explore this important point is to tag along with the quality tour that Mr. Jones was taking a fictional Xerox manager on—the one we met back in Chapter 9 as he introduced us to leadership tools. One of the stops on this quality tour story Xerox uses in its training is the office of a Jane Smith, who has something to say about benchmarking.

ON WITH THE QUALITY TOUR

Jones conducted me to the office of the Field Manager for Customer Service, Jane Smith. She was on the phone. It crossed my mind—not for the first time—that much of Xerox spends much of its life on the phone.

> *"I see," Smith concluded. "Thanks for taking the time to answer my questions. We at Xerox, of course, are eager to have you change your mind."*

> *After the call was finished, Jones made the introductions and explained my presence to Smith. Then he asked her,*

"Was that call part of your competitive benchmarking project?"

"Yes." She turned to me. *"We've been losing too many service contracts to a local third-party dealer. I've been trying to find out why."*

Jones said, *"Jane's been calling customers who have cancelled contracts and asking what made them go with our competitor. What she's really doing is benchmarking how we're meeting customer requirements against how they are."*

Smith smiled, *"Very informal benchmarking."*

Jones said, *"Very natural benchmarking. Because you really want to know."*

"Well, of course I want to know. After we decide what customer requirements the other guy is meeting better, we can decide how to meet the benchmark. Make an action plan to improve our process to better conform to customer requirements."

I blurted out, *"Isn't that time-consuming? How do you fit it in with all your regular job duties?"*

"Actually, it's not that time-consuming," Smith said. *"So far, I've just been making phone calls, a few at a time, and writing down the findings. When I know what specific things in the service-contract area the competition is succeeding at, I can focus on benchmarking those in greater detail. Then the whole Service Team will devise a plan to deal with the situation. Meanwhile, I'm cutting windows."*

I didn't understand the reference, and my face must have shown that.

"Competitive benchmarking is a tool to cut windows in our Xerox box," Jones said. *"So often we get so caught up*

in our job demands that we forget that Xerox functions in a much larger economic environment. We build a box around ourselves. By looking hard and systematically at what the competition is doing—and even at the business practices of firms that aren't our competitors—we can incorporate elements of their successes into our operations. And cut some windows in the box."

I said, "You make competitive benchmarking sound very easy and natural, whereas other people I talk to seem to see it as a mysterious burden."

"Competitive benchmarking is natural," Jones said, "because everyone is curious about others' business practices, and especially about competitors'. Benchmarking merely uses that curiosity to lead to action—which in turn can lead to very practical business results."

"Yes, I see," I said. "Good luck with your benchmarking, Jane."

"Oh, it won't succeed by luck," Smith said. "It will succeed by action. We're going to beat that dealer in obtaining service contracts."

"Using the right tool," Jones said, looking significantly at me. Smith, I saw, wasn't listening; she had already returned her attention to her benchmarking.

Go get'em Jane, *I thought. I was confident she would.*

INFORMAL BUT NOT UNGUIDED

Informal benchmarking has proven so valuable that in recent years Xerox has developed—don't laugh—a formal methodology for informal benchmarking. It is a three-step process:[1]

---

[1]Ibid., p. 6–7.

1. Awareness; discovering that another company is doing something particularly well.

2. Research; learning more about what they do through background reading, talking to people, and other simple research methods.

3. Action; incorporating the useful practices you have discovered into your operation.

To help employees perform these three steps, Xerox distributes worksheets listing the types of questions one might ask at each step. While at first glance it may seem silly to create a formal methodology for informal benchmarking, it is a practical necessity if you want to train employees in the practice. What is informal about the method is that it is conducted casually, out of curiosity, entirely at the initiative of the individual employee or team and without formal management oversight and approval. It is an example of moving from conscious to unconscious use of quality tools, and thus a worthy benchmark for any company engaged in the pursuit of quality.

Both informal and formal benchmarks are powerful quality tools because of their ability to keep an organization's map of the competitive terrain up to date now that it has become essentially unstable. But they are also important for another reason: their impact on corporate culture. Benchmarking leads to an unprecedented level of within-company cooperation and sharing of ideas. It breaks down the many barriers that prevent one department, factory or office building from sharing practices and insights with another. At Xerox, internal benchmarking is encouraged through a benchmarking network, as Robert Osterhoff, a quality manager for Xerox's General Service Division explains. He believes "The network has been the glue that has held benchmarking together. The 400 Xerox people who form this internal network meet twice a year" to "exchange stories of how these practices have actually worked in their operations."[15] This internal exchange of benchmarks and benchmarking practices is another way in which the tools of benchmarking contribute to the transformation of the organization on a day-to-day basis. Both formal and informal benchmarking, like other hands-on quality tools, tend to transform an organization from the bottom up as an almost accidental artifact of their routine use.

EXHIBIT 12-1 COMMONLY USED METRICS FOR BENCHMARKING

Xerox uses the term 'metric' to describe the specific, quantitative measures against which it benchmarks. Here is a list, provided by Xerox, of the metrics that have been used most commonly in the benchmarking efforts of its operating units.[16] To use one of these metrics it is necesssary to standardize measurement technique with the benchmarked group or company, and, of course, to share comparative data on the metrics at both companies.

Cost and Cost-Related Metrics

- Percent of sales, service, customer administration, distribution, or general and administrative costs to revenue

- Labor overhead rate (percent)

- Material overhead (percent)

- Manpower performance ratio

- Months of supply

- Cost per order

- Cost per engineering drawing

- Occupancy cost as percent of revenue

- Return on assets

---

[15]Conference Board Report No. 990, p. 25.
[16]From *Competitive Benchmarking: What It Is And What It Can Do For You,* Xerox Corporate Quality Office, 1987, p. 17.

Exhibit 12-1 Commonly Used Metrics
for Benchmarking (continued)

Quality Metrics

- Percent of parts meeting requirements
- Percent of finished machine quality improvement
- Number of problem-free machines
- Internal and external customer satisfaction results
- Billing error rate

Service Metrics

- Work support ratio
- Cost per SACAT hour (Standard Available Call Activity Time)
- First time fix of service call problem
- Percent of supplies delivered next day on time
- Percent of parts available for the technical representative

MEASUREMENT

The SQI index [FedEx's quality measure] has helped us change our thinking.
—*Fred Smith, CEO,*
Federal Express Corporation[1]

Cost of Quality changes its nature as a quality culture is institutionalized. As the culture matures, the tools are bound to change.
—*Mac McDonnell, vice president and general*
manager, Industrial Systems Division,
Texas Instruments[2]

We measure everything. I'm telling you that if you went to the bathroom one extra time, it would show up on a Milliken chart.
—*Thomas J. Malone, president and chief*
operating officer, Milliken & Company[3]

[1]Speech to employees, December 5, 1990, provided courtesy of Federal Express Corp.
[2]Harvard Business School Case No. 9-189-029, p. 1.
[3]Speech, "Quest for Excellence," Georgia Tech, April 10, 1990.

"Measurement? You can't be serious. Isn't that the problem of quality control engineers and accountants? (Or perhaps, at Milliken, plumbers?) Why in the world should managers bother with the details of measurement systems?"

This is the most common reaction to the statement that measurements are absolutely critical to quality improvement, and must become the serious concern of everyone—from project team members to chairmen and CEOs. But listen to John Evans, European quality manager, Dow Corning Ltd., discuss the role of measurement in his company's quality program.

> After seven years of quality improvement efforts, it is sobering to examine our achievements. We have both micro- and macro-measures because the sum of the micro-measures adds up to the macro-measures. Our internal test methods are a typical micro-measure. Because our tests for finished products were not reliable, we have worked on improving these.
>
> One crucial macro-measure: We measure complaints carefully. The more closely a company measures complaints, the more the numbers rise. Now we have the process under control and the numbers are coming down. On-time delivery and cost effectiveness are improving.
>
> Customer awareness in R&D is difficult to measure, but we try. In the technical reports from Europe, we scan for both generic and specific references to customers, we look for the use of experiment design, and we watch for statistical methods. In 1986, I found few of these references, but awareness improved in 1987 and 1988. For the European area as a whole, we now ship 94 percent on-time, compared to a starting base of shipping 64 percent on-time.[1]

Evans talks about measurements with a passion that few managers can muster. He speaks of details such as counting the number of references to customers in his company's technical reports—an onerous task, no doubt—because dramatic

---

[1] John Evans, "A Three-Pillared Approach to Quality Management," speech at The Conference Board's Third Annual Quality Conference, April 2–3, 1990, New York.

changes in the corporation's culture can be effected through such measurements. How else can a manager know whether technical reports are motivated by a customer orientation, but to create a measurement of customer orientation in technical reports?

Evans' reference to testing of finished products is reminiscent of Dow-Corning's problems in 1992 with leaking breast implants. It is interesting to speculate that the unreliability of tests for finished products that Evans refers to may be behind the failure of some of the silicone breast implants the company manufactured. In any event, it now appears likely the company will experience exceptionally high costs for this quality problem (since the costs to customers with leaking implants are potentially high). The case, though no doubt unwelcome, may be a confirmation of Evans' concern for better measurement of finished product quality.

You Are What You Measure

Customer orientation is a constant theme in quality programs, and in every chapter of this book, for that matter. Part of the new quality culture is a *customer* culture, as we saw in Chapter 4. The best way to incorporate the customer perspective into every process of a company is to measure it. The surveys and root cause analyses described in Chapter 4 can be thought of as a form of measurement. Just as the measurement of profits helps a company make profits, the measurement of customer perceptions helps a company please customers (the first and most vital step in making profits). Allan Jacobson, chairman and CEO, 3M Company, describes the role of measurement in his company's pursuit of a customer perspective. He equates awareness with measurement, and indeed, measuring something is a powerful way to create awareness of it. Here is Jacobson of 3M's approach:

We hope to integrate customer expectations into all operations in a systematic way. 3M's goal is total quality awareness and measurements throughout all company functions. To facilitate this, we have conducted extensive interview programs with many customers to determine how different people view our products and services. In Europe, for example, we did 28,000 interviews to find out what customers thought about every aspect of our business. Our objective was to forge a measurement and to create a positive influence on customers in each contact. Ultimately, 3M wants to provide the best customer service of any company of our kind in the European market.[5]

Jacobson sees the need to "forge a measurement" in order to achieve the goal of superior customer service. The ability to pursue an ambitious service-quality goal such as this is dependent upon the ability to measure progress toward the goal. (By the way, that is not a typo in the quote—3M really did do *28,000* interviews, an order of magnitude more than the standard market research effort would entail.)

Of course a customer orientation is only one of the important elements of any quality program. It is important to develop macro-level measures, as Evans of Dow Corning Ltd. terms them, measures that give as clear a snapshot of quality progress as the standard financial statements give of bottom-line results. But there is broad agreement as to what the key macro-level measures of a firm's financial performance ought to be. Quality practitioners have no such guidelines, and even if they did, it would be inadvisable to follow them. Financial measures are designed to serve a common set of customers, the investors, and their information needs are fairly similar across a wide variety of companies and industries. Not so with quality measures. They tend to be more company-specific, as each company is concerned about a unique set of consumers, the customers who purchase and use its products or services. And each company is also concerned about progress toward

[5]Allen F. Jacobson, "Customer Expectations in the New Decade," speech at The Conference Board's Third Annual Quality Conference, April 2–3, 1990, New York.

its unique vision and goals. As a result, every company must define its own macro-level measures of quality.

Focusing on the Pulse Points

The 'pulse point' concept is helpful in visualizing this task. At Westinghouse's Commercial Nuclear Fuel Division, a handful of the hundreds of measures used throughout the company have been designated pulse points, or key quality measures. Like pulse points on the human body, these measures are the most obvious and important general measures of the health and well-being of the company's quality initiative, and thus of the company itself. They are represented visually on a diagram of the human body. (A simple, powerful visual image like this is especially helpful in communicating quality measures throughout a large company.) Exhibit 13-1 is the pulse point diagram used at Westinghouse's Commercial Nuclear Fuel Division.

The pulse points "provide standards for our quantitative evaluation system and address internal productivity and quality issues as well as customer satisfaction," according to James Fici, manager, total quality planning, for Westinghouse's Commercial Nuclear Fuel Division. He explains how the pulse point measures are used: "Along with hundreds of other yardsticks that employees measure their performance against, the primary pulse points are posted at all our locations, to remind us that continuous quality improvement is important to the future success of the business."[6]

Jack Fooks, (previously) vice president, corporate productivity and quality, for Westinghouse Electric Corp., emphasizes the focusing power of pulse points. His remarks tie measurement systems back to the need for focus we first discussed in the context of planning and management processes, in Chapter 5. According to Fooks, "A company can't do everything; you must zero in on the survival issues. In our

[6]Conference Board Report No. 937, p. 86.

Exhibit 13-1 Pulse Points Westinghouse Commercial Nuclear Fuel Division

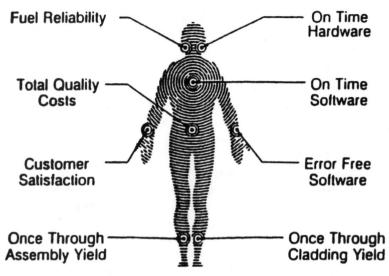

Fuel Reliability

On Time Hardware

Total Quality Costs

On Time Software

Customer Satisfaction

Error Free Software

Once Through Assembly Yield

Once Through Cladding Yield

Source: Westinghouse Electric Corp.

Commercial Nuclear Fuel Division, for example, they focus on pulse points, which they believe are some of the measures of the key issues in their business. These issues will impact the movement toward their vision. There are monthly measures and the results are posted throughout the division. Accordingly, every employee is keenly aware of the results." The Westinghouse case demonstrates that measures can be a powerful device for focusing employee efforts on the company's quality vision.[7]

MEASUREMENTS DRIVE CHANGE

Measurements can be used to drive the continuous improvement process—in fact, some quality practitioners have actually

Jack H. Fooks, "Culture Change and the Quality Organization," speech at The Conference Board's Third Annual Quality conference, April 2–3, 1990, New York.

used measurement as the *cornerstone* of their quality programs. Metropolitan Life Insurance Company is one. The company based its quality measures on academic research concerning service delivery. Academic research pointed toward five factors the company expected to be especially important indicators of service quality in its business. These factors provided the basis of an elaborate measurement system which now drives the company's quality improvement efforts. John Falzon, senior vice president of Met Life, explains:

> The researchers were able to identify five significant types of factors that influence the overall evaluation of service quality:
>
> 1. Reliability, the ability to perform the promised service dependably and accurately;
> 2. Responsiveness, the willingness to help customers and provide prompt services;
> 3. Tangibles, physical facilities, equipment, and appearance of personnel;
> 4. Assurance, the knowledge and courtesy of employees and their ability to convey trust and confidence;
> 5. Empathy, the caring, individual attention provided to customers.
>
> Each of these five classifications can be expressed as a series of "expectations" statements, which are further refined so that more meaningful customer data can be collected. . . . The gap between expectations and perceived level of service delivery represents the extent of a service problem.
>   . . . Our initial directive from the Quality Steering Committee was that our quality effort should be line driven, with minimal staff support. Our challenge, as a corporate staff, was thus to communicate the results of this research in an easily understandable way, showing the line organizations how they could apply the principles to their own operations.

The approach the company chose was to train line managers to develop and use their own expectations/perceptions surveys based on the academic research. The work was done by 'Policy Issue Teams' at each location. For example, the Policy Issue Team at one of Met Life's administrative offices used the methodology to measure service quality to the internal customers it served. Falzon explains,

> The team developed a series of expectation statements, making sure that all five of the service quality dimensions noted in the research were covered . . . In addition to the expectation statements, other questions tested the adequacy of standards the team had established—such as turnaround time for "rush" cases. Customer reaction was overwhelming. Eighty-seven percent of the sales managers surveyed responded and the Policy Issue Team became aware of the potential for some rather "painful gaps." The result led the team to institute procedural changes designed to help meet their customer expectations.[8]

In this story of a service improvement team's efforts at Met Life, measurement is a constant theme. A conceptual structure for measuring service quality provided the starting point for the team's work. Performance gaps were identified and prioritized based on the results of the measurement effort. And, presumably, improvements were monitored and more improvements made over time, using the measurement system the team established.

Measurement was also key to achieving the company's goal of a quality process that is administered through the line organization, rather than the corporate office. The quality process was implanted in the line organization by giving line managers new measures of service quality and training them in how to use the measures. Yet we do not usually think of something as simple as a new measurement technique as having the power to transform an organization. How does this approach work? Can it be generalized to other companies?

Met Life's measurement-driven transformation *can* be generalized, precisely because of how it works. It works because measurements have hidden power. The measurement

[8]Conference Board Research Report No. 909, pp. 54, 56.

system that was transferred to the line organizations harnessed the transforming power of *information*; information is the end result of measurement. When you train line managers to measure service performance gaps, you ensure that they will be confronted with new information about *their* service performance gaps. Once the information is there, in black and white, it cannot be ignored. It is only because quality and service gaps are hidden from view in the traditional organization that they are permitted to exist. The right measurement technique can shed daylight on performance gaps, forcing the organization to confront them and drawing everyone into the effort to close these gaps. Measurements are transforming because of the power of the information they reveal.

For example, IBM calculates that a 0.99 percent error rate—considered desirable at most manufacturers—would produce, across the United States, 20,000 pieces of lost mail every hour and 5,000 incorrect surgical procedures every week. Within IBM's own manufacturing facilities, this error rate translates into 10 defects out of every 1,000 solder joints on the motherboard of a computer. Most of those computers would require more time to fix than it took to make them in the first place![9] These examples demonstrate convincingly the problem with an 0.99 percent error rate, a rate that sounds awfully good until you peak beneath the surface. Measurement of percentage error rates does not capture the high cost of such errors accurately. In fact, measurement systems often fail to measure cost of poor quality.

THE HIGH COST OF BAD QUALITY

One of the most transforming things a company can do in the early days of its quality process is to measure the cost of quality—of bad quality, that is. Fici reports that, "In 1984 we

---

[9]Shawn Clark, "Quality Isn't Enough; Programs Need to be Market-Driven," *Marketing News,* June 10, 1991, p. 15.

started to track and report on quality failure costs." 1984 was the second year of the Commercial Nuclear Fuel Division's quality program.[10] With the new measurements as ammunition, the quality program was able to portray cost-of-quality more accurately, and it was a lot higher than anyone had expected.

Frederick Reichheld, a director at Bain & Company, and Earl Sasser, a Harvard Business School professor, recently wrote that, "If companies knew how much it really costs to lose a customer, they would be able to make accurate evaluations of investments designed to retain customers. Unfortunately, today's accounting systems do not capture the value of a loyal customer." Reichheld and Sasser go on to explain that, according to their analysis of various service industries, "customers generate increasingly more profits each year they stay with a company. Across a wide range of businesses, the pattern is the same: The longer a company keeps a customer, the more money it stands to make . . . For one auto-service company, the expected profit from a fourth-year customer is more than triple the profit that same customer generates in the first year. When customers defect, they take all that profit-making potential with them."[11]

DEFECTS MEAN DEFECTIONS

Defect is just what customers do when they experience defective products or services. The machine that breaks down, the package that is delivered late, the information that is delivered wrong—whatever the problem, it is likely to precipitate a change of vendors. Customers will exercise their right of choice and shift from competitor to competitor as long as they

---

[10]Conference Board Report No. 937, No. 85.

[11]Frederick F. Reichheld and W. Earl Sasser, Jr., "Zero Defections: Quality Comes to Services," *Harvard Business Review*, September-October 1990, p. 106.

Exhibit 13-2 Profit Growth from a 5% Reduction in Customer Defections

Auto-service chain	30%
Branch deposits	85%
Credit card	75%
Credit insurance	25%
Insurance brokerage	50%
Industrial distribution	45%
Office-building management	40%
Software	35%

Source: Frederick F. Reichheld and W. Earl Sasser, Jr., "Zero Defections: Quality Comes to Services," *Harvard Business Review,* September-October 1990, p. 110.

are dissatisfied with quality. Along the way, the costs of trying to solve quality problems are high—for both the company and its customer. Efforts to fix problems after they have occurred often account for 20–40% of total costs at manufacturing companies, although few accounting systems reveal this fact. And when the customer defects, the impact on profits is dramatic. Almost unbelievable. To illustrate this point, Exhibit 13-2 gives the statistics Reichheld and Sasser obtained by analyzing specific industry profit data. The exhibit shows how much profit increases, as a percent, when customer defections are reduced by just 5% (profit is defined as the net present value of future profit streams for the average customer life). There is a huge multiple. In software, a 5 percent reduction in customer losses increases profits by 35 percent. In the area of retail banking they studied, 5% fewer defections gives profit an 85 percent boost!

In measuring the cost of poor quality, or of mistakes and sub-optimal performance, one can either look at the direct financial costs to the company, or one can look at costs from a *customer* perspective. This is what FedEx now does. It's measurement systems are designed to illuminate the customer's

experience of poor service, not the company's. Here is how
the system works, and how it evolved, as described by Fred
Smith, CEO of Federal Express.

> We have long sought to measure service delivery from the
> *customer's* point of view. Out SQI (Service Quality Indicator)
> index has helped us make extraordinary improvements in actu-
> al service. And there is no question that we measure service
> with a more reliable and timely process than any of our compet-
> itors. The SQI index has also helped us change our thinking,
> from looking at quality as a *percentage* of on-time deliveries, to
> looking at it as the *actual* number of service failures that occurs
> on a given day. I believe this change in thinking has made a
> profound difference in our own perceptions of how we are
> performing, and as a result we have radically improved our
> delivery of service to the customer.[12]

The switch from a percentage basis to an actual basis
brings home the cost in customer ill will. Each copy of the
company's monthly in-house newsletter, *Customer Satisfaction,* displays the actual SQI numbers on its front page. In a
recent issue, for example, readers can see that 931 packages
were lost, 878 pickups missed, and 9,289 invoices had to be
adjusted on average every day over the last month. On a
percentage basis, these numbers are inconsequential. On-time
performance is over 99 percent in the system, for example—
but the system is so large that this still means tens of thousands
of people receive their packages late. To these individual
customers, service quality is dreadful. Their perceptions of
Federal Express are shaped by their individual experiences (as
we saw first in our discussion of transaction analysis in Chapter
6), not by the system average. Only a system that never delivers
anything late can be considered perfect from the customer's

---

[12]Speech to employees, December 5, 1990, provided courtesy of Federal
Express Corp.

point of view. The new actual-basis service quality indicators guarantee that this fact will not be forgotten at Federal Express.

COST-OF-QUALITY SYSTEMS MUST EVOLVE

The new measurement system that stimulates quality improvement can, as it ages, turn into an impediment to further improvement. Measurement is not a static activity, but must constantly evolve if it is to lead change rather than hold it back. This is the experience of Texas Instruments, whose cost-of-quality system, first instituted in 1983, "served as the language for the cultural change" required by the quality process, as Mac McDonnell, vice president and general manager of Texas Instrument's Industrial Systems Division, described it.[13] The initial system measured costs of poor quality in four categories: prevention costs, appraisal costs, internal failure costs, and external failure costs. The trouble with the system, according to Werner Schuele, vice president, people and asset effectiveness, at Texas Instruments, was that "the Cost of Quality Figure probably includes only half of all the costs associated with quality and may no longer provide sufficient incentives to drive further improvements." He believes that "Cost of Quality numbers should be as high as possible to aid in identifying areas for improvement."[14]

Now TI is expanding its cost of quality measures to include more of these indirect costs. McDonnell goes on to explain that "Cost of Quality changes its nature as a quality culture is institutionalized. As the culture matures, the tools are bound to change." And this statement can safely be generalized to all quality-related measures. If measurements are to drive change, they must receive on-going and creative management attention.

[13]Harvard Business School Case No. 9-189-029, p. 1.
[14]Harvard Business School Case No. 9-189-029, p. 1.

Applying Measurements: Quality Function Deployment

The power of measurements is clearly visible in applications of quality function deployment, or QFD, a Japanese import used to make product designs better reflect customer requirements. In QFD, a multi-functional team measures and analyzes both customer attitudes and product attributes in great detail. Then the team creates a visual matrix in order to find ways to modify product attributes (engineering characteristics) so as to improve the product on the customer-based measures of product performance. Along the way, the team must develop a series of measures of several different types.

First, it must measure the customer's perceptions. This includes not only how the product is ranked on various attributes versus competitors, but also what all the specific, often painfully specific, attributes are and how important each is to customers. Second, the team must define each of the engineering characteristics, the specifics of what and how the product is made, and devise tangible measures of them that relate to customer perception. This can be tricky. For example, it may not be meaningful from the customer's perspective to measure a car door by the weight or cost of the components, even though these measures are no doubt collected by the engineers who design and build the car. More useful are measures of the force needed to close it, the sound made when it closes, and how steep a hill it can be opened on without falling shut accidentally. Third, the team must attempt to measure the potential impact of possible design changes on customer perception. Does a change in the door hinge improve customer perception of the car on one of the customer attributes? Further, does it interact with other elements of the design in a negative way that might cancel out the intended benefit?

Cars, and many other products and services, are complex systems requiring a holistic approach to quality improvement. It is difficult to improve them without a great many careful measures and a way to relate all of the measures to each other. QFD and the detailed measurement systems it requires allow a quality improvement team to look at the big picture instead of trying to tackle individual components of the product or service on a one-at-a-time basis. As such, QFD can be thought of as a way to integrate measurements into a holistic model of the product or service as system in all its richness and complexity.

The systems approach underlies the new process perspective which companies are bringing to their work processes, and it also underlies QFD and the holistic approach to product design and development. Measurement plays an important part in this shift from traditional reductionist management to more holistic approaches. Decision-makers must learn not only to measure better; they must also learn to integrate many more measures into individual decisions. To truly manage any system (whether process or a product), one must have a sense of the many variables, the many causes and effects, and the many possible interactions when any one of them is altered. Strategic decisions can no longer be based on a few simple ratios, and neither can product development decisions. QFD is a higher-order technique for integrating and using the more complex measurement systems that become necessary in the quality management approach, and as such is probably an example of the kind of methods that will come into wider use as total quality management progresses. It is therefore interesting to examine briefly how QFD is actually implemented in product design.

However, it is only fair to say that most companies report difficulties with QFD. People are not naturally systems thinkers. It is hard to juggle dozens and dozens of variables and their measures, whether for QFD or for any other methodology. This is an important frontier for managers and their companies, but it may not be reasonable to expect rapid progress on this frontier.

Earl Conway, Director, Corporate Quality, for Procter & Gamble, introduced quality function deployment to his company in 1988 (it was developed by a Japanese professor, Yoji Akao, in the 1980s). According to Conway, "It's been one of the most powerful methodologies we've used. It represents tremendous untapped potential although there's a lot of misunderstanding about what it is intended to do." (Both of these statements are borne out by the comments of many managers I spoke to while researching this book. The majority of companies trying QFD find it difficult and frustrating, but a few, including P&G, have developed sufficient skill that they are able to produce wonderful results with it.) Part of the problem companies have with QFD comes from misunderstanding its intended use. Conway explains that "It is actually a design planning methodology for multi-functional teams to translate what is known about customer requirements into the actual design of products and systems." He warns that, "Like the TQM movement itself, QFD as a methodology requires management understanding and commitment before teams can begin to apply the methodology, and it takes a lot of time and patience." Further, "it is not for all situations. It is only applicable to complex product and system design projects."[15] But when complex design projects need to be tackled by multi-functional teams, it is the best technique available. Here is how it works.

Step 1.   Customer attributes (CAs) are defined. These are descriptions of what the customer wants, often in their own words and phrases. There may be dozens of them, and it may be expedient to group them into bundles of related attributes. CAs are also given relative importance weightings, often through trade-off analysis and other forms of survey research (usually weightings are in relative percents such that they total 100 percent).

Step 2.   Competitive position customer evaluations of competing products are obtained for each of the CAs determined

---

[15]Discussion with the author, May 29, 1992.

in step 1 (usually survey research is needed). Competitive position is often measured on a relative scale where 1 = worst and 5 = best. This comparative data helps product engineers and managers understand how best to achieve competitive advantage through their work on the CAs.

Step 3.   Engineering characteristics (ECs) that may affect CAs are listed. Usually the design team does this after reviewing CAs in detail (in order to help them develop descriptors that are meaningful from the customer's perspective). Some ECs affect more than one AC. Some of the proposed ECs will not appear to affect any ACs, which means they may be unnecessary, or that there may be a flaw in the customer research. ECs are described quantitatively: weight, length, number, and so forth. This exercise presents a good opportunity for rethinking both the design and the existing quality measures for it.

Step 4.   The extent of the impact of each EC on each AC is determined or estimated. This is often done on a four-point scale in the body of the matrix such as:

1   Strong positive impact
2   Medium positive impact
3   Medium negative impact
4   Strong negative impact

Step 5.   All this information is summarized in a chart, often called the house of quality (the reason is obvious when you look at the diagram), that shows customer attributes on the vertical, and engineering characteristics on the horizontal dimension. The resulting grid is filled in with the relationship scores from step 4. See Exhibit 13-3.

Step 6.   The impact of changes in any EC on other ECs is evaluated (a scale such as the one in step 4 can be applied to this step). Interactions among EC's in which changes in one EC have an impact on another are represented in a "roof" diagram above the matrix (see Exhibit 13-3).

Exhibit 13-3 Simplified House of Quality Diagram

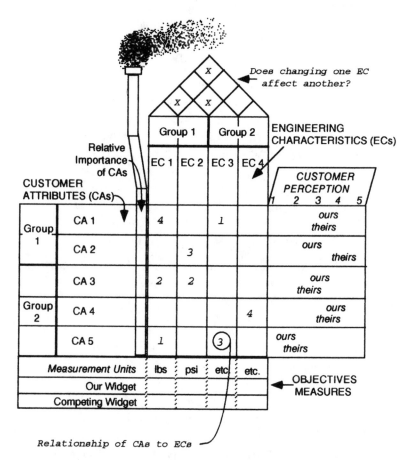

Source: Copyright © 1992 Alexander Hiam & Associates

Step 7. As the team develops the measures and fills in the matrix, it naturally begins to focus on CAs on which the product appears weak and also begins to develop ideas concerning how to improve various ECs. Now that the matrix is complete, the team turns its attention completely to the task of redesign, using the house of quality diagram as a guide. Because the diagram integrates a great many measures having to do with customer perception, competitive position, and engineering characteristics, the team is far better able to keep all these considerations in mind during redesign than it could without this tool.

A brief example helps make the benefits of QFD more tangible. Here is one from two professors who described the method in an academic journal when it was first introduced to the U.S.:

> Consider the location of an emergency break lever in an American sporty car. Placing it on the left between the seat and the door solved an engineering problem. But it also guaranteed that women in skirts could not get in and out gracefully. In contrast, Toyota improved its rust prevention record from one of the worst to one of the best by coordinating design and production decisions to focus on the customer concern. Using the house of quality, designers broke down "body durability" into 53 items covering everything from climate to modes of operation. They obtained customer evaluations and ran experiments on nearly every detail of production, from pump operation to temperature control and coating composition. Decisions on sheet metal details, coating materials, and baking temperatures were all focused on those aspects of rust prevention most important to customers.[16]

QFD is thought of as a technique for product design, but in fact its measurements and its visual representation of their interactions can also be useful in the processes that follow, or come downstream from product design. It is used in parts deployment by building a matrix with ECs on the vertical axis and product characteristics on the horizontal. It is used in process planning by building a matrix with parts characteristics on the vertical and key process operations on the horizontal. And it is also used in production planning by rolling parts

---

[16]John R. Hauser and Don Clausing, "The House of Quality," *Harvard Business Review*, May-June 1988, p. 64.

characteristics to the vertical axis and adding production requirements to the horizontal. Each of these planning steps is necessary along the way from product design to actual production of the product in a factory, and each would normally be pursued in isolation from the initial customer research. However, by building a house of quality for each step on the foundation provided by one of the axes from the step before, the fundamental customer orientation is retained and the needs of internal customers are incorporated.

Of course, the end result is also a surprisingly complex system of measurements, one that cannot really be used by any one individual decision-maker but instead requires considerable effort by a series of multi-functional teams. More and better measurements require more and better decision-makers, and the many new measurements now under development in companies with quality programs will no doubt necessitate the development of new, more holistic approaches to understanding and working with information. QFD is probably a forerunner of such methods, and in another decade there may well be similarly complex techniques in place for many other tasks, from strategic planning to management of customer service interactions. The thought is both frightening and exciting. It is exciting because it suggests that there are new and unexplored levels for total quality management, but it is frightening in the sense that most employees (and authors!) are not yet ready to make the leap to complex systems-oriented decision-making. There is considerable need for innovation and learning in this area, and there is also considerable opportunity—more than enough to justify management attention to measurement systems.

14

PROCESS MANAGEMENT METHODS AND TOOLS

> Processes adapt, if left unregulated; over time the usual result is an adaptation for comfort rather than competitiveness.
> *—Edward Kane, vice president, quality and management systems, D&B Software*[1]

The reason there is a quality gap in companies (and other types of organizations) is that, when left to their own devices, business processes produce suboptimal results. As Edward Kane of Dun & Bradstreet Software (DBS) observes in this chapter's opening quote, they adapt for comfort rather than competitiveness. The reason is because, in his words, "The individuals who work in these processes—and particularly those who manage them—seek self-control in place of environmental control." Their instinct is to optimize their personal control (and reduce personal risk) through their management of the process, rather than to let the process be shaped by the demands of its environment. As a result, most processes are

---

[1] Edward J. Kane, "IBM's Quality Focus on the Business Process," *Quality Progress,* April, 1986.

built for comfort, not for speed—and so, too, are the companies which are composed of them. This is why it is necessary not only to recognize the process perspective in a general way (as we did in chapter 5), but also to systematically attack each process within the firm and modify it until it is truly competitive.

Modifying processes is very much a hands-on effort. It is the blue-collar component of quality improvement. It is where values and goals meet reality. You have to roll up your sleeves and put on your rubber boots to work on a company's processes in a constructive manner.

When it comes to hands-on process improvement, there are two fundamental issues: What to do, and how to do it. And when the topic of process improvement is addressed, in books and training sessions, the tools and techniques of process management are generally front and center. Statistical process control, cause-effect charts, and design of experiments are among the sophisticated new tools available for managing processes. But it is important to recognize that these are the *how to's*. Master these tools, and you know how to do it—but you still do not know *what* to do.

At Conference Board companies that make process management the main focus of their quality initiatives, such as IBM, FPL, Ford, and DBS, there is less emphasis on the specific tools and more on what the key steps in the process improvement cycle should be. (Tools are taught and used, to be sure, but only in the context of *method*.) If you think about it, this bias makes good sense. There is nothing to be gained by giving employees hammers, saws and levels and telling them to start building a house. Far more progress will be made if you start by defining what each person must do, in what sequence, in order to get the house built. When one asks a question such as, "How do you build a house?", one does *not* want to hear about the pros and cons of different weights of hammers—one wants to hear what each step is, from designing and blueprinting, to pouring the foundation, to framing, to sheathing, to finishing—and one needs to know *who* does each step and *how* the steps should be managed to produce a well-designed, well-built house. Not that the details of specific tools are unimportant—they are just secondary to the big-picture issue of method.

With this thought in mind, I have turned the typical presentation of process management upside down. This chapter starts by describing a process management methodology, one that can be used to identify, analyze, and modify any process so as to improve the quality of its result. This, like the plans for building a house, is the least visible but most important of all the tools. As the process management methodology is described, we will stop to look at several of the most important hand-tools it requires. The chapter will end by describing the process managers' toolbox and the tools it contains, keeping in mind that mastering the specifics of each tool is less important than mastering the process improvement methodology itself. After all, if you know what to do, you can generally figure out how to do it—a quick trip to the library or a phone call is all that is required to obtain the details of using most of the process tools. But if you know how to do it, but have no idea *what* to do, you are in deep trouble. The most important tool is therefore the method itself.

THE DBS EIGHT-STEP PROCESS MANAGEMENT SYSTEM

When Edward Kane came to DBS as vice president, quality and management systems, he instituted a formal process management approach that has helped the company reduce the time required to develop new software, and has also improved customer service and field support processes. Kane came from IBM, where he had been instrumental in developing that company's 12-step process management methodology.[2] The eight-step process that he designed for DBS is, according to Kane, not only simpler but better. It was also developed "to handle any kind of process,"[3] according to Kane. I have chosen to profile it for these reasons. It is simple and clear, but sufficiently robust to be applicable in any process improvement effort. Companies with their own process management methods will find it a useful benchmark (since existing methods can and should always be improved), and companies without a formal methodology will find this one a useful starting point.

DBS has not been using the method for very long, but nonetheless has been able to show some significant results from it. The most impressive results are in the area of new software development, as this is a lengthy, complex process and one that is central to the continued competitiveness of any software company. Because of the complexity of the process, Kane explains that "It took two years to complete the new methodology including training, implementation of the new tools and standards, and the establishment of certification and management review." Results include a reduction in defects reported and an increase in deadlines met. Kane explains that, "Results, while expected to evolve slowly, have been strongly in evidence. A dramatic improvement in the ability to meet schedule dates occurred during the first two years. In addition, early results show a sharp drop in field service requests [concerning problems] for products using the new methodology."[4]

But perhaps the most striking change is in the length of time it takes DBS to design and develop a new product. Exhibit

[2]For details of this method, contact IBM or see Edward J. Kane, "IBM's Quality Focus on the Business Process," *Quality Progress,* April, 1986.

[3]Conversation with the author, February 1992.

[4]Edward J. Kane, "The Ascent of Quality in a Software Company," manuscript dated August 19, 1991, provided by the author. Quote from p. 12. (This manuscript appeared as "Process Management Methodology Brings Uniformity to DBS," *Quality Progress,* June 1992, pp. 41–46.

EXHIBIT 14-1 DBS PRODUCT DEVELOPMENT TIME

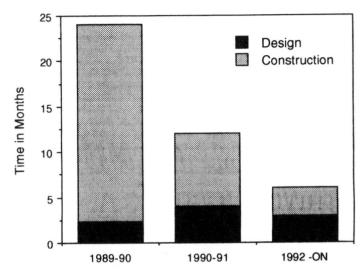

Source: Dun & Bradstreet Software

14-1 illustrates the impact of the process improvement effort on the development cycle of D&B's software products. Total product development time has been cut in half, and is now being cut in half again. This reduction in development time reflects significant changes in the development process, as evidenced by the fact that design time actually increases, rather than decreases—evidently more and better design is one of the keys to reduced development time.[5]

The DBS process management system consists of eight phases that are performed consecutively, and together make up a process improvement cycle (the cycle can be repeated for continued process improvement). Here are the eight phases

[5]From D&B's 1991 ADAPSO (now ITAA) award application, reprinted with permission of the company.

with a brief discussion of how they are performed, assuming a process has already been picked for improvement.[6]

1. IDENTIFY PRIORITIES AND ORGANIZE

Management of line organizations should take responsibility for setting priorities for process improvement. They should look at problems, opportunities to redesign obsolete processes, all activities central to the organization's mission, and critical success factors as they think about what priorities should provide the focus for the process improvement effort. After management has set priorities, cross-functional teams are formed that represent all key areas. Responsibility for the team is assigned to an individual.

2. DEFINE THE PROCESS AND DETERMINE CUSTOMER REQUIREMENTS

While the process in question may be clear enough in a general sense, a formal, detailed definition of it often proves elusive. Where does it begin and end? What should be included or excluded? What processes connect with it? As these questions are resolved, the processes' boundaries become clear.

Further definition is provided by specifying who the suppliers are and what their input is, and by determining what the process' output is and who the customers are. Every process is a customer of other processes, since it consumes their input—and every process has customers, the people or processes who consume *its* output. At DBS, these customers are studied with the same care the marketing department might give to the company's external customers. Interviews, surveys and other research methods are used to determine customer requirements and learn more about competitors.

[6]This discussion follows Edward J. Kane, "The Ascent of Quality in a Software Company," and various company documents provided by Mr. Kane.

3. SET OBJECTIVES, MEASUREMENTS AND TARGETS

Specific objectives flow from the general priorities defined in phase one, and provide formal, measurable benchmarks whereby progress can be judged. Objectives need to be defined such that, when all have been achieved, the mission is complete. Measurements of the effectiveness and efficiency of the process are also important, as they will make it possible to track performance benefits resulting from process improvements. I assume that measurements are begun as soon as the measures are defined, so as to provide base-line data on the performance of the process against which progress can be tracked.

4. DOCUMENT THE PROCESS

How exactly does the process now work? Management traditionally took a 'black box' approach to most processes. Before processes can be improved, the inside of the black box must be mapped. In fact, the improvements flow from the deeper understanding of the process that results from this and the previous steps.

Kane and DBS use process *flowcharting* in this phase, and it is a sufficiently valuable technique that it is worthwhile to look at a brief example of it in action. In Exhibit 14-2, the process for handling an incoming express package is flowcharted. This flowchart, provided by DBS, was probably prepared as one of a number of charts of subprocesses within the overall process of handling mail at the company (in flowcharting it is often helpful to break down the process in question into smaller, and more easily-understood, subprocesses). This flowchart illustrates the basic elements of all flowcharts. Each step in the process is symbolized with a box. Each decision or choice is symbolized with a diamond. Connections among the various steps and decisions are indicated with lines, and arrows at their ends show which direction the activity flows.

EXHIBIT 14-2 FLOWCHART FOR AN INCOMING OVERNIGHT PACKAGE

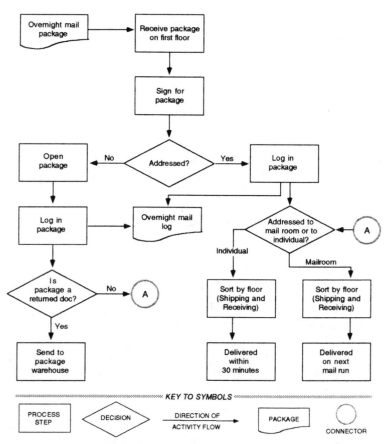

Source: Dun & Bradstreet Software

(Where connections are awkward to draw, circular, code-lettered connectors are used in place of the lines.) It is also common to identify the control points in the process by labeling them on the flowchart. (In addition to these symbols, you will sometimes see an oval used on a flowchart to symbolize the beginning or end of a process.)

The end result is something like a blueprint, showing what happens over time as the process unfolds. It is the *lingua franca* of all who study business from the systems perspective, and can provide the basis for computerized modeling and other sophisticated applications. However, most companies will find the flowchart an end in itself, and will be able to identify a great many opportunities for improvement simply by examining a process through its flowcharts.

Sometimes a flowchart is laid out on a sheet with rows symbolizing the different departments that participate in the process, and each activity is placed in the appropriate row based on which department performs it. Time is represented as flowing from left to right. The resulting *cross-functional flowchart* is helpful in understanding how different departments interact in the execution of the process. Problems usually arise whenever the process crosses department boundaries. See Exhibit 14-3 for an example.

Flowcharting can seem like a rather obscure, technical activity, best left to quality control engineers. Not so! When W. Edwards Deming introduced quality concepts to Japan in the 1950s, he brought with him a simple antecedent to the modern flowchart. And, in his words, "I think now, as I look back, that the flow diagram was the most powerful individual piece in Japan . . . the flow diagram in my lectures gave an overall view. It put the customer into the production line. I think that helped Japan to forge ahead."[7]

5. ANALYZE

Note that we have come halfway through DBS's process management method without actually making a single *change* in the process. The first half of the phases in the DBS method focus simply on understanding and documenting the existing

---

[7] As quoted in Rafael Aguayo, *Dr. Deming: The Americans Who Taught the Japanese About Quality*, Simon & Shuster, 1990, p. 120.

Exhibit 14-3 Cross Functional Flowchart

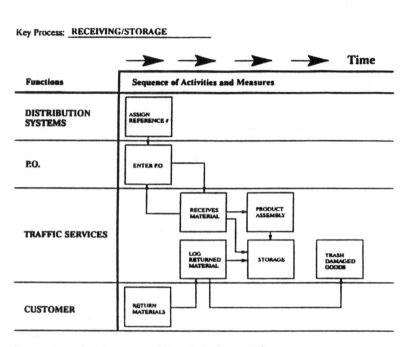

Key Process: RECEIVING/STORAGE

Source: Reproduced courtesy of Dun & Bradstreet Software

process, because the better this understanding and documentation is, the more effective efforts to improve will be.

In the analysis phase, the team starts modifying the process, but really only as a stop-gap until the process can be redesigned from the ground up. Therefore the focus is on identifying major problem areas, finding the root causes of these problems, and fixing any that can be readily fixed and that seem likely to have an impact on the customer. None but the most urgent problems need be addressed through process modifications right now. The rest are analyzed to identify causes and plans are prepared for their ultimate solution. The reason for delaying is that reactive modifications, made as soon as problems arise, will never produce as clean a process as a thoughtful redesign from the ground up.

To say that the root causes of a problem should be identified in this phase is to dismiss much of what makes the process approach unique—something we do not want to do. *How* root causes are identified, and how various companies go about the difficult task of analyzing their processes in general, is a particularly important issue. The analysis phase of process management demands considerable analytical skills, and in fact much of the quality training done in Conference Board companies focuses on the analytical skills needed in this stage. Conventional quantitative analytical tools, from control charts to histograms, are often helpful as the team tries to understand the extent and nature of variation in the process outcome and attempts to make causal inferences. The statistical concept of variability is of considerable importance in process management, and will be taken up shortly. However, most readers will find it helpful to look at two specialized analytical tools at this point.

The *Pareto chart* is a vertical bar chart that is used to compare the significance of various problem types or causes. For example, at DBS, Customer Complaints can easily be broken down into five specific areas: shipping problems, installation problems, delivery problems, clerical problems, and other problems. DBS wishes to minimize the number of complaints its field service receives from customers (perhaps a better way to put this is to say DBS wishes its customers to have fewer problems). But what are the major sources of customer complaints? A simple frequency analysis by complaint type reveals that 42% of all complaints concern shipping problems. Graphing complaint types by frequency (number of complaints received in a specific period), then placing them in descending order of frequency from left to right, gives you a clear visual ordering with the most important causes to the left. The customer complaint example from DBS is illustrated in Exhibit 14-4.

EXHIBIT 14-4 PARETO CHARTS

DBS FIELD SERVICE CUSTOMER COMPLAINTS

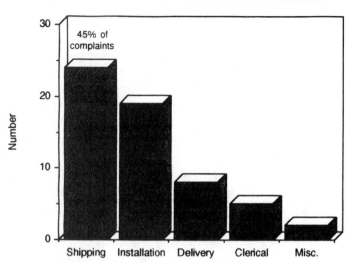

Source: Dun & Bradstreet Software Services, Inc.

XEROX CUSTOMER SERVICE COMPLAINTS

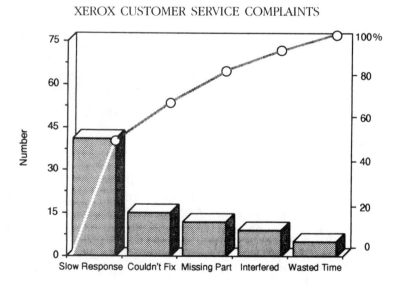

Source: Multinational Customer and Service Education, Xerox Corp.

The fishbone drawing traces its history to the work of the Japanese statistician, Kaoru Ishikawa. He developed it for Kawasaki Iron Fukiai Works in 1952, and it is now commonly referred to as the *Ishikawa Cause-Effect Diagram*. Exhibit 14-5 is a generic version of the diagram drawn by Ishikawa, showing some of the most common causes found in manufacturing applications. The diagram is generally used to identify and explore the most important causes via a group process involving the people who are most familiar with the process. Ishikawa explains,

> While there are many cause factors, the truly important ones, the cause factors which will sharply influence effects, are not many. If we follow the principle set by Vilfredo Pareto[8], all we have to do is standardize two or three of the more important cause factors and control them. But first these important factors must be found. In searching for these important cause factors, people who are familiar with a particular process, such as workers, engineers, and researchers, must all be consulted. They must be able to discuss the process openly and frankly, and the session can be conducted as a brainstorming session. The opinions presented in this session must be analyzed statistically and must be checked scientifically and rationally against the data available.[9]

The use of a cause-effect diagram in *brainstorming* is particularly helpful. It provides a skeleton that gives structure and meaning to the creative efforts of the group or team, and

---

[8]"The Pareto principle states that it is possible for many performance measures, such as scrap, machine failures, vendor problems, inventory costs, and product development time, to separate the "vital few" causes resulting in unacceptable performance from the "trivial many" causes. Historically, this concept has become known as the 80/20 rule, which states that a performance measure can be improved 80 percent by eliminating only 20 percent of the causes of unreliable performance." Source: Victor E. Kane, *Defect Prevention: Use of Simple Statistical Tools*, New York: Marcel Dekker, Inc., p. 344.

[9]Kaoru Ishikawa (David J. Lu, Translator), *What Is Total Quality Control? The Japanese Way*, Prentice Hall, 1985, p. 64.

Exhibit 14-5 Ishikawa Cause and Effect Diagram

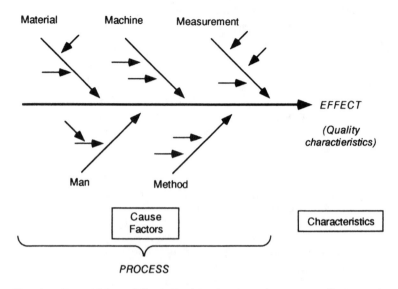

(Based on Kaoru Ishikawa, *What Is Total Quality Control?*, Prentice Hall, 1985, p. 63)

helps keep them focused on the problem at hand. But, as Ishikawa emphasizes, the resulting model must be verified and detailed through careful, quantitative measurement and analysis.

After analysis has been performed, the team working on a process will have considerable insight into how it works and, of particular importance, what causes the major quality problems, such as delays or variation in results. According to Kane, "At the conclusion of this phase, the team should have solved all of the urgent issues (problems) affecting process results and analyzed desired improvements. The output consists of a

---

[10]Edward J. Kane, "The Ascent of Quality in a Software Company," manuscript dated August 19, 1991, provided by the author. Quote from p. 7.

statement listing potential improvement items."[10] These will provide the input needed to redesign the process.

6. REDESIGN THE PROCESS

It may be that someone on the team will wake up in the middle of the night with a brilliant new vision of the process in mind, and will simply draw a new flowchart that solves all the problems and makes everyone happy. But I doubt it. Better to stick to systematic method. Kane recommends a more incremental approach. Start by identifying all the opportunities for constructive change within the process; all the areas where a change seems likely to increase the competitiveness of the process by improving effectiveness (Kane defines this as adding value or eliminating defects), or by improving efficiency (defined as eliminating or simplifying nonvalue-adding activities).

Next, analyze each of these potential changes by examining their impact on other elements of the process. When you change one thing in a process, many things are affected. Kane recommends looking for interactions in the broad areas of "people, organization, information systems, and technology," and observes that "information systems improvement is a basic consideration at this point and may be the major enabler of change."[11] The end result of this should be a list of specific changes and a good understanding of what impact each change has on the entire system. Before implementation, test the proposed changes as much as is possible—just in case!

Kane says that "the minimum output from this phase is a re-engineered process including simplified flowcharts and procedures. Other outputs are updated performance plans and a plan to communicate changes to customers and suppliers."[12]

[11]Ibid.
[12]Ibid.

7. IMPLEMENT, TRACK
AND EVALUATE PROGRESS

Now is the time to actually change the process. This transition requires careful management, and a specific series of steps are followed at DBS:

a. Develop a step-by-step *action plan* for the change-over to the new process that specifies what should be done, how and when, and identifies the resources needed.

b. Gain commitment from the people who are critical to successful implementation.

c. Develop and implement measurements of progress, including a customer feedback system.

d. Stabilize the process by documenting it, educating all affected, and establishing a feedback mechanism.

e. Establish a management plan for continuous improvement of the process; institute and distribute a regular status report.

At DBS, the team responsible for modifying a process prepares a report describing what they have done, and it covers points a through e above.

8. REVIEW IMPLEMENTATION
AND RATE THE PROCESS

This step is performed by management, after it receives the report generated by the team in step 7. (At DBS, a sponsoring executive is always designated so that there is someone at a high level who is responsible for the work of the team.) In this step, management reviews what the team has done, performs an audit of the implementation (DBS has developed a formal rating system for this purpose), and, to close the loop, reevaluates the priorities generated in step 1.

OK, that is the end of DBS' process management method. But it is only the beginning of process management. Once one change cycle is complete, another can be initiated. In practice, processes should flow through the eight phases of this methodology repetitively, improving with each cycle. That is what continuous improvement means, after all. And with each iteration, project teams and managers become more proficient at process improvement and, perhaps, find opportunities to apply new and more advanced process tools.

THE PROCESS MANAGEMENT TOOLBOX

We reviewed several critical process management tools as we discussed the methodology of process management. Histograms and Pareto Charts help identify the most significant causes so as to focus improvement efforts on them. The Ishikawa Cause and Effect Diagram gives groups a useful skeleton upon which to build a causal model and thus to understand quality characteristics of the process. Flowcharts are used to define and analyze processes, and they provide useful blueprints of the processes. These are probably the most important tools in the process management toolbox, but there are many others that are put to good use at Conference Board companies. It is helpful for anyone actually engaging in hands-on process improvement efforts to have a quick look at the entire toolbox. Exhibit 14-6 lists all the tools in common use at DBS, and also at FP&L and Xerox to make sure our toolbox is truly representative of the leading quality practitioners.[13]

This is not to say that people at Xerox do not know how to use some of the tools that DBS uses, or vice versa. What Exhibit 14-6 shows is the tools that employees are commonly

---

[13]According to D&B Software's *Leadership Through Excellence* Reference Guide, Xerox's *Leadership Through Quality Processes and Tools Review* and *USMG Partnership: A Guide to Work Process Improvement,* and the FPL Quality Improvement Story in Exhibit 2 of Harvard Business School Case 9-688-043.

Exhibit 14-6

Tool Used at?	DBS	FPL	Xerox
Action plan		÷	
Brainstorming	÷	÷	÷
Check Sheet	÷	÷	÷
Control Chart	÷	÷	÷
Countermeasures Matrix		÷	
Critical Activity Chart	÷		
Cross-functional Flowchart	÷		
Flowchart	÷	÷	÷
Histograms	÷	÷	÷
Ishikawa Cause/Effect Diagram	÷	÷	÷
Nominal Group Technique	÷		
Pareto Chart	÷	÷	÷
Process Capability Chart			÷
Project Planning Worksheet		÷	
Run Chart	÷		
Scatter Diagram	÷		÷

trained to use at each company—the line employees and middle managers who often make up the working teams that analyze and improve processes. And two striking points emerge from a survey of the tools commonly used at these three companies. First, there are a lot. More than I care to present in this chapter, and probably more than the reader cares to study in one sitting. And in fact, this is just scratching the surface—there are probably hundreds of analytical tools and techniques that can be applied to process management. The point is that more and better training in analytical tools and techniques is in general a very useful thing for companies that wish to pursue continuous improvement. Second, the companies do not agree completely on what the basic toolbox should contain.

Does this mean one has the best approach, and the others are behind? No. Rather it seems to be the case that which tools are taught and used in what order is not very important. It does not have a dramatic effect on the outcome of process improvement efforts. Teams at Xerox and FPL, and at IBM, Ford, and many other Conference Board companies, have achieved dramatic improvements in a wide variety of processes. DBS has no monopoly on process improvement. I think the lesson is that the specific tools used are not too important, as long as the methodology is pursued with enthusiasm.

Having said that, I still wish to bring the reader's attention to two methodologies—one, design of experiments, because it is new, innovative and difficult, at least in this country. It represents the next level of sophistication, or next step, for many companies that have become proficient with the existing toolbox. However, I will not discuss methods of experimentation, as this involves the equivalent of several semesters of academic training. The key point to recognize is that 'design of experiments' means just that, and nothing more—it simply applies the scientific principles of experimental design to business processes, using them to create controlled experiments that help tease out difficult-to-find causes. The other, the control chart, for just the opposite reason—it is so basic and fundamental that every company uses it; and I think this is true because it represents some of the key concepts behind statistical control of processes. Let's look briefly at this tool and the concepts it represents.

Control Charts and the Concept of Variation

The recognition and control of small variation in parts has been critical to the success of quality improvement efforts in industry, making component parts truly interchangeable for the first time. The same can be said of variation in all sorts of process outcomes and quality effects. Minor variations, undetected and uncontrolled, can combine and interact to produce miserable quality, whether in products or services (this is

EXHIBIT 14–7 CONTROL CHARTS FOR AVERAGES AND RANGES

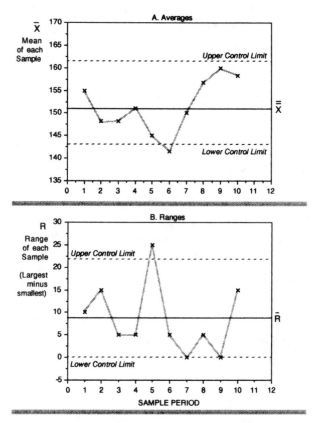

Explanation: This process was analyzed by taking samples of several products once every hour for ten hours. Each time sample measures were made they were averaged, and these averages are plotted above. The smallest measure was also subtracted from the largest, and the range plotted below. A mean of the means was calculated—the dark line above. A mean of the ranges was plotted with the dark line below. Upper and lower control limits were determined using a standard chart of R Factors and formulas (see sources, below, or any quality control handbook). The limits were set at three standard deviations from the mean.

This process is out of control. The charts show it varies more than might be expected according to chance. The root causes of the outliers need to be identified and the process improved.

Sources: Thomas Pyzdek, An SPC Primer, Quality Publishing, Tucson, AZ, 1984. Harvard Business School Case No. 9-686-118.

termed tolerance stack-up by statisticians). Variation is a formal statistical concept, and is best understood from the statistician's perspective. The control chart gives a process management team, or anyone working within an ongoing process, the power to understand variation of two kinds—the total amount of variation, or spread, in the outcome, and also the extent to which the various outcomes are centered on the target or specification. One way to visualize this is to imagine a bell-shaped curve on a graph. It represents a great many samples of some measure important to quality—it could be any measure. How wide is the bell? If it is low and wide, then the measurements are spread out. There is wide variation. If control limits have been defined, the bell will spill over both the upper and lower limits. This causes quality problems, of course. Now imagine another bell, this one tall and narrow because most of the measurements are very close to each other. So far so good. But, the center of the bell, the statistical mean or average of the measurements, is way off to one side of the targeted center. The bell spills over one or the other side of the control limits. This also leads to poor quality. The only acceptable output of any process is a narrow bell, centered on the target measurement. Both spread and centering must be controlled. The control chart, or charts, give users the power to diagnose problems in both areas—two closely-related charts are actually needed. Both are illustrated in Exhibit 14-7.

We opened this chapter with the observation that processes tend to adapt for comfort rather than competitiveness. The purpose of process management tools is to seize control over the adaptation of a company's processes. When this is done, both the direction and rate of their adaptation prove surprisingly manageable.

15

CONCLUSION

We began this book with the sobering observation that our traditional notions of excellent management are no longer viable. The magic stopped working at many companies. It is hard to say whether this is due to the opening of global markets and the challenges of foreign competitors, due to the gradual saturation of many markets and a resulting shift to more customer-oriented competition, or perhaps due to other factors not yet clear to us. What is clear is that a new management paradigm is needed, and total quality management certainly fits the bill. Here is a new magic that really works, as the experiences of various Conference Board companies attest.

We reviewed the elements of successful U.S. quality programs. Their management requires the creation of an appropriate vision and planning process, plus a rediscovery of the customer and a new focus on managing the processes inside those 'black boxes' of the traditional organization chart. These four elements allowed management of companies as diverse as Florida Power & Light, IBM, GTE, Corning, Xerox, American Express, Maytag, Ford, Hewlett-Packard, Hoechst Celanese, and Dun & Bradstreet to achieve improved, often outstanding, results. The elements of quality management are allowing these and other companies we reviewed, including small companies such as Baldrige winners Globe and Zytec Corp., to close the quality gap and achieve world-class leadership.

We also reviewed the factors that seemed critical to these companies as they undertook the transformation of their own corporate cultures. An emphasis on innovation, not just in technology but in everything; a drive toward employee participation in management-level decisions; a reduction in intracompany competition combined with a shared drive toward marketplace competitiveness; strong, unambiguous quality leadership from the top; and an unprecedented investment in employee training and development—these elements combined to transform the nature of the workplace, the roles played by employees and managers, and the quality of the work they perform. The total quality improvement programs we reviewed did transform the cultures of companies, often far beyond the initial vision of their executives. And it is clear that the transformation is ongoing—corporate culture is still evolving even at companies whose quality programs date back to the early eighties. The end result of this process may be a company so different from the traditional model that we still do not have a clear vision of it.

Third, we examined the fundamental tools needed to put individual employees and managers to work on the day-to-day tasks of continuous improvement. Teams are essential to this transformation of daily work, and companies give teams more responsibility as they travel farther down the quality path. The quality vision gives companies a wider view of their world, and leads many to 'cut windows' into unfamiliar industries and organizations in the effort to benchmark their processes against world leaders. The drive toward continuous improvement requires a host of new measurements to insure that customer views are fully represented, to track progress in quality improvements, and to better understand the costs of poor quality—lost customers, reworked or scrapped products, ill will, and other costs that are not captured in the traditional accounting system. Finally, we reviewed a model of process

management and some of the tools needed to work on processes. These tools range from the simple to the highly complex, and while it is not essential that a company master all of
them, it is important that it begin to apply some of them to the
work of diagnosing and modifying its many processes. Combined, these activities provide the follow-through for management's vision of total quality, harnessing the hands and minds
of every employee in the drive for continuous improvement.

In a sense this book has been a quest for understanding
of what makes the best U.S. quality programs work. Now that
we have emerged from this quest, sleeves rolled up and
visions of flowcharts dancing in our heads, it is a good idea to
step back and see where the journey has taken us. Like a
canoeist who has taken an uncharted fork in the river, it is
necessary to emerge from the rapids long enough to climb the
bank and see what lies ahead. The journey is inspiring, but
does it end in a swamp or the ocean? Does it offer passage
through the wilderness, or will it return us to where we
started? The evidence we have reviewed is encouraging, to say
the least, but it needs to be held at arm's length before we can
proclaim certainty. One good way to do this is to look for an
historical context.[1]

STEPPING BACK

When I look at the emergence of quality programs, and the
dramatic productivity increases they make possible, I am
struck by the thought that their impact on the world may
parallel the impact of the industrial revolution. The industrial
revolution was, after all, the result of innovations in the organi-

---

[1]The great advantage of not being an historian is that it is so easy to see bold
patterns in the sweep of history. One lacks that clutter of facts that makes the
professional historian hesitate to draw parallels and conclusions. Of course, one also
lacks the richness of information that insures conclusions are accurate—but life is full
of trade-offs! In any event, I find it useful to put the current quality revolution into
historical context, and I think the readers will too.

zation and management of work combined with rapid increases in the technology of production. And we certainly are in another period in which technology develops very rapidly and in which new and better approaches to the organization and management of work are emerging.

The industrial revolution brought production-line methods to many industries, and by so doing allowed productivity increases of several hundred percent and more. These seem so dramatic it is hard to imagine any modern innovations that could eclipse them. Yet in this book we have reviewed cases where cost-time profiles have shrunk so dramatically that similarly rapid quality and productivity improvements are becoming possible again. It is probably too early to say whether total quality management has as great a potential for productivity gains as the industrial revolution had, but it is clear that it has extraordinary potential, and therefore it seems likely it too will have a broad, transforming effect—not only on the practice of management, but on the nature of economies and cultures around the world. History teaches us that productivity gains do not occur in a cultural or economic vacuum.

The industrial revolution spread through Europe starting in the 1840s, about thirty years after the Great War, as it was then known, of the late 1700s and early 1800s. Napoleon was exiled to the history books, peace predominated, world trade expanded, and British industrial development catapulted it to the leading position in the world's economy. And here we are today—in a period of relative peace and heightened world trade, coming on the historical heels of our own great wars—apparently on the verge of a similar expansion in both industrial productivity and international trade.

My recollection of the industrial revolution, somewhat faded by the many years intervening since I last sat in a history class, is as a dramatic, sudden leap in production technologies and in productivity itself. I believe it is taught this way—the historical perspective tends to simplify such events. It is easy to assume that the new industrial methods were so far superior to the old they must have displaced them at once. Not so, according to historian Paul Kennedy—suggesting an interesting parallel to the modern quality movement. English industrialization and the resulting rapid growth of their productivity and exports "did not produce a sudden burst of modernization" throughout Europe:

> There simply was not enough capital, or local demand, or official enthusiasm, to produce a transformation; and many a European merchant, craftsman, and handloom weaver would bitterly oppose the adoption of English techniques, seeing in them (quite correctly) a threat to their older way of life.[2]

EXHIBIT 15-1 THE INDUSTRIAL REVOLUTION

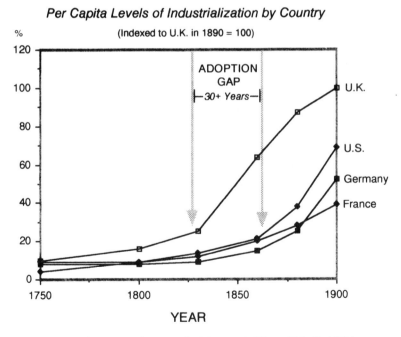

Per Capita Levels of Industrialization by Country

(Based on Data from Bairoch, *Journal of Economic History* Vol. 43, 1983.)

[2]Paul Kennedy. *The Rise and Fall of the Great Powers*, Vintage Books, 1989, p. 159.

As a result, U.S. and European national economies lagged behind the U.K. by 30 or 40 years, at least according to data compiled by another historian and summarized in Exhibit 15-1. Industrialization took off on a rapid growth curve in England beginning around 1825, but similar acceleration in growth curves is not seen in other countries until almost 1875. This adoption gap seems to explain why the industrial revolution resulted in the emergence of England as the leading world power (much as current Japanese economic successes can be attributed in part to their leadership in total quality management).

THE ADOPTION GAP

Is a similar adoption-gap effect at work right now in the global economy, with U.S. and European economies lagging behind Japan as it innovates in the area of total quality management? It seems as if history will repeat itself. But the evidence we have reviewed in this book shows that successful U.S. (and Canadian and European) quality programs are emerging, that individual firms and managers are scrambling to close the gap and put themselves on the new growth curve along with the early adopters of TQM. In fact, it is here that the historical parallel begins to break down. At least among Conference Board members, leading quality practitioners can be found in many countries—Japan and other Asian countries, Europe, Canada and the U.S. The early leaders were predominantly Japanese companies, as this is where the constellation of management methods we now call total quality management (and they call *kaizen*) first emerged. As we observed in the introduction, the U.S. adoption curve is about 15 or 20 years behind Japan's, and there certainly is resistance from those who, like the "merchant, craftsman, and handloom weaver" of the Industrial Revolution, bitterly oppose the adoption of total quality management techniques. But pockets of innovation and leadership are expanding all around the industrialized world, and I believe the adoption gap is shrinking as the rate of learning accelerates in various companies, industries and countries.

There is in fact no good reason why the current adoption gap cannot be closed, allowing all nations to benefit from the productivity gains TQM offers. History offers us the comforting conclusion that, once the U.S. and Europe caught up with the industrial revolution, they experienced economic benefits similar to England's. Kennedy tells us that, "When other European states and the United States followed the path to industrialization, their shares [of world markets] also rose steadily, as did their per capita levels of industrialization and their national wealth."[3]

ARE INDUSTRIAL REVOLUTIONS POSITIVE-SUM GAMES?

In other words, the industrial revolution offered economic advantage to all who joined it, not just to the early adopters. We are not used to games that work like this—there are supposed to be losers as well as winners. Games with clear winners and losers are called zero-sum games, meaning there is a fixed pay-off, and a gain for one side means a corresponding loss for the other (thus the sum of the winnings is always zero). Competition over market share, collective bargaining between unions and management, the trade negotiations of nations, and many other strategic situations share the common logic of zero-sum games. But any leap in the fundamental methods of production creates the potential for a win-win situation, one in which new markets are created, more profits become available to share among stockholders and employees, and standards of living increase on both sides of the Atlantic and Pacific. The Industrial Revolution fueled economic growth and expansion, allowing *all* participating countries to gain. That this potential also exists for the quality revolution means much of the conventional wisdom on how to address

[3]Ibid., p. 148.

ventional wisdom on how to address strategy and competition at the firm, industry and national levels is now inappropriate.

However, the game remains a zero-sum one for any companies or countries that do not join the revolution. Others' gains will be at their expense. History tells us, by way of example, that countries not participating in the Industrial Revolution fell dramatically behind those that did. In fact, the Industrial Revolution marked the beginning of the now-familiar division between first-world and third-world nations. Before the Industrial Revolution, per capita income was not widely different among most European, Asian and African countries. But countries whose populations grew without a corresponding adoption of high-productivity industrial methods fell rapidly behind industrializing nations, and most have fallen farther behind since. This gap proved extremely hard to close, and it seems important now, not only that industrial development continue to be pursued by Third World countries, but that they not miss the boat on the quality revolution as well. It is also interesting to speculate whether any new divisions could emerge as a result of the quality revolution—for instance, might a lower, second tier of industrialized nations be created if some fail to embrace TQM? This is in fact what Lester Thurow of MIT's Sloan School of Management forecasts—and he believes the U.S. will be among the second-tier countries, not the first.[4] It seems likely that the speed and enthusiasm with which the U.S. adopts TQM will determine whether this bleak view is fulfilled or not.

MAKING HISTORY

History provides an illuminating view on the quality revolution, but on the other hand it must not be allowed to steal the spotlight from the dramatic current events we witnessed in earlier chapters of this book. It is very exciting to see compa-

---

[4]Lester Thurow, *Head to Head: The Coming Economic Battle Against Japan, Europe, and America*, William Morrow, 1992.

nies pick themselves up, turn around, and discover that they had been going in reverse instead of forward all along. (As one CEO quoted earlier observed, "We had been looking at the horse from the wrong end, and it was not a pretty sight.") And when individual companies do make this discovery, and start to act on it, they often startle themselves and their industries with the results. As Douglas Swanson, manager of the quality program at Baldrige-winner IBM Rochester, recalls,

> There is a value in doing all this. Based on the quality efforts led by some of our leaders, we've enjoyed a two to three times improvement in product reliability, a 60 percent reduction in product development cycle, a five-point increase in customer satisfaction for our main system product [in a single year], a greater than two times revenue growth versus the industry. In short, the 8,100 people in IBM Rochester have taken this from a nice little business in the cornfield to the second-largest computer company in the world—of course, that is if we were separate from IBM.[5]

The implications are staggering should TQM offer as much value to all practitioners. What if most companies in the U.S. (or the world) were to succeed in adopting the principles and practices of total quality management, and were to see improvements of the sort experienced by IBM Rochester? It is a simple exercise of mathematical imagination to visualize improved process management, more rapid individual and organizational learning, increased productivity, and resulting higher-value products and services rippling through the world economy like a rising tide, lifting regional and national economies onto a faster growth curve. It is more difficult to provide iron-clad evidence that this will happen, or to say exactly how high or fast this tide might rise. As a matter of fact, we have not yet presented any firm evidence that the innovations that benefit the handful of companies covered in this book have

[5]Conference Board Report No. 990, p. 11.

had any generalized impact on the performance of U.S. companies and the U.S. economy. How well do the revolutionary practices of TQM translate from the corridors of the few handfuls of companies we have discussed in these pages to the macro-economy as a whole? The prognosis will be encouraging if we can be certain, first, that this new management paradigm does have a measurable impact on the bottom line, and second, that this paradigm can be disseminated widely throughout our society.

Much of the evidence for success on the company level is circumstantial or anecdotal, making it hard to know exactly how large the impact might be. What is the appropriate multiplier to use when projecting the potential impact of TQM on an entire industry or economy? Xerox attributes its turnaround to its quality program, and many other Conference Board members have attributed dramatic results to TQM as well. It is certainly encouraging to hear individual companies attribute bottom-line performance gains to TQM, and to note that these companies represent a broad range of industries. But are there any hard numbers to substantiate this circumstantial evidence? Do they really achieve superior bottom-line results that can be replicated across whole industries and economies?

SUPPORTING EVIDENCE

The U.S. General Accounting Office recently conducted a survey of 20 U.S. companies which have scored well on Baldrige criteria in an effort to address this very issue. While this is really just the beginning of a formal answer, based on a relatively small number of companies, it is nonetheless very encouraging. It provides an independent second opinion that verifies the conclusions drawn from our Conference Board sample. The GAO survey indicated significant improvements in a number of performance measures at U.S. companies with quality programs. First, there are measurable improvements in employee satisfaction, attendance, turnover, safety and health,

EXHIBIT 15-2 EMPLOYEE-RELATED INDICATORS

Average Annual Improvement

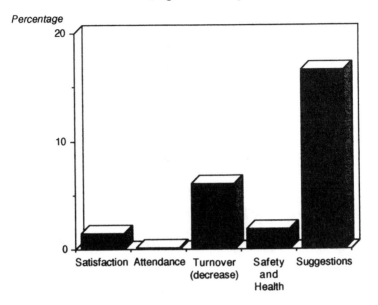

Source: U.S. General Accounting Office survey of companies with quality programs, 1991.

and the contribution of suggestions (Exhibit 15-2). The quality programs of surveyed companies can be shown to have benefitted the workforce on these measures. Some of the changes are small—a few percentage points—and others are larger, but the point is that the numbers support the many qualitative and quantitative assessments of the managers whose voices we have listened to in the pages of this book.

Customer attitudes have changed measurably too (Exhibit 15-3). Complaints are down an average of about 12 percent in the GAO survey, and customer satisfaction and retention are both up measurably. The reasons for these positive trends are probably revealed in the improved operating indicators in Exhibit 15-4. Five to ten percent improvements in measures of reliability, defects and errors, on-time delivery and order pro-

EXHIBIT 15-3 CUSTOMER SATISFACTION INDICATORS

Average Annual Improvement

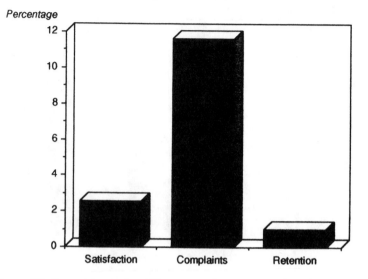

Source: U.S. General Accounting Office survey of companies with quality programs, 1991.

cessing times reflect improved employee attitudes and performance and no doubt increase the customer's satisfaction.

Do these changes make it all the way to the bottom line? Exhibit 15-5 shows that surveyed companies have been able to grow their market shares through quality programs, that sales per employee (a good general measure of the efficiency and effectiveness of the company's operations) are up significantly, and that measurable improvements in both return on assets and return on sales have resulted. That means the companies are enjoying direct financial benefits from their efforts.

Does improved quality pay off? Most of the managers interviewed in this book, and perhaps most of the readers, would say "Of course." Perhaps they might add, "Don't ask stupid questions." But the return is not as straightforward or proximate as many managers expect and hope. Recall that

EXHIBIT 15-4 OPERATING INDICATORS

Average Annual Improvement

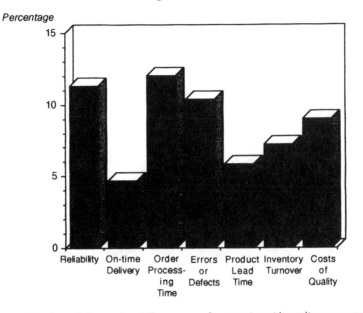

Source: U.S. General Accounting Office survey of companies with quality programs, 1991.

most of the Conference Board companies studied have had large-scale quality programs for five years or more—and that their managers reported a variety of difficulties and false starts in the early years of these programs. To be honest, I was surprised, despite my enthusiasm, that the GAO's survey indicated any measurable improvement in return on assets at all. Individual companies have certainly increased market shares, revenues and profits as they have implemented their quality programs. But, on average, quality programs are in their early years. (By the time this book is published, there will probably be hundreds of one and two year old programs across the U.S.) Most are teenagers, still lacking confidence and momentum, and sometimes common sense as well (hence the conclu-

EXHIBIT 15-5 FINANCIAL PERFORMANCE INDICATORS

Average Annual Improvement

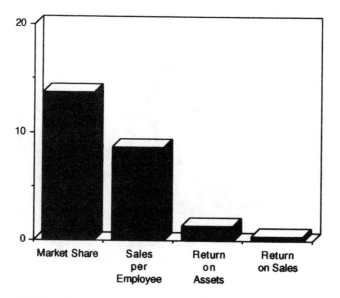

Source: U.S. General Accounting Office survey of companies with quality programs, 1991.

sion of the Ernst & Young survey, cited in the introduction, that the majority of quality programs have not "reached lasting and meaningful levels.") And many of them are growing up in the context of hostile environments, both internal and external, that make it difficult to compare their performance after they start a quality program with their performance in a more sheltered prior period.

EXTERNAL CHALLENGES
AND INTERNAL BARRIERS

Externally, many companies are facing heightened competition at home and abroad. Quality programs are often conceived of as a response to external threats. William Lesner of

Cadillac Motor Cars tells a story that is fairly typical of many quality initiatives:

> In 1985, our first priority was not to change the culture. The background of our leadership group—the executive staff—was well-grounded in top-down management by objectives leadership, and they weren't necessarily unhappy with the culture that resulted. But as Dr. Samuel Johnson once said, "Nothing so heightens a man's senses as the prospect of being hanged in the morning."[6]

Many companies find themselves embracing TQM and the far-reaching cultural changes it requires because, and only because, they are eager to avoid being hanged in the morning. This means many companies might have posted significant *declines* in profits and return-on-assets had their management not taken remedial steps. It is not necessarily fair to compare financial performance before and after the initiation of a company-wide quality program and expect the difference to be a direct measure of the positive impact of total quality methods on performance. There are too many other factors at work, many of them negative.

Internally, many companies find their quality programs in conflict with established practices. As we saw time and again in the pages of this book, total quality management stands in opposition to our traditional notions of management excellence. This produces roadblocks and internal conflict, and makes it difficult for management to send consistent signals throughout the workforce. For a simple example, take Caterpillar and its 1992 dispute with the United Auto Workers over a labor contract. When the UAW called off a bitter five-month strike and sent the strikers back to work, the story might have been considered a happy one from the traditional viewpoint. But the labor-management relationship that framed this conflict was certainly built on the traditional zero-sum approach to

[6]Conference Board Report No. 990, p. 13.

management. Each side had prescribed roles and goals in a distributive bargaining game designed to allow each to fight for the largest piece of the given financial pie. The end result seemed destined to produce a winner and loser.

But what about Caterpillar's investment in total quality, and its efforts to involve this same workforce in participative process management, teamwork, and many of the other activities associated with total quality management? A newspaper reported at the time that "strikers expressed anger at both the company and union officials for what many now view as a wasted effort. Their frustration indicates that Caterpillar could face a huge task in trying to rebuild goodwill within its workforce."[7] Is it possible that the loss of goodwill could set back the quality improvement process? Of course. Any bitter dispute is likely to produce a workforce that is angry and cynical, prepared only to 'put in their time' rather than to pursue continuous improvement. Perhaps the clearest message to emerge from the experiences of Conference Board quality practitioners is that quality cannot be pursued or gaps closed when employees do no more than put in their time. Conformance to minimum expectations is the antithesis of quality improvement, whether it describes employees on the production line or the products they produce.

TRIPPING ON HISTORY

Employees read all the signals a company gives them, the unintended ones as well as the intended ones. As a result, a quality program can bump into major setbacks like labor-management disputes, and it can bump into smaller but more common setbacks like evaluation and promotion practices that conflict with quality goals. As we have seen, successful U.S. quality programs require companies to move toward workforce participation in management—of their own work, and,

---

[7] "Caterpillar Says That Some Strikers May Not Be Allowed to Return to Work," *The Wall Street Journal*, April 16, 1992, A3.

eventually, of the company as a whole. And they require a shift toward participative leadership styles. But it is not yet clear whether this means a complete abandonment of the traditional labor-management relationship. For instance, when a company decides that it's employees ought to be given more responsibility and control, does it also need to make a stronger personal commitment to those employees? Are the greatest benefits of TQM only attainable when accompanied by job guarantees? If not, how else can the greater trust required be created? This issue has not been dealt with, at least not definitively. I do not know the answer, but I suspect, and the Caterpillar case seems to indicate, that it will eventually be pushed onto the agendas of managers who follow the quality path. While the history of the Industrial Revolution offers valuable lessons, the history of individual companies and of management practices as a whole is a serious obstacle to successful adoption of TQM. History can teach lessons, but tradition can trip those who try to learn from the lessons.

There are many reasons to question whether U.S. quality programs, or any quality programs, have been followed through to their end. Even the leading practitioners seem to have one foot in the new quality paradigm and the other still in the old management paradigm. Remember the Conference Board survey indicating that leading practitioners consider themselves, on average, about halfway to Baldrige standards? Of course, some have presumably achieved those standards, as they have won the award. But even the Baldrige standards do not presume a complete turnaround in the way a company is managed and its work performed. One indication that Baldrige is not an end-point for TQM is provided by the difference between the attributes of successful Conference Board quality programs, reported in this book, and the seven criteria used to judge the Baldrige Award:

1. Leadership

2. Information and Analysis

3. Strategic Quality Planning

4. Human Resource Development and Management

5. Management of Process Quality

6. Quality and Operational Results

7. Customer Focus and Satisfaction

When compared to the factors emerging from our study of best practices, this Baldrige list looks familiar—but not completely. Leadership, measurement (under the heading 'information and analysis'), planning, and a customer focus are on both lists, and are all essential parts of successful quality programs. But on the management level, Conference Board companies emphasize vision and the process perspective more than do the Baldrige Award categories. (Both elements are measured in the scoring for the award, but only as sub-headings.) In the area of corporate culture, Conference Board companies emphasize innovation in a way that the Baldrige criteria do not. They also emphasize training, the creation of a participative style of work (including teams), and the management of intracompany competition. These issues are interwoven into some of the Baldrige criteria (especially number 3), but are not highlighted to the degree they are in successful Conference Board programs. This difference suggests that the Baldrige criteria are not designed to catalyze the transformation of corporate culture, at least not to the degree that many companies are finding necessary.

Does this mean the Baldrige criteria are flawed? Not at all. The point is that they obviously do not define an ending to the quality journey. That best practices in Total Quality Management may go farther than even the Baldrige criteria in transforming corporate culture is no surprise. We should expect practice to continue evolving, hopefully at an even faster rate in the future. It will move beyond current Baldrige criteria (one reason the administrators of this award modify the criteria every year), and it will even move beyond anything currently imagined by the leading practitioners we have profiled in this book. The quality revolution is probably still in its earliest stage—in fact, that is the most exciting news anyone can bring back from the front. There is incredible potential for economic benefit as the existing programs advance, and as new programs are initiated at an accelerating rate. It is as the adoption curve moves into a high-growth phase that we can expect to see dramatic, measurable benefits from the practice of total quality management. It is therefore impressive to see *any* measurable financial benefits for the average U.S. practitioner at this early stage. I think it is fair to say that we do not yet have a clear understanding of the extent to which TQM can and will change the organization and management of work—or the extent to which it can increase productivity and benefit the world economy in general. My belief is that we are in for a surprise; that the full impact of a new management paradigm has not yet dawned on management or society as a whole.

To say that the quality revolution is in its inception raises the question of how we should track its growth. It will be important to track adoption of TQM by industry, as well as in the public sector, and—as TQM practitioners do on the organization level—to measure the impact of quality on the economy. This is not an easy task, however. We do not measure 'cost of quality' in society as a whole, for example. What is the cost of failures in the education system? Of a health system that does not deliver effective prenatal care to all pregnant mothers, and that, in general, emphasizes treatment of disease over prevention? How many crimes, and criminals, are preventable and what is the cost of our failing to prevent them? How many business failures might be preventable—for example, what would the relative costs have been of managing S&L's sufficiently so as to avoid the current crisis? How much smaller could the Pentagon's budget get if it were focused on prevention and conflict resolution rather than after-the-fact military intervention? Without an accurate understanding of the cost of poor quality, it will be difficult for society to determine how and how much it benefits from improved quality. Just as a company cannot see the return on building quality into processes until it improves its cost-of-quality measures, economies and societies are blinded to the costs of quality and unable to justify prevention without accurate cost-of-quality measures.

HOW WILL WE KNOW WHEN WE'RE SUCCEEDING?

But I am jumping the gun a bit by raising issues such as quality in education, public health and the criminal justice system. Eventually TQM may be seen as a solution to the federal deficit and a way to make social programs of all sorts more effective. But the first challenge is simply to bring the quality banner to the bulk of U.S. companies and to both anticipate and track whatever economic benefits this provides. How should the nation measure quality improvement in companies and other organizations? We do not measure quality at present, at least not in any way that allows an industry- or country-wide assessment of it. On the rare occasions when it is measured experimentally, as in the long-term Profit Impact of Marketing Strategy database (which tracks performance of business units over time for hundreds of companies), quality is strongly correlated with higher market share and higher return on investment.[8] (The database was originally developed at Harvard Business School and is now maintained by the nonprofit Strategic Planning Institute.) The measure of quality in this database is customer-defined: How good are a company's products or services relative to competitors', according to *customers*? This is a difficult measure, and so far not one that companies feel confident about putting in their annual reports. The GAO survey referred to above ran into the difficulty that some

---

[8]Robert Buzzell and Bradley Gale, *The PIMS Principles: Linking Strategy to Performance*, New York: The Free Press, 1987, p. 9.

participants refused to release customer survey data even when they had it. It is difficult to imagine collecting and synthesizing enough customer survey data to rate the relative quality of the nation's products and services!

Further, while it makes sense in the short term to think about how your quality stacks up to competitors', in the long run the industry standards for quality ought to move, and they ought to move faster as the rate of continuous improvement increases. Any relative measure fails to capture this movement. To say a horse won by three lengths tells you nothing about the speed at which it ran. It is very hard to imagine any absolute measure of quality that could show us how fast individual companies, let alone whole industries or nations, are improving. Direct macro-level measures of quality progress may never be available.

THE IMPACT ON PRODUCTIVITY

Another way to think about the problem of tracking progress is to look at productivity. We saw, in the chapters addressing the process perspective and the methods of process management, that quality improvement is associated with reductions in the cost-time profile of any process. In other words, when people work alone or in teams to redesign their own processes and jobs, they are able to produce the same or a better product using less time and money. This should produce significant productivity gains. Why not track productivity as a measure of the progress of U.S. quality improvement?

Conventional wisdom has it that the productivity of U.S. factories lags behind that of many other countries. Why else export all those manufacturing jobs? How else to explain the ability of foreign producers to invade the U.S. market over the last few decades? And this was certainly true in the seventies, when U.S. productivity grew at a little over 1 percent while productivity grew almost four percent on average among our major trade partners. The U.S. was falling behind steadily every year. But in the eighties, this gap began to close. U.S. factory productivity grew at the same rate as other countries on average: Three and a half percent.[9] In other words, the U.S. is no longer falling behind its major trading partners in productivity growth, and is actually decreasing the gap on a percentage basis.

However, two qualifications have to be added. First, this is in manufacturing only—23.3 percent of the nation's output—and does not include service and white-collar work. White-collar productivity is not growing at a significant rate. This, along with the recession, means that the U.S. started the nineties with overall annual productivity growth for all sectors in the range of one percent or less. However, the up-tick in manufacturing productivity is certainly encouraging.

While quality programs are now applied to all sorts of processes, not just manufacturing processes, they started in the manufacturing sector and on the manufacturing side of most companies. The oldest U.S. quality programs are by and large in manufacturing, some going back to the early 1980s. Could they be responsible for the gains in manufacturing productivity?

Unfortunately, the statistics suggest that another factor was largely responsible for the gains of the 1980s: Automation and the loss of jobs that results from it. Productivity is measured in output per worker, and so can be increased either by learning how to produce more per employee or by eliminating employees. As a *New York Times* analysis of the productivity figures concludes, "Industries like textiles have reversed their fortunes by automating, but far lower employment is the result." Another report has it that the many announced downsizings of public companies traded on Wall Street resulted in

---

[9]Data from 1973-79 and 1979-89. Compares growth in U.S. factory productivity with growth in factory productivity of Britain, Canada, Denmark, France, Germany, Italy, Japan, Netherlands and Sweden. Source: Bureau of Labor Statistics; reported in *The New York Times,* February 10, 1991, p. F2.

"amputation of a record half-million jobs" in 1991.[10] There are benefits to automation, of course, but it seems only a partial solution from an economic perspective. What happens to the people who lose their jobs and the factory towns that lose their factories? Automation without continuous process improvement provides only a one-time gain in productivity for the company, and when the dust settles the payoffs follow the rules of a zero-sum game again.

It is likely, however, that widespread adoption of TQM will lead to automation and other forms of innovation in the context of a new 'win-win' game that benefits productivity and the labor force simultaneously. Automation combined with, or driven by, on-going learning and process improvement seems much more likely to produce on-going productivity improvement over the long term. It promises to make it more feasible for companies to overcome new competitors and grow their businesses, increasing the productivity of the existing workforce rather than pruning that workforce down. The productivity gains of the eighties were in too many cases the result of cut-backs and scale-downs. Ideally, TQM makes it possible to replace these end-game strategies with strategies for regeneration and new growth. And that means productivity figures ought to go up in response to the spread of total quality management, without a corresponding cut in employment or other offsetting factors. While it is probably still too early to see a significant impact on the nation's productivity, we can expect, and hope, to see a dramatic impact in coming years. In fact, this will provide the best evidence that TQM is living up to its current promise.

There is more than one way to automate; or innovate, or manage teams, or lead employees, or listen to the customer. We have looked at many of these activities in the context of

---

[10]Don Boroughs, "Amputating Assets," *U.S. News & World Report,* May 4, 1992, p. 50.

quality programs, and in this context they take on a new meaning. When infused with the vision of continuous improvement, and the benefits this provides to customers, employees, managers and stockholders, any of these activities has the potential to create an end result that is more than the sum of the parts. The quality vision brings magic back into the equation at a time when it is sorely needed. Yet we must also remember that this magic is not recaptured easily.

As President Bush warns on the cover of the 1992 application for the Malcolm Baldrige National Quality Award, "Quality management is not just a strategy. It must be a new style of working, even a new style of thinking." Whichever speechwriter penned that line will get my vote in the next election, because it cuts right to the central issue, one that presents a problem as well an opportunity.

That quality management is more than a new strategy explains its transforming potential. That it demands new ways of working and thinking explains why it can be so wrenching for those who pursue it. The adoption of new ways of working and new ways of thinking is naturally a slow process. But we face a critical gap—not only in the performance of our economic institutions, but more fundamentally in our adoption of new ways of working and thinking. It is therefore imperative that we work to close this gap as rapidly as possible. The progress of the Conference Board companies and others reported in these pages is most encouraging, suggesting that the U.S. is fully capable of rekindling its own fires and recapturing any magic its economy may have lost. The gap has been closed at a number of companies, and their experiences mark the path for the larger-scale effort to come.

INDEX